REFUGEES FROM SLAVERY

AUTOBIOGRAPHIES OF FUGITIVE SLAVES IN CANADA

BENJAMIN DREW

Introduction to the Dover Edition by

TILDEN G. EDELSTEIN
WAYNE STATE UNIVERSITY

DOVER PUBLICATIONS, INC.
Mineola, New York

Bibliographical Note

This Dover edition, first published in 2004, is an unabridged republication of
the work originally published in 1969 by Addison-Wesley Publishing Company,
Reading (Massachusetts) under the title *The Refugee: A North-Side View of
Slavery.* Please note that the running heads herein reflect this original title. The
introduction by Tilden G. Edelstein from the 1969 edition has been
specially revised for this reprint.

Library of Congress Cataloging-in-Publication Data

Drew, Benjamin, 1812-1903.
    [Refugee]
    Refugees from slavery : autobiographies of fugitive slaves in Canada /
Benjamen Drew ; introduction to the Dover edition by Tilden G. Edelstein.
        p. cm.
    Originally published: The refugee: a North-side view of slavery. Reading
Mass. : Addison-Wesley, 1969, in series: Fugitive slave narritives. With a
revised introduction.
    ISBN 0-486-43448-6 (pbk.)
    1. Fugitive slaves—United States—Biography. 2. Fugitive slaves—
Canada—Biography. 3. Slaves—United States—Social conditions. 4. African
Americans—Biography. 5. Blacks—Canada—Biography. 6. Canada—
Biography I. Title.

E450.D77 2004
973.7'115'092—dc22

2004041352

Manufactured in the United States of America
Dover Publications, Inc., 31 East 2nd Street, Mineola, N.Y. 11501

CONTENTS

viii   *Contents*

INTRODUCTION TO THE DOVER EDITION

For the last fifty years, historians of American slavery have relied upon Benjamin Drew's *A North-Side View of Slavery* as a revealing source. The paucity of antebellum accounts provided by the mass of unknown slaves makes it a rare one. Published in 1855, Drew's book had a central place in the abolitionist crusade.

Drew, employed by the Boston public schools for twenty years, was a forty-three-year-old school principal and part-time journalist whose ancestors had settled in Plymouth, Massachusetts in 1660. As a member of a group of writers congregating at The Shades, a Boston saloon in Cornhill Square, he shared the convivial company of the humorists Artemus Ward, Miles O'Reilly, and Benjamin Shillaber. All were interested in folk language and folk wit. Shillaber, at this time, was the best known of the group, being the author of *The Life and Sayings of Mrs. Partington* (1854)—a widely read book filled with Yankee moralizing and popular malapropisms. He was also editor of a humor magazine, *The Carpet Bag*, which included among its contributors, Drew, Ward, O'Reilly, and Mark Twain (whose first published humorous essay appeared in the magazine). Drew and Shillaber wrote folk genre essays for the Boston *Post*, the city's most sophisticated newspaper. Such essays were the prose counterparts to James Russell Lowell's *Bigelow Papers* and the forerunner of American regional fiction. Drew used the cognomen Ensign Stebbings, which was probably derived from a Shillaber character. (Ensign Stebbings was mockingly described as the hero of Maine's bloodless Aroostook War of 1839 who was wounded by tripping over a commissary wagon.)[1] Prior to writing *A North-Side View of Slavery*, Drew's association with antislavery agitation had been indirect: his cousin, Thomas Drew, was editor of the Worcester *Spy*, the major antislavery daily in Massachusetts.[2]

Benjamin Drew's book was an immediate response to a deep crisis in northern antislavery sentiment exemplified by the 1854 appearance of *A South-Side View of Slavery* by the Reverend Nehemiah Adams of Boston. An early opponent of antislavery preaching from the pulpit, Adams subsequently led a petition campaign against the extension of slavery into the territories.[3] After returning from a tour of the South, however, he published observations challenging major assumptions about the evils of slavery and the need for its abolition. Instead of regarding slave owners "as holding their fellow-men in cruel bondage," Adams suggested that they be viewed as "the guardians, educators, and saviors of the African race in this country."[4] Because of the social control exerted by the master class, African American slaves seemed to him less dangerous than lower-class foreigners in the North—a persuasive comparison in the context of the era's powerful anti-immigrant prejudices. Granting that the slave's personal liberty was restricted, Adams saw "no reason to dissolve the union to abolish slavery." African Americans, he concluded, were happy to be slaves. The South gradually would eliminate the worst features of slavery (which were best known to southerners) if the North ceased its antislavery agitation.[5]

Some of Adams' arguments had been heard before, but to have them repeated by a distinguished Boston minister after so many years of antislavery agitation—and especially during the discouraging events of 1854—disturbed antislavery advocates. Furthermore, his book was not simply the restatement of old arguments. Adams specifically challenged the veracity of *Uncle Tom's Cabin* (1852) by suggesting that it was impossible for fiction to be accurate. Mrs. Stowe, in appealing to emotions, had grossly distorted the reality of slavery, he asserted.[6] By questioning this enormously influential book, and by implication, the validity of its author's subsequent effort to document it in *A Key to Uncle Tom's Cabin* (1853), Adams urged those who had been moved to sympathy for the slave to support sectional reconciliation and depend upon the masters' benevolent paternalism. *A South-Side View of Slavery* added to the heavy barrage of proslavery literature aimed at *Uncle Tom's Cabin*.[7]

Antislavery forces sought to counterattack. William Lloyd Garrison, appalled by *A South-Side View of Slavery*, reprinted in the *Liberator* a thorough critique which originally appeared in the *Christian Examiner*, a magazine known for supporting antislavery but opposed to Garrison's radical abolitionism. "All the facts float in the air," said the *Examiner*'s reviewer in rebuttal to Adams' claim that antislavery advocates were blindly theoretical about the South's "peculiar institution."[8] The significance of *A South-Side View of Slavery* was deepened by other events of 1854. Observations similar to Adams' appeared in George Fitzhugh's book of the same year: *Sociology for the South; or the Failure of Free Society*. Fitzhugh, a southern critic of northern capitalism, claimed that the slave "was as happy as a human being could be" and in better condition than members of the northern lower classes.[9] The issues raised in these two widely discussed books went beyond the battle of polemical literature, for they were reflected in surrounding events. While the Compromise Acts of 1850 had disheartened antislavery advocates, even more ominous to their cause was the passage of the Kansas–Nebraska Act of 1854.

It sought to end antislavery agitation forever by allowing the existence of slavery in each new territory to be decided by the voters of that territory. Moreover, it appeared that antislavery sentiment had received another setback in May 1854 when a runaway slave, Anthony Burns, was captured in Boston and summarily convicted under the provisions of the Fugitive Slave Law of the Compromise of 1850. A few militant abolitionists sought to free the imprisoned Burns from the Boston Court House, and large and boisterous antislavery meetings were held supporting him. But the futility of these efforts was underscored by the arrest of several abolitionists and the dispatch of a large force of federal and state troops, accompanied by artillery, to ensure Burns' return to slavery.[10] If the observations of Adams and Fitzhugh gained increased acceptance, then slavery, supported by congressional compromise and armed force, might indeed become further entrenched.

In response to this antislavery crisis, Benjamin Drew departed for Canada in 1855; in the same year *A North-Side View of Slavery* was published by John P. Jewett and Company—the publishers of *Uncle Tom's Cabin* and *A Key to Uncle Tom's Cabin.*

Canada had not always been a haven for the slave. As early as the seventeenth century, slavery had been legal; from 1787 to 1793, some slaves from Canada, seeking sanctuary, had fled south to New England and the Northwest Territory. Many years after most northern states had ended slavery within their borders, slavery remained legal, if little practiced, throughout British North America. Although Canadian slavery was not abolished until 1833, local antislavery action was evident by 1793 when the first Lieutenant Governor of Upper Canada, Colonel James Simcoe, convinced his executive council to pass a bill declaring that no African American slave could be brought into the province, and that every child born to a slave mother would be freed upon reaching the age of twenty-five. Comparable to these efforts at gradual abolition, judicial decisions in Lower Canada and in the Maritime Provinces further undermined slavery's existence. By the beginning of the nineteenth century, it was apparent that Canada could serve as an asylum for American slaves. Canadian authorities repeatedly rejected American demands for the extradition of fugitive slaves; on several occasions Canadian governmental organizations invited fugitives to Canada in open defiance of the United States.[11]

Benjamin Drew estimated that there were close to 30,000 fugitive slaves in Canada when he arrived there in 1855. Most had settled in the inter-lake portion of Upper Canada (present-day Ontario)—bounded on the south by Ohio and Pennsylvania, on the east by New York, and on the west by Michigan. But freedom did not mean equality. Canadian prejudice and discrimination against black people, while less than in the United States, would grow as their numbers increased.[12]

Although it is clear from *A North-Side View of Slavery* that most fugitive slaves were in Canada to escape the hardships of southern slavery, to a lesser extent they testified that they were there because the northern United States practiced legal and extra-legal discrimination against African Americans—free or fugitive. Northern states nearest the South, fearing the influx of fugitive slaves, had passed restrictive legislation. Illinois and Indiana added anti-immigration provisions to their constitutions. Ohio required bonds from $500 to $1,000 from all African Americans as bail for their good behavior. From the time Maine was admitted to the Union in 1820, to the outbreak of the Civil War, every new state ratified a constitution with various restrictions on African American suffrage. Ninety-three percent of the northern African American population lived in states where suffrage either was constitutionally limited to white men or had special requirements for black men. In addition, five states prohibited court testimony by African Americans in cases involving whites, and only in Massachusetts could African Americans serve as jurors. Not until 1855 were Boston public schools desegregated, while in most of the North segregated schools continued to exist. Migration to Canada noticeably increased as discrimination heightened. In Cincinnati, for example, when the Ohio bond law was enforced in 1829 and mobs of whites simultaneously attacked the black section of the city, some 2,000 African Americans departed for Canada where about 500 of them established the Wilberforce Settlement. The greatest wave of northern African Americans fleeing to Canada followed the passage of the Fugitive Slave Law of 1850.[13]

To gather information for his book, Benjamin Drew carried letters of introduction from William Lloyd Garrison, Theodore Parker, and other Massachusetts antislavery leaders.[14] Perhaps his most valuable Canadian contact was a white man, the Reverend Hiram Wilson, formerly one of the group of students and teachers at Lane Seminary in Cincinnati who had withdrawn from the school when antislavery preaching was forbidden. Wilson, the Reverend Theodore Weld, and others settled at Oberlin College and became early religious leaders of the antislavery crusade. Wilson helped establish the Canada Mission for blacks; the Dawn settlement, near Dresden in Canada West—the former Upper Canada—became the site of a manual labor school. Wilson later served at the fugitive slave settlement in St. Catharines.[15]

Another white leader to whom Drew was indebted for access to Canadian fugitives was the Reverend William King, founder, in 1849, of the Elgin Settlement in Buxton—the most successful of the organized black communities in Canada. An Irish-born Presbyterian minister, King had inherited slaves from his southern wife. He soon freed them by bringing them to Canada.[16]

Other issues besides slavery and discrimination concerned Drew. A central interest was how fugitives were performing as free men. Underlying this theme were broader observations about the nature of African Americans. Drew tried to answer the momentous question troubling even those men most committed to emancipation: what would happen in North America once slavery was abolished? Since the 1830s, American abolitionists had assailed all emancipation plans that looked to African colonization. Migration of fugitive slaves to Canada, on the other hand, was advocated by many antislavery men. The geographic proximity of Canada to the United States was less important, perhaps, for maintaining this view than the long-held feeling of most Americans that Canada was not a genuine foreign country but rather a potential appendage to the United States. Annexation sentiment dated back to 1775 when the American colonies tried to conquer Canada; Benjamin Franklin later sought to have Britain cede it to the United States as part of the peace treaty ending the American Revolution. Annexationist attitudes remained throughout the nineteenth century.[17] Canada, therefore, seemed to be an excellent place for training fugitives for freedom and for their eventual assimilation into American life.

In gathering evidence and writing about African Americans in Canada, Drew understood that criticism of previous fugitive slave accounts was directed against their failure to be authentic and typical. To their critics, the narratives of Frederick Douglass, Josiah Hensen, or William Wells Brown seemed unrepresentative for several reasons: these fugitives had such exceptional leadership qualities and other outstanding personal characteristics that their very uniqueness belied the claim that they represented four million oppressed southern slaves. Given the relatively small number of slaves who had escaped from the South, any fugitive, by definition, was atypical, and most fugitives came from border-states and therefore did not reflect the slavery experience of those from the Deep South. The polemical quality of abolitionists and their literature meant that any account published under their auspices could be judged untrustworthy, necessarily reflecting their strong biases and projecting their propaganda.[18] Finally, could it be expected that blacks, so accustomed to assuming roles dictated by white society, would be able or willing to speak truthfully to a white interviewer and to white readers?

Drew, aided by his reputation for honesty and by the fact his name could not be immediately associated with the better known and more radical antislavery advocates, tried to meet these criticisms in several ways. What was unique and most important, however, were the sources and scope of his information. Drew recorded the testimony of more than one hundred fugitive slaves who, except for Harriet Tubman, were unknown to the public. He claimed to have randomly interviewed African Americans in both cities and settlements of Canada West, seeking to transcribe their words accurately and making less than "a dozen verbal alterations" during his subsequent editing.[19] His book includes statements taken from black men and women in fourteen Canadian communities who had been enslaved or free in the South. Represented are prosperous and poor fugitives who, before reaching Canada, had held a variety of occupations: field hand, house slave, cooper, blacksmith, barber, storekeeper, and bartender. Most impressive is the diversity of testimony found in *A North-Side View of Slavery.* There are kind masters and cruel ones; easy escapes from slavery and difficult ones; suspicion of all white men and trust in some of them; fugitives wishing to remain in Canada and those who wanted to return to the United States if slavery were abolished; successful individual and community efforts and discouraging failures; praise for Canadian and northern racial attitudes as well as evidence of prejudice and discrimination.

Drew's sampling and editing methods have several limitations that prevent his book from being a microcosm of the life of all slaves and fugitives. The people appearing in it are mostly young men from border-states—a representative sample of fugitives but certainly not of slaves. Former field hands and craftsmen predominate, while there are few house servants. Among the one hundred and thirteen African Americans whose testimony appears, there are only sixteen women, fourteen of whom are married. And there are some sensitive issues to northern public opinion that remain either absent or disguised: the book does not candidly treat marriage, sexual promiscuity, and miscegenation. Unlike Drew, a major twentieth-century historian of slavery has suggested that sexual monogamy was rare under slavery because marriages between slaves were severely restricted by the master and were not legally binding.[20] Northern fears of emancipation and the possible migration of African Americans to the North were strongly related to this issue. It seems, in retrospect, that the impact of *Uncle Tom's Cabin* upon northern readers had been more dependent upon the threat to family stability caused by slavery (with the novel's agonizing scenes of forced family separation) than upon any other aspect of the slave's plight. Similarly, in *A North-Side View of Slavery,* slaves are depicted merely as white men with black skins, except when families are actually divided by sales or by individual slaves fleeing the South. Otherwise, family patterns and values are unaffected by the strictures of slavery. No relevance is given to an African heritage.

Historians continue to reexamine the extent to which slave families existed and how they were structured where they did exist. Evidence suggests both a greater degree of family stability than previously believed, and also the presence of slave families resembling many nineteenth-century white families. Family stability also appears evident in both the predominantly patriarchal and community-structured slave relationships.[21] *A North-Side*

View of Slavery, nevertheless, remains suspect in recording a high percentage of slave marriages; neither variety nor complexity characterizes Drew's account of slave families. Largely absent are indications of slave families' matriarchal configurations. Either Drew deliberately or unconsciously shaped the fugitives' testimony to accommodate white values about marriage and family stability, or when faced by the complexity of slave family relationships, he simplified them and thereby distorted the testimony by making all slave families correspond to the norms of nineteenth-century white society. Perhaps the fugitives themselves similarly sought to meet these standards when relating their stories. (Exiles, of course, often are nostalgic for a type of stability that they never possessed.) Although some slaves undoubtedly had become fugitives when family units were threatened by sale of their members, it is unlikely that only the faithful family men escaped to Canada. And while some intermarriage with white Canadian women actually occurred once fugitives had settled there, Drew's lack of candor about such matters is forcefully illustrated by his silence regarding racial intermarriage and by his discussion of miscegenation solely in relation to southern slavery (and then exclusively between black women and white men), not in the context of freedom.[22]

A *North-Side View of Slavery* is also silent about the issue of political equality for the free African American. Fugitives eloquently attack various forms of racial discrimination, especially school segregation in Canada, but are mute about whether they are voting or wish to do so in the future. In reality, fugitives were voting in local Canadian elections and achieving some success in placing in office candidates sympathetic to their cause.[23] Again, Drew avoided an issue that would disturb many northerners.

While there is much that is distinctive and valuable in *A North-Side View of Slavery,* particularly the description of life in Canada (not exclusively accounts of slavery and the escape from it), Drew's technique generally followed the pattern of previous fugitive slave narratives. The reader expecting incidents of suspenseful flights from slavery was not disappointed. Rubbing a red onion on the soles of shoes to kill the scent for pursuing hounds ranks high on a list of ingenious devices previously known. But most evident, even overwhelming, is the sheer quantity of cruelty endured by the southern slave. If this era's sensitivity to tales about whipped and shackled slaves may in time have become dulled by repetition and by charges of exaggeration, Drew's book provided a chilling return to reality. There is nothing abstract about the sadism and barbarism of slavery in this account. Especially to readers nurtured on delicate Victorian novels and family magazines, the slave narrative at times must have seemed prurient. Witness the scene depicted by Drew of a slave woman being forced to bend over, lay her head on a basket of cotton, and have her tunic raised to hide her face before being whipped by the white overseer. And there is the slave forced to get out of his wife's bed to allow his owner to take his place.[24] Ironically and unfortunately, Drew chose to follow the pattern of previous slave narratives by transmuting the language of the fugitive into educated prose. Selected for the task partly because of his interest in folk language and folk wit, he nevertheless failed to record African American imagery and dialect. Perhaps his desire for clarity and the poignancy of what he heard and saw in Canada moved Drew to try to avoid nuances and humor in his account. The starkness of the prose does result in a powerful and credible book, but it could have been a richer one.

John P. Jewett and Company first announced publication of *A North-Side View of Slavery* in the *Liberator* of November 16, 1855. Also included in the nine-inch-high advertisement was a notice of *An Inside View of Slavery; or a Tour Among the Planters* by Dr. Charles G. Parsons, with an introduction by Harriet Beecher Stowe. Jewett and Company was simultaneously attacking Nehemiah Adams' *A South-Side View of Slavery* and defending *Uncle Tom's Cabin* by publishing Drew's slave testimony and Parsons' views of the slave-owner. The advertisement declared: "These volumes are not works of fiction, or stories of the imagination, but true records of what these intelligent travelers . . ." saw and heard. It noted that Drew traveled from town to town, from cabin to cabin, recording the statements of fugitive slaves.

> He has given them to the world, nearly verbatim, in this soul stirring volume. Men and Women of America! you may learn much, if you will, from these THIRTY THOUSAND CANADIAN SLAVES. They can take you behind the curtain and tell you the practical workings of the slave system—*the beautiful, Christian, Democratic institution of America*, which finds so many apologists and defenders.

The publisher asked one thousand antislavery advocates to see to it that both books would be "placed in the hands of every intelligent reader." The cost of *A North-Side View of Slavery* was one dollar, postage included.

The *Liberator* commended this "highly interesting work" and devoted three columns to the publication of the entire account by John Holmes, the longest and one of the most pointed statements in the book: "I was black, but I had the feelings of a man as well as any man." Several weeks later (the advertisement ran for nine weeks), a letter from the Reverend Hiram Wilson of St. Catharines appeared in the newspaper, declaring that the book was "perfectly reliable" because it had tapped the "solid matter of experience" of Canadian fugitive slaves.[25]

The appearance of *A North-Side View of Slavery* can be viewed as a watershed in the methods and concerns of American antislavery advocates. The culmination of the innumerable fugitive slave autobiographies that preceded it, the book portrays the results of years of effort to provide freedom for the slave in Canada. It was written in response to the antislavery crisis caused by the discouraging events of 1854 and the fear that the slave power might forever hold the initiative in the battle over abolitionism. But the events during the year were to stimulate other antislavery action, not stifle it. The emergence in 1854 of the Republican Party, which initially opposed slavery only in the territories, eventually would reshape politics and the nation itself. The Kansas–Nebraska Bill would not end antislavery agitation but would move militant northerners to send arms to Kansas in the fight against proslavery forces. And soon another northerner would go to Canada to speak with fugitive slaves. But unlike Benjamin Drew, John Brown would visit Chatham, Buxton, and Hamilton, all in Canada West, to recruit African Americans for his raid on Harpers Ferry.[26] More immediately, the increased public repugnance to the Fugitive Slave Law generated by the government's success in returning Anthony Burns to slavery ended attempts to enforce that law in Boston. A federal marshal, attempting to seize a fugitive slave in Worcester, Massachusetts, was assaulted by an antislavery mob and forcibly driven out of town. One militant Worcester abolitionist minister exhorted his congregation: "No longer conceal Fugitives and help them on, but show them and defend them. Let the Underground Railroad stop here . . . ! *Hear O Richmond! And give ear Old Caroline! Henceforth Worcester is Canada to the Slave!*"[27]

A North-Side View of Slavery looked to the future to the extent that it provided evidence for those concerned with the African American's eventual emancipation, economic opportunity, and racial integration. Less visible are some of the obstacles to realizing these goals. A revealing sequel to Drew's book appeared in 1864 when the American Freedmen's Inquiry Commission issued its Canadian report. Secretary of War Edwin M. Stanton had appointed the Commission, which included Benjamin Drew, soon after the Emancipation Proclamation. The Commission was empowered to investigate the conditions of emancipated African Americans in order to suggest what measures would "best contribute to their protection and improvement. . . ." Stanton had chosen Samuel Gridley Howe, Robert Dale Owen, and Colonel James McKaye to head the Commission because they were all antislavery men and could be expected to view the problem sympathetically. McKaye, who did most of the work, had visited freedmen in the South and issued a report before investigating the Canadian situation.[28] The resulting *Refugees from Slavery in Canada West* illuminated both those themes that Drew had stressed and those he had omitted.

Like Drew, McKaye noted that Canadian blacks were earning a living, accumulating property, and maintaining stable marriages. "Sober, industrious, and thrifty," they had proved themselves capable of living in freedom. African Americans needed emancipation and legal protection—not charity or guardianship. Segregated schools and segregated neighborhoods were bad because they were inferior to integrated ones and only served to increase white racial prejudice.[29] McKaye, who had studied *A North-Side View of Slavery* and interviewed some of the same people, agreed with many of

Drew's observations. Writing, however, near the end of the Civil War, when four million slaves were likely to be freed, he was even more concerned than Drew about their eventual migration to the northern United States and how this would influence post-war reconstruction policies. He was especially apprehensive about miscegenation. Observing that the Canadian fugitives were "for the most part hybrids," McKaye blamed this fact primarily on slave-breeding in the South. But he used terminology indicating that he viewed miscegenation as pathological to predict the impact of the shortage of African American women in Canada: "Natural tastes and dispositions, unduly thwarted, are perverted into morbid and monstrous passions— if uncultured black men cannot find black mates, they will find white ones. . . ."[30] Seeking to allay fears of white northerners about the future, McKaye asserted that mulattoes, unfavorably affected by cold climates, were infertile, and likely to "decrease and disappear in a few generations." They were physically weaker, he claimed, than pure-blooded African Americans. The latter's greater ferocity would abate, McKaye assured all Americans, once the black man inevitably returned to his "natural" home—the tropical South. The North, therefore, need not expect black paupers, racial inter-marriage, or aggressive black men. (By 1871, some 40,000 fugitive slaves were reduced to fewer than 15,000 by migration from Canada West.)[31]

Granting some weaknesses, *A North-Side View of Slavery* remains a com-prehensive antebellum account of slavery's impact upon African Americans. And it is an invaluable depiction of fugitive life in the North and in Canada. Only Theodore Weld's *American Slavery As It Is* (1839), which heavily relied for evidence on advertisements for runaway slaves in southern newspapers, is comparable in documenting slave conditions. The abundance of testimony Drew gathered is later rivaled only by James Redpath's 1859 book, *The Roving Editor, or Talking With Slaves in the Southern States. A North-Side of Slavery* also provides an essential comparative source for utilizing the mam-moth 1930s WPA project, which interviewed former slaves; a large portion was published in 1972 and edited by George P. Rawick in *The American Slave: A Composite Autobiography.* Drew's book remains sufficiently sophis-ticated and multi-dimensional to refute past and present critics of the aboli-tionists who have charged them with a simplistic view of the South's "pecu-liar institution."

T.G.E.

NOTES

1. Sketches of Drew are in obituaries in the following newspapers: *Old Colony Memorial*, Plymouth, Massachusetts, July 25, 1903; Boston *Globe*, July 20, 1903; Boston *Evening Transcript*, July 21, 1903. Also see William T. Davis, *Memories of an Octogenarian*, Plymouth, 1906, pp. 291–293. Accounts of *The Carpet Bag* are in James T. Trowbridge, *My Own Story*, Boston, 1903, pp. 179–187, and in Cyrus Clemens, *Shillaber*, London, 1946, p. 83.

2. Davis, *Memories*, p. 230. After his book's publication, Benjamin Drew returned to teach in Boston and later moved to St. Paul, Minnesota where he became Superintendent of Schools. Subsequently, he was employed as a proofreader for various publishers, including Harvard University Press. He also was a proofreader in Washington, D. C. for the Government Printing Office. Considered an authority on typography, he published a manual, *Pens and Types*, Boston, 1891. His last book, *Burial Hill, Plymouth Massachusetts*, Plymouth, 1894, was a compilation of inscriptions and epitaphs found on the monuments and gravestones in the Plymouth cemetery. He died in 1903 at age 91.

3. Wendell Phillips Garrison and Francis Jackson Garrison, *William Lloyd Garrison*, Boston, 1885, II, 133; Nehemiah Adams, *A South-Side View of Slavery; or Three Months at South in 1854*, Boston, 1854, p. 9.

4. Ibid., p. 141.

5. Ibid., pp. 25, 48, 89, 99, 118.

6. Ibid., pp. 160, 165. Also see pp. 158–179.

7. Ibid., p. 200. Among the rebuttals are: John W. Page, *Uncle Robin in His Cabin in Virginia and Tom Without One in Boston*, Richmond, 1853; Mrs. Mary H. Eastman, *Aunt Phillis's Cabin; or Southern Life As It Is*, Philadelphia, 1852; Charles Jacobs Peterson, *The Cabin and Parlor; or Slaves and Masters*, Philadelphia, 1852.

8. *Liberator*, Jan. 12, 1855. *Liberator* (Sept. 22, 1854) printed an exchange of letters between Virginia's Governor Henry Wise and the Reverend Mr. Adams in which the minister again urged cooperation between North and South to reform some features of slavery. Wise responded that slave ownership was a fundamental property right immune from northern interference; the foreign slave trade should cease to be prohibited by the federal government. Southern slavery, the governor conceded, might end through colonization to Africa in about two centuries. On the other hand, Benjamin Drew called for the constitutional abolition of slavery and defiance of the law until this occurred: *A North-Side View of Slavery*, pp. 10, 11, 13.

9. Richmond, 1854, p. 240.

10. Samuel Shapiro, "The Rendition of Anthony Burns," *Journal of Negro History*, XLIV, Jan. 1959, pp. 34–51.

11. Robin W. Winks, "A Sacred Animosity: Abolitionism in Canada," *The Antislavery Vanguard*, Ed. Martin B. Duberman, Princeton, 1965, pp. 301–303; John Hope Franklin, *From Slavery to Freedom*, New York, 1967, pp. 363–370; Jason H. Silverman, *Unwelcome Guests: Canada West's Response to Fugitive Slaves, 1800–1865*, Millwood, 1985.

12. Dwight Dumond, *Antislavery: The Crusade for Freedom*, Ann Arbor, 1961, pp. 335–336; Drew, p. v.

13. Leon Litwack, *North of Slavery: The Negro in the Free States, 1790–1860*, Chicago, 1961, pp. 70, 72, 73, 75, 79, 92, 93.

14. Boston *Evening Transcript*, July 21, 1903.

15. Drew, pp. 18, 238; William H. and Jane H. Pease, *Black Utopia: Negro Communal Experiments in America*, Madison, 1963, pp. 14, 64.

16. Drew, p. vii; Pease and Pease, pp. 84–86.

17. Louis Filler, *The Crusade Against Slavery*, New York, 1960, pp. 20–22, 61–62; Thomas A. Bailey, *A Diplomatic History of the American People*, New York, 1950, p. 27; David Herbert Donald, *Charles Sumner and the Coming of the Civil War*, New York, 1960, p. 367.

18. U. B. Phillips, who reflects this skepticism about the authenticity of the ex-slave narratives, has become one of the few twentieth-

century historians of slavery not employing Drew's book as a
source. See *Life and Labor in the Old South, Boston,* 1929, p. 219.
The best defense of the historical use of fugitive slave accounts is
John W. Blassingame, *The Slave Community: Plantation Life in the
Antebellum South,* New York, 1979, pp. 370–376.

19. Drew, p. vi.

20. Kenneth Stampp, *The Peculiar Institution: Slavery in the
    Ante-Bellum South,* New York, 1956, pp. 150, 198, 346–347.

21. George P. Rawick, *The American Slave: From Sundown to Sunup,*
    Westport, 1972, pp. 9, 89–93; Eugene D. Genovese, *Roll, Jordan
    Roll: The World the Slaves Made,* New York, pp. 482–494, Herbert
    G. Gutman, *The Black Family in Slavery and Freedom,* 1750–1925,
    New York, 1977, pp. 461–463.

22. Stampp, pp. 112, 343; S. G. Howe, *The Refugees from Slavery in
    Canada West,* Boston, 1864, p. 29; Drew, pp. 351–352.

23. Drew, pp. 137, 159, 247, 306, 313, 347; Winks, "Abolitionism in
    Canada," pp. 316–319.

24. Drew, pp. 64, 141, 162.

25. *Liberator,* Nov. 23, 1855, Jan. 11, 1858; Drew, pp. 198–223.

26. Oswald Garrison Villard, *John Brown: A Biography After Fifty
    Years,* Boston, 1910, pp. 327–328.

27. Worcester *Spy,* Nov. 30, 1854; Thomas Wentworth Higginson,
    Massachusetts in Mourning, Boston, 1854. For a discussion of mil-
    itant abolitionism, see Tilden G. Edelstein, *Strange Enthusiasm: A
    Life of Thomas Wentworth Higginson,* New Haven, 1968.

28. Silverman, p. 75; Willie Lee Rose, *Rehearsal for Reconstruction: The
    Port Royal Experiment,* Indianapolis, 1964, pp. 208–209; James M.
    McPherson, *The Struggle for Equality: Abolitionists and the Negro
    in the Civil War and Reconstruction,* Princeton, 1964, pp. 182–186.

29. Howe, *Refugees,* pp. 79, 94, 101–103.

30. Ibid., pp. 18, 29, 101.

31. Howe, *Refugees,* pp. 25–27, 57, 101, 103; Silverman, p. 159.

A NORTH-SIDE VIEW OF SLAVERY

THE REFUGEE:

OR THE

NARRATIVES OF FUGITIVE SLAVES IN CANADA

RELATED BY THEMSELVES

WITH

AN ACCOUNT OF THE HISTORY AND CONDITION OF THE
COLORED POPULATION OF UPPER CANADA

BY

BENJAMIN DREW

BOSTON:
PUBLISHED BY JOHN P. JEWETT AND COMPANY
CLEVELAND, OHIO:
JEWETT, PROCTOR AND WORTHINGTON
NEW YORK: SHELDON, LAMPORT AND BLAKEMAN.
LONDON: TRÜBNER AND CO.
1856

PUBLISHERS' ADVERTISEMENT

The work here offered to the public will be found, we venture to say, one of the most instructive and interesting that has yet appeared on the subject of American Slavery. It is original in design and scope, and has been executed with the most conscientious care and fidelity. The author is a gentleman of high character, whose statements may be implicitly relied upon, and whose intelligence is not likely to have been deceived. As for the statements of the Fugitives from Slavery, they speak for themselves. Nowhere else can be found such a mass of direct and unimpeachable testimony as to the true character of the Peculiar Institution, by witnesses who have had the best opportunities of knowing its nature, and who occupy a point of view from which its characteristic lineaments can be most distinctly discerned.

We are confident that "A North-side View of Slavery" will prove to be not only one of the most effective Anti-slavery arguments ever issued from the press, but a valuable and permanent contribution to American Literature.

JOHN P. JEWETT & CO.

AUTHOR'S PREFACE

The colored population of Upper Canada, was estimated in the First
Report of the Anti-Slavery Society of Canada, in 1852, at thirty
thousand. Of this large number, nearly all the adults, and many of
the children, have been fugitive slaves from the United States; it is,
therefore, natural that the citizens of this Republic should feel an
interest in their fate and fortunes. Many causes, however, have
hitherto prevented the public generally from knowing their exact
condition and circumstances. Their enemies, the supporters of
slavery, have represented them as "indolent, vicious, and debased;
suffering and starving, because they have no kind masters to do the
thinking for them, and to urge them to the necessary labor, which
their own laziness and want of forecast, lead them to avoid." Some
of their friends, anxious to obtain aid for the comparatively few in
number, (perhaps three thousand in all,) who have actually stood in
need of assistance, have not, in all cases, been sufficiently discrimina-
ting in their statements: old settlers and new, the rich and the poor,
the good and the bad, have suffered alike from imputations of
poverty and starvation—misfortunes, which, if resulting from idleness, are akin to crimes. Still another set of men, selfish in purpose,
have, while pretending to act for the fugitives, found a way to the
purses of the sympathetic, and appropriated to their own use, funds
intended for supposititious sufferers.

Such being the state of the case, it may relieve some minds from
doubt and perplexity, to hear from the refugees themselves, their
own opinions of their condition and their wants. These will be found
among the narratives which occupy the greater part of the present
volume.

Further, the personal experiences of the colored Canadians, while
held in bondage in their native land, shed a peculiar lustre on the
Institution of the South. They reveal the hideousness of the sin,

which, while calling on the North to fall down and worship it, almost equals the tempter himself in the felicity of scriptural quotations.

The narratives were gathered promiscuously from persons whom the author met with in the course of a tour through the cities and settlements of Canada West. While his informants talked, the author wrote: nor are there in the whole volume a dozen verbal alterations which were not made at the moment of writing, while in haste to make the pen become a tongue for the dumb.

Many who furnished interesting anecdotes and personal histories may, perhaps, feel some disappointment because their contributions are omitted in the present work. But to publish the whole, would far transcend the limits of a single volume. The manuscripts, however, are in safe-keeping, and will, in all probability, be given to the world on some future occasion.

For the real names which appear in the manuscripts of the narratives published, it has been deemed advisable, with few exceptions, that letters should be substituted.

To those persons mentioned in the course of the work as having given him assistance and aid, the author acknowledes his obligations: and he feels, likewise, that his thanks are due to Thomas Henning, Esq., Secretary of the Anti-Slavery Society of Canada; F. G. Simpson, Esq., Agent of the same Society, and S. Walton, Esq., of Toronto; John Doyle, Esq. City Clerk, London; Rev. Mr. Peyden, of Hamilton; Rev. William King, Buxton; John Hatfield, Esq., Amherstburg; John Fairfield, Esq., Canada West.

Boston, 1855.

INTRODUCTION

When in any State, the oppression of the laboring portion of the community amounts to an entire deprivation of their civil and personal rights; when it assumes to control their wills, to assign them tasks, to reap the rewards of their labor, and to punish with bodily tortures the least infraction of its mandates, it is obvious that the class so overwhelmed with injustice, are necessarily, unless prevented by ignorance from knowing their rights and their wrongs, the enemies of the government. To them, insurrection and rebellion are primary, original duties. If successfully thwarted in the performance of these, emigration suggests itself as the next means of escaping the evils under which they groan. From the exercise of this right, they can only be restrained by fear and force. These, however, will sometimes be found inadequate to hold in check the natural desire of liberty. Many, in spite of all opposition, in the face of torture and death, will seek an asylum in foreign lands, and reveal to the ears of pitying indignation, the secrets of the prisonhouse.

The escape of slaves forms the most irritating subject of discussion between the North and the South.

If on this, as on all other evils connected with or growing out of slavery, a common man of plain common sense, were asked his opinion, he would probably say—"remove the cause and the effects will cease; remove the oppression which induces to emigration, and a fugitive slave will be an impossibility." But this "would only excite a smile at the South." How mistaken is common sense!

The South are taking measures, (when was it otherwise?) to preserve, extend, and perpetuate slavery. The problem must be solved, if solved at all, without the oppression being removed.

By the combined influence of ignorance and fear, the amount of emigration has been reduced to a minimum. We could wish the South would adopt a mode of reasoning sometimes presented to us,—

something of this sort;—in all kinds of business, losses are inevitable. Men at the North lose by fall of stocks, by consignments, by fires, and in a great variety of ways. If a Yankee loses a ship worth twenty thousand dollars, he does not expend one hundred thousand in endeavoring to fish it up. He simply enters it in his account of profit and loss. And if a slave runs away, we might as well make the same entry quietly, as to wound the feelings and sensibilities of our northern friends; magnifying and increasing "the deep sectional difference of inborn feeling;" and filling whole cities with grief, shame, and an indignation irrepressible, except by marines and detachments of artillery.

Meanwhile the fugitive slave law continues to be enforced.

Gloss the matter over as much as we may, and take "south-side views" through a multiplying glass,—yet we must admit, that the slave's is a cruel lot.

We may compare King James's or the Douay Bible with the Hebrew and the Septuagint; we may find there, and in all recensions, polyglotts, and translations extant, the history of Abraham and Hagar,—yet we must allow, that an American slave, in his best estate, is a man badly educated, and systematically ill used.

We may study the New Testament and become conversant with the proceedings of Paul in regard to Onesimus; we may wade through the commentaries of pro-slavery and anti-slavery writers thereupon,—yet the truth will remain, that an American slave is deemed "a chattel personal,"—"the property of a master to whom he belongs,"—that he is liable to be flogged, sold, and divorced, as the interest, caprice, or spite of his master may dictate.

It may possibly be the case that the denunciatory language which the South has used in speaking of abolitionists, may have "irritated" them, and that, under this irritation, they have manifested more zeal in the cause of emancipation, than they would otherwise have done. Still we deem it undeniable, that if there is any situation on earth in which a man can be placed, which should stir up from its depths, the most active sympathies of the human heart, it is the deplorable situation of an American slave.

If these things are so, how can it be wrong to assist a slave who is making his escape? Surely, to aid the unfortunate is a duty, which no power on earth can legislate into a crime.

But at this late day, the question is forced upon us, whether it is an unfortunate thing for a man to be a slave? This "excites a smile" at the North,—but as this book is destined to be read at the South as well as at the North, we will examine the question a little.

Slavery, we are told, has its bright as well as its dark parts. In southern cities, there is good order, the streets are quiet in the night, and there is an absence of mobs. In that portion of southern society which is under the highest cultivation, the slaves smile, laugh, are happy,—one must see that they are happy. Religion has gained a wonderful ascendency among the colored people. The number of communicants among them is very large. "The only difference between them and us, as to religious instruction is, they cannot generally read." "As responsibility, anxiety about the present and future, are the chief enemies to cheerfulness, and, among mental causes, to health, it is obvious that if one can have all his present wants supplied, with no care about short crops, the markets, notes payable, bills due, be relieved from the necessity of planning and contriving, all the hard thinking being done for him by another, while useful and honorable employment fills his thoughts and hands, he is so far in a situation favorable to great comfort, which will show itself in his whole outer man. Some will say, 'This is the lowest kind of happiness.' Yet it is all that a large portion of the race seek for; and few, except slaves, obtain it." "If the colored people of Savannah, Columbia, and Richmond, are not, as a whole, a happy people, I," says the reverend author from whom we quote, "have never seen any." We are told, indeed, that "Cases illustrating the opposite of almost every agreeable statement now made could also be multiplied; still the things just described are as represented, and he is not in a healthful state of mind, who cannot appreciate them. Our error has been in mixing the dark and bright parts of slavery together. This is wrong. We should never lose sight of distinct moral qualities in character, as we do of different colors in mixing paint. Let us judge slavery in this manner; let us keep her different qualities distinct—abhor that in her which is evil, rejoice in that which is good."

Damocles sits at the royal banquet, surrounded with gold and silver plate; the table is loaded with delicacies of every kind. "Happy fellow that Damocles," says Mr. South, "he is in a broad laugh!"

"Yes;" answers Mr. North, "but look—do you not see that glittering sword hanging over his head by a single hair?"

"Never mind the sword,—you are mixing together the bright and the dark. This is wrong. Let us, at present, consider only the dinner. What splendid fare! Judging from the gold and silver plate, from the chaplets of roses, from the handsome pages about him, from the mingled flavors of the roast and the boiled, and from the appetite of Damocles himself, one must see that he is a happy man."

"If he is happy it is either because he is ignorant of his condition,—or knowing 'the day of trouble and of treading down,' he has adopted the philosophy spoken of by the prophet, 'let us eat and drink, for tomorrow we shall die.' As happy as Damocles appears, there is the sword,—who would want a good dinner with such an accompaniment?"

"You are wrong. The dinner is good—let us rejoice over that. Damocles fares well. It is a pity that the hungry, dirty, rascally, riotous Celts cannot have just such a dinner every day at the table of Dionysius. Now we will examine the sword a little—but let us handle it gingerly."

If slavery causes an "absence of mobs," let slavery have all due credit on that score. Give it joy that it prevented the destruction of Cassius M. Clay's press, the murder of Lovejoy, the expulsion of Judge Hoar, the lynching of Amos Dresser, and the thousand and one acts of violence and outrage which have caused some unreflecting men to deny that the South is tenanted by a civilized people: more recently that it prevented a mob of armed Missourians from interfering in the Kansas election, and spared the office of the Parkville Luminary. We presume that the absence of mobs of colored persons must have been intended.

A strong police must watch the motions of the oppressed—prevent them from meeting together unless some of the oppressors are present—keep them in their quarters at night, etc. This system of police usually answers its atrocious purpose very well. It wields the lash against offenders, and instils into the oppressed the fear requisite to suppress any overt act toward gaining their rights as human beings. Incidentally, it hinders the commission of crimes, prevents mobs [of colored persons], and keeps the streets quiet, and is so far beneficent in its action. Yet it cannot be denied that the cause of liberty in the world has been much indebted to mobs.

"Oppression driveth a wise man mad." The oppressed, then, must not be made wise. If they do not know that a laborer can be a free man, the thought of freedom for themselves will not, perhaps, enter their heads. If they can be *raised,* so ignorant as to believe that slavery is the proper and natural condition of their being,—that they cannot take care of themselves, they will probably, be contented with their lot. The more infantile their minds are suffered to remain, the less will they comprehend the absolute wretchedness of their estate; the less opportunity will they have to learn of lands where all are free,—the less capable will they be of putting forth exertion to resist oppression or to escape from it. The intention of the slaveholders in this respect, seems to be approximately realized. Unaware of the delights of mental cultivation, of the proper growth and expansion of the human soul many of the oppressed class will appear in good humor and often in a "broad laugh." The manhood of this portion of the sufferer has not, indeed, been "crushed out of them:"—it has never been developed. They are little children in every thing but bodily maturity. "The slaves in Savannah," says Patrick Snead, a fugitive slave from that city, "are poor, ignorant creatures,—*they don't know their condition.*"

A class of men retained in the lowest form of bondage, hopeless of any thing higher and better on earth,—at the best dividing their earnings with masters, but more often urged to hard and prolonged labor, through the influence of fear,—incapable of obtaining any degree of cultivation of dignity here below,—will be peculiarly interested in representations of a better life hereafter. A religion which insists on obedience to masters and mistresses, and which inculcates forgiveness of injuries, will find many teachers among those whose domestic cares lessen, and whose profits rise in proportion to the number of proselytes, and whose codes legalize the grossest wrongs: a faith which promises heavenly rewards to humility, obedience, and patience,—which admonishes him that is smitten on one cheek to turn the other also, will find many converts among those who are glad to escape a sense of their indignities and incessant humiliations, by believing that servility itself is a Christian grace. "Suppose a family [of slaves] bound to their master by affection and respect. Whatever he can make appear to their understandings and consciences to be right, he has as much power to enforce upon them as ever falls to the power of moral suasion." "If the numbers of pious slaves are an indication, it must be confessed that slave-owners, as a body, have performed their Christian duties to their slaves to a degree which the masters of free apprentices and the employers of free laborers have as yet hardly equalled." What knowledge the slaves have of the Scriptures is obtained by the ear, for "they are generally unable to read." While we would hope that many among the class of oppressors are faithful in proclaiming the whole counsel of God, it must be admitted that there is a strong temptation on the part of the masters to use the Scriptures mainly as an auxiliary to the overseer.

The South-side View of Slavery says, "The gospel which is preached to them [the slaves], so far as I heard it, is the same gospel which is preached to us." But the prayers of the slaves [p.54 and 55] and the hymns they selected, [p.55] Watts' Ps. 51, Hymns 139, B. I. and 90, B. II., seem to confirm the view we have presented; while the address of the superintendent of the colored Sabbath school, [p. 85] by no means contradicts it: nor does the hymn sung by slaves [p.212].

To magnify the benefits which incidentally and casually grow out of the system of slavery, and to represent them as vast enough to sink its direct enormities into comparative insignificance, is, as if a man were to point to an abundant harvest of corn, on the blood-enriched field of Waterloo, as a sufficient reason for involving the world in the horrors of war.

If, as we have said, the slave's lot is a cruel one,—if, in his best estate, the enslaved American is a man badly educated, and systematically ill-used,—if, by law he is "the property of a master to whom he belongs"—liable to be flogged, sold, and robbed of his wife and children, as the interest, or caprice, or spite of the master may dictate—it appears to us that to assist him if he endeavors to escape from bondage, is a binding duty which not all the constitutions, laws, and sophistries in Christendom can erect into a crime.

But before you render assistance, you should know "whom you are helping and for what reason he has fled." Perhaps he is running away to get rid of a scolding wife,—or he may be an ungrateful man,—nay, he may be a thief or a murderer.

And where am I to go for information on these points? To his pursuers? They will not tell me the truth. Patrick Snead, a fugitive from Savannah, as white as nine tenths of the men of the north, and not therefore "a fugitive *black* man," was arrested on a false charge of *murder*. Sims and Burns, both "*black* men," were kidnapped in

Boston on charges of *theft*. By taking the word of a pursuer, I may "plunge a shipmate into the jaws of a shark." Proceedings are "summary,"—and by the time I could obtain reliable intelligence, the fugitive might become the victim of an incensed tyrant, whose malice is protected by written atrocities denominated laws. In any particular case, the probabilities are, that the fugitive slave is an innocent man,—a wronged and suffering brother, to hear whose prayer it would be perilous for a Christian to refuse. But if, in one case out of a thousand, it should subsequently appear, that he had committed larceny, or had even "killed an Egyptian,"—it might quiet our consciences to reflect that in judging of a slave's guilt, allowances ought to be made for the peculiar privations and wrongs, incident to a slave's life, and on the score of the abject ignorance, to which he has been condemned by an unjust law,—that if the same crime had been perpetrated by a white man, in order to effect his escape from wrongful captivity among Patagonians or Arabs, he would be acquitted both in conscience and law,—and that it were better to aid ten, nay, ten thousand poor, unenlightened, uninstructed creatures to escape hanging, than to incur the tremendous responsibility of consigning an innocent man to a doom worse than death itself.

But even in cases where the fugitives bring proof that they are fleeing from brutal treatment, "no rule was ever made that could determine a man's duty." We must "return to the Constitution!" Return to the gospel, rather. "Lord when saw we thee, *a stranger,* and did not minister unto thee? Then shall he answer them, saying, Verily, I say unto you, Inasmuch as ye did it not to one of the least of these ye did it not to me." Could not an ingenious clergyman manage to construct from this passage a rule to determine a man's duty in case of a fugitive stranger? To suppose that one on the left hand might urge in reply, "Lord, the least of thy brethren came to my door, hungered, and athirst, a stranger, and naked; it offended my moral sense to have him taken back to involuntary servitude: but there were other interests for moral sense to be concerned about besides those of a fugitive black man. I lived in a Union, under a Constitution, which contained a 'simple provision' that he must be delivered up,—and there was a law of the land, which made it penal to minister to thy brother,—and I chose to obey man, rather than to obey God, therefore place me among the sheep." To suppose that this might be urged in reply, were taking a south-side view of the day of judgment.

A certain man on his way from Jerusalem to Jericho "fell among thieves which stripped him of his raiment, and wounded him, and departed, leaving him half dead." Leaving *him!* They were quite merciful compared with slave-hunters,—these take man and all. The priest and the Levite saw him but had no compassion on him,— perhaps they wanted to know whom they were helping, before they lent their aid,—or perhaps they had constitutional scruples. But a certain Samaritan put him on his own beast, and brought him to an inn. "Which now of these three, thinkest thou, was neighbor unto him that fell among the thieves? And he said, *he that showed mercy on him.* Then said Jesus unto him, *Go, and do thou likewise.*" This is in illustration of the LAW, "Thou shalt love thy neighbor as thyself,"—a LAW rather "HIGHER" than the Blue Ridge, or the Black Code: and considering the source from which it emanated, possibly somewhat higher than any form of Constitution in any human government whatever: nay, than that embodiment of American civilization, that flower of human wisdom, that rarest union of exact justice and gentle mercy, the unconstitutional fugitive slave law. But until the "law of the land" is repealed, all appeals to a "higher law" are "fanaticism!" Let us strive to amend the Constitution, and to repeal the obnoxious statute,—for Constitution, and laws, and the Republic itself must come to nought, if the people subscribe to the doctrine, that the enactments of man, however unjust and abominable, are paramount to the merciful laws of the Most High God.

But with whatever tint of words oppression may be decked: with what zeal soever it may strive to bring a clean thing out of an unclean, and to prove that ignorance and degradation and man-chattelism are productive of happiness to their victims, and pregnant with some immense good in some unknown way to Africa, and to those persons in this country having less or more African blood, and who are of all shades and colors, "from snowy white to sooty;" it is a positive fact, that many thousands have fled from the "happiness" of southern servitude, and found freedom in Canada. From the ties of a common humanity and a common nationality, we feel a deep interest in those exiled men. Why have they left a government which acknowledges that "all men are born free and equal," and given their allegiance to another which does not recognize so democratic a doctrine? What circumstances have led them to prefer a monarchy to a *republic?* Why have they exchanged the genial clime of the south for a realm where winter holds half the year? Why have they abandoned friends and kindred, kind masters and mistresses who were willing to take care of them, [wives, children, and home, we would add, were it not that the idea would "excite a smile at the South"] to live a life of exile among strangers? What are their views of the patriarchal institution? Which condition do they find best suited to the African race, or rather to a race partly African, partly Saxon,—slavery or freedom? Should a contest with England arise, would they enlist under the cross of St. George, or under our stars—and stripes? What is their present condition? What are their prospects for the future?

These and similar questions can be most satisfactorily answered by the refugees themselves.

The history of their sufferings and their wrongs, of their bondage and their escape, may excite in some heart hitherto unmoved a glow of sympathy for our colored brother, yet fraudulently deprived of his birthright,—it may furnish the true friends of our country,—the friends of liberty and equal rights,—additional means toward over-throwing the slave power; that scandalous aristocracy which has hitherto been allowed to a great extent to sway the destinies of our nation.

The opinions and views of those who have been held in bondage in the United States may enable us to obtain a clearer insight into the nature of American slavery,—may prompt us to perform more energetically than hitherto, our duties to the oppressor and the oppressed,—to the North and to the South,—to the national government, and to the State in which we dwell.

The writer of these pages intends to visit those Americans who have fled from the North and the South into Upper Canada to escape the oppression exercised upon them by their native countrymen. He will assure them that they have the sympathies of many friends in the United States, and advise them that their good conduct and success in life may have an important bearing on the destinies of millions of their brethren, colored and white, in this country, who have the misfortune to be descended from slave mothers. He will endeavor to collect, with a view to placing their testimony on record, their experiences of actual workings of slavery—what experience they have had of the condition of liberty—and such statements generally as they may be inclined to make, bearing upon the weighty subjects of oppression and freedom.

Objections may be urged to the testimony of the refugees on the score of their ignorance. We may naturally expect errors and mistakes in regard to dates, ages, proceedings at law, and other matters to know which would require an amount of information not vouchsafed to American slaves. But errors of this sort are of secondary consequence, and should rather be imputed to those who have from interest or necessity (the tyrant's plea) placed their candle under a bushel, that it might not give light to all who were in their house. With this qualification there appears to be no reason why the statements of the colored Canadians should not be received as readily as any human testimony whatever.

If verbal alterations are required care will be taken to preserve the meaning: and if any portion of the narrative is found to trench upon affairs having no connection with slavery, or is likely to involve any good Samaritan in trouble, it will receive no other attention from the writer than to be studiously omitted.

And now we will make the best of our way to Canada. From that point let us survey the institution which entails many "domestic evils deplored by the whites,"—which "impoverishes a State,"—"stays the development of its natural resources,"—is "a great curse"—"a blot on our holy religion,"—"a curse in all its relations of master and servant," exerting a "bad influence," says a slaveholder, "upon our passions, upon our children, destroying that sense of moral responsibility which ought to bear upon us:" and let us indulge a hope that the cause of emancipation may receive a new impulse from a North-Side View of Slavery.

ST. CATHARINES

Refuge! Refuge for the oppressed! Refuge for Americans escaping from abuse and cruel bondage in their native land! Refuge for my countrymen from the lash of the overseer, from the hounds and guns of southern man-hunters, from the clutches of northern marshals and commissioners! Rest! Rest for the hunted slave! Rest for the travel-soiled and foot-sore fugitive.

Refuge and Rest! These are the first ideas which arise in my mind in connection with the town of St. Catharines.

I might mention here its pleasant situation, its commercial advantages, the Welland Canal, its telegraphic wires, its railroads, its famous mineral springs, and other matters interesting to the tourist; but we will step aside from these, and look at St. Catharines as the peaceful home of hundreds of the colored race.

Of the population of about six thousand, it is estimated that eight hundred are of African descent. Nearly all the adult colored people have at some time been slaves.

The name, too, of a distinguished, self-denying philanthropist comes into my mind with the recollection of St. Catharines, the Rev. Hiram Wilson. With him the refugee finds a welcome and a home; the poor stranger is pointed by him to the means of honorable self-support, and from him receives wise counsel and religious instruction. The lady of Mr. Wilson warmly seconds his benevolent exertions. The wayfarer, however forlorn, degraded, or repulsive even, shares her hospitality, and is refreshed by her words of kindness and her cheerful smile.

I have seen the negro—the fugitive slave, wearied with his thousand miles of travelling by night, without suitable shelter meanwhile for rest by day, who had trodden the roughest and most unfrequented ways, fearing, with too much cause, an enemy in every human being who had crossed his path; I have seen such arrive at Mr. Wilson's, bringing with him the subdued look, the air of sufferance, the furtive glance bespeaking dread, and deprecating punishment; I have seen such waited on by Mr. and Mrs. Wilson, fed and clothed, and cheered, and cared for. Such ministrations give a title to true greatness, a title recognized by Divine wisdom, and deriving its authority from revelation itself: "Whosoever would be great among you, let him be your minister."

The houses occupied by the colored people are neat and plain without; tidy and comfortable within. Through the kindness of Mr. Wilson and other friends, I was enabled to visit many families, and was invariably received with courtesy and kindness. Such narratives and statements as I received in St. Catharines, it is now my purpose to spread before the reader.

JAMES ADAMS

I was raised in Virginia, about twenty miles above the mouth of the Big Kanawha. At the age of seventeen, I set out to seek freedom in company with Benjamin Harris, (who was a cousin of mine,) and a woman and four children. I was young, and they had not treated me very badly; but I had seen older men treated worse than a horse or a hog ought to be treated; so, seeing what I was coming to, I wished to get away. My father being overseer, I was not used so badly as some even younger than myself, who were kicked, cuffed, and whipped very badly for little or nothing. We started away at night, on the 12th of August 1824. After we had crossed the river, alarm was given, and my father came down where we had crossed, and called to me to come back. I had not told my intention to either my father or mother. I made no answer at all, but we walked three miles back from the river, where we lay concealed in the woods four days. The nights we passed at the house of a white friend; a friend indeed. We set out on a Monday night, and on the night following, seven more of my fellow-servants started on the same race. They were overtaken on Wednesday night, while they were in a house on the Ohio side. One jumped from a window and broke his arm; he stayed in the woods some days, and then he returned. The other six, two women and four children, were carried back, and the man we stopped with told us that the two women were whipped to make them tell where we were, so they could come upon us. They told their master as near as they could. On Thursday five white men came to the house where we had been concealed, but we were then in the woods and mountains, three miles from the friend's house. Every evening, between three and four o'clock, he would come and bring us food. We had nothing to give him—it was the hand of Divine Providence made him do it. He and others on the river see so much abuse of colored people that they pity them, and so are ready to give them aid; at least it was so then. He told the white men he knew nothing about us, and nothing of the kind. They searched his premises, and then left, believing his story. He came to us and said, "Boys, we are betrayed, they are coming now round the hill after us." We picked up our bundles and started on a run; then he called us back, and said he did it to try our *spunk.* He then told us of those who were carried back, and of the searching of his premises. We lodged in his barn that night. On the morning of Friday, he took us twelve miles to a place where the woman would have to leave her children, because he could conceal her better without them. He pointed out a house occupied by a family of Methodists, where she could go and tell them she was going back, and so leave her children there. But when she reached the house the father and mother were absent, so she went at a venture to another house. As it was raining and dark, she was guided by a white boy, a stout lad, and a girl with a lantern. At this house, she slept on a pallet on the floor; and when all else were asleep, she put her baby, which she had all along kept in her arms, into her oldest boy's care, crept to the door and went out. We had bidden her good-by, not expecting to see her. When the boy and girl had come back from guiding her, I heard the boy say, "Now we shall get fifty dollars for giving her up, and she'll get a good fleecing into the bargain." The man where we had stopped intended to take her to his house after she had got rid of her children, and when opportunity offered, send her to Canada. We went to a fire which we saw burning in a clearing, and Ben slept while I kept watch. Presently the woman came towards us. I heard the cracking of sticks as she came, and awoke Ben. He raised a sort of tomahawk he had made, intending to strike the person approaching, supposing it was an enemy. Said she, "Oh Ben, don't strike me, it is I." This made me cry to think Ben was so near killing the woman. Then she begged us not to leave her until the man should come to

find her. He not coming so soon as we expected, we all steered back
the twelve miles through the woods. Towards night, we heard his
cow-bells; we drove the cattle before us, knowing that they would go
home. Just as they had guided us there, the man, who had also
followed the bells, came up. He told us that the children had been
carried back to their master. We supposed the boy—guide—had
betrayed them, but do not know. We stayed in his barn all night, and
left on Sunday morning, the woman remaining behind.

At about noon, we were near a village. He pointed out a haystack,
where we were to rendezvous at night, to meet another man whom
our friend was to send to take us further along on our way. At night
we went to the haystack; a road ran by it. Instead of keeping watch
by the stack, we were so jaded that we crossed the road and lay
down to rest on the bare ground, where we fell asleep. The man, as
we afterwards learned from him, came as agreed upon, whistled and
made signals, but failed to wake us up. Thinking we had been
pursued away, he went back without us. The next morning, when we
awoke, the sun was rising red, right on the public road. We saw a man
at his door some two hundred yards from us. I went to ask him how
the roads ran; Harris told me to inquire the way to Carr's Run, near
home, so we would go the contrary. By the time I got back, Ben,
who had watched, saw the man leave his house with his gun, and take
a circle round to come down on us; but before he could head us, we
were past him in the road running. We ran and walked about four
miles barefoot; then we took courage to put on our shoes, which we
had not dared stop long enough to do before, for fear the man with
the gun would get ahead of us.

We were now on the top of a high hill. On our right was a path
leading into the woods. In this path we descended, and after walking
a few minutes, we arrived at a house by the main road. We went in to
ask for a drink of buttermilk. Only the woman of the house was at
home. Said she, "Boys, you are the very ones my husband was
looking for last night." We denied it, being right on the road, and
afraid. She insisted, "for," said she, "the man who came to tell my
husband, said there was a big one and a little one." I was the little
one. She gave us crackers, cheese, and onions. Against her advice, we
left the house and moved on. Presently we came to a toll-gate, about
which there were standing several white men. We walked up boldly
to the gate; one of the men then asked us, "Where are you going?"

Ben answered, "We are going to Chillicothe to see our friends there."
Then he made answer and said, "You can't go any further, you must
go back with me, you are the very boys I was looking for last night."
We told him we wanted to go on, but he said, "There are so many
buckskin Yankees in these parts that you will be taken before you
get half through the town." We then went back to his house, but we
did not stop more than ten minutes, because it would be dangerous
for him as well as for us if we were caught on his premises. He stuck
up a pole close to his house and tied a white cloth on it; then he led
us up to the top of the hill (this was Monday, quite early in the
morning), and showed us a rough place of bushes and rocks where we
could lie concealed quite pleasantly, and so high up that we could see
the main road, and the toll-gate, and the house, and the white flag.
Said he, "If there's any danger, I'll send a child out to throw down
the white flag; and if you get scared away from here, come back at
night and I'll protect you." Soon after he left us, we saw five white
men come to his house on horseback; they were the five who had
carried back the others that tried to escape. Two of them went into
the house; then we saw a little girl come out and climb up on the
fence, as if she were playing about, and she knocked down the
flag-pole,—which meant that we were to look out for ourselves. But
we did not feel that there was any immediate danger, and so we kept
close under cover. Pretty soon the two came out of the house, and
they all rode forward very fast, passed the toll-gate, and were soon
out of sight. I suppose they thought to overtake us every minute, but
luckily I have never seen them since. In the evening the man came
and conducted us to his house, where we found the men we had seen
at the toll-gate in the morning. They were mostly armed with pistols
and guns. They guided us to a solitary house three miles back among
the mountains, in the neighborhood of which we remained three
days. We were told to go up on the mountain very high, where was
an Indian cave in the rocks. From this cave we could look a great
distance around and see people, and we felt afraid they would see us.
So instead of staying there, we went down the mountain to a creek
where trees had been cut down and branches thrown over the bank;
we went under the branches and bushes where the sand was dry, and
there we would sit all day. We all the time talked to each other about
how we would get away, and what we should do if the white folks
tackled us; that was all our discourse.

We stayed there until Friday, when our friends gave us knapsacks full of cakes and dried venison, and a little bundle of provision besides, and flints and steel, and spunk, and a pocket-compass to travel through the woods by. We knew the north-star, but did not travel nights for nearly a week. So on Friday morning we set out, the men all bidding us good-by, and the man of the flag-staff went with us half a day to teach us the use of the compass; we had never seen one before. Once in a while he would put it on a log to show us how to travel by it. When he was leaving us, he took his knife and marked on the compass, so that we should steer a little west of north.

During the six days succeeding, we traversed an unbroken wilderness of hills and mountains, seeing neither man nor habitation. At night we made a fire to sit by. We saw deer on our way; we were not annoyed by wild animals, and saw but one snake, a garter-snake. The first sign of man we met with was a newly-made road; this was on the seventh day from the time we left the house in the mountains. Our provisions held out well, and we had found water enough. After crossing the road, we came out from the mountains to a level cleared place of farms and houses. Then we were afraid, and put ourselves on our guard, resolving to travel by night. We laid by until starlight, then we made for a road leading to the north. We would follow a road until it bent away from the north; then we would leave it and go by the compass. This caused us to meet many rivers and streams where there were no bridges; some we could wade over, and some we crossed by swimming. After reaching the clearings, we scarcely dared build a fire. Once or twice we took some green corn from the fields, and made a brush fire to roast it. After lighting the fire, we would retire from it, as far almost as we could see it, and then watch whether anybody might come to it. When the fire had gone out, the corn would be about done.

Our feet were now sore with long travelling. One night we came to a river; it was rather foggy, but I could see a ferry-scow on the other side. I was afraid of alligators, but I swam over, and poled the scow back and ferried Ben across,—his ancle was so sore, that he did not like to put his foot in the water if he could help it. We soon reached an old stable in the edge of a little town; we entered it and slept alternately one keeping watch, as we always managed while in the neighborhood of settlements. We did not do this in the wilderness,— *there* we slept safely, and were quite *reconciled*. At cock-crowing in the morning we set out and went into the woods, which were very near; there we stayed through the day.

At night we started on and presently came into a road running north-west. Coming to a vine patch we filled our knapsacks with cucumbers; we then met a white man, who asked us, "Which way are you travelling?" My cousin told him "To Cleveland, to help a man drive a drove of cattle." He then said, "I know you must be runaways,—but you needn't be afraid of me,—I don't want to hurt you." He then told us something that we knew before—that the last spring five fugitives were overtaken at his house by my master and two other men; that the fugitives took through his wheat-field,—one of them, a little fellow, could not run so fast as the rest, and master called to him to stop, or he'd shoot him. His answer was, "shoot and be d—d!" The man further told us, that he took through the wheat-field as if he would assist in catching the slaves, but that when he got near enough, he told them to "push on!" Ben and I knew about the pursuit, and what the little fellow had said; for it got round among the servants, after master got back. That little fellow's widow is now my wife. We went to the man's house, and partook of a good luncheon. He told us to hurry, and try to get through Newark before daylight. We hurried accordingly, but it was daybreak when we crossed the bridge. We found the little toll-gate open and we went through—there were lights in a tavern window at the left of the gate, and the windows had no curtains. Just as we were stepping off the bridge, a plank rattled,—then up started after us a little black dog, making a great noise. We walked smartly along, but did not run until we came to a street leading to the right,—then we ran fast until we came to a left hand turn, which led to the main road at the other side of the town. Before sunrise, we hid in a thicket of briars, close by the road, where we lay all day, seeing the teams, and every thing that passed by.

At dark we went on again, passed through Mount Vernon in the night, and kept on until daylight. Again we halted in concealment until night, then we went on again through Wooster. After leaving Wooster, we saw no more settlements, except one little village, which we passed through in broad day. We entered a store here, but were asked no questions. Here we learned the way to Cleveland. In the middle of the afternoon we stopped for a little rest. Just before night we moved forward again and travelled all night. We then stopped to rest until four in the afternoon, meanwhile roasting some corn as before. At about four, we met a preacher, who was just come from Cleveland. He asked us if we were making our escape,—we told him "No." He said, "You need not be afraid of me,—I am the friend of all who travel from the South to the North." He told us not to go into Cleveland, as we would be taken up. He then described a house which was on our way, where, he said, we might mention our meeting him, and we would find friends who would put us on board a boat. We hid until dark,—then we went to the house, which we recognized readily from the preacher's description. We knocked at the door, and were invited in. My cousin told them what the minister had said. The man of the house hid us in his barn two nights and three days. He was a shoemaker. The next night after we got there, he went to Cleveland himself to get a berth for us aboard some boat for Canada. When he returned, he said he had found a passage for us with Capt. B., who was to sail the next Thursday at 10, P.M. At that hour we embarked, having a free passage in a schooner for Buffalo. On board this boat, we met with an Englishman whom we had often seen on a steamboat at the plantation. He knew us, and told us a reward of one hundred dollars was offered for each of us, and he showed us several handbills to that effect. He said they had been given him to put up along the road, but he had preferred to keep them in his pocket. Capt. B. took away our knives and Ben's tomahawk, for fear of mischief.

We reached Buffalo at 4, P.M. The captain said, that if there was any danger in the town, he would take us in his yawl and put us across. He walked through the town to see if there were any bills up. Finding no danger, he took us out of the hatchway,—he walked with us as far as Black Rock Ferry, giving us good advice all the way, how we should conduct ourselves through life in Canada, and we have never departed from his directions,—his counsel was good, and I have kept it.

I am now buying this place. My family are with me,—we live well, and enjoy ourselves. I worship in the Methodist church. What religious instruction I received on plantation, was from my mother.

I look upon slavery as the most disgusting system a man can live under. I would not be a slave again, except that I could not put an end to my own existence, through fear of the punishment of the future.

Men who have never seen or felt slavery cannot realize it for the thing it is. If those who say that fugitives had better go back, were to go to the South and *see* slavery, they would never wish any slave to go back.

I have seen separations by sales, of husbands from wives, of parents from children,—if a man threatens to run away, he is sure to be sold. Ben's mother was sold down South— to New Orleans—when he was about twenty years old.

I arrived in Canada on the 13th September, 1824.

WILLIAM JOHNSON

I look upon slavery as I do upon a deadly poison. The slaves are not contented nor happy in their lot. Neither on the farm where I was in Virginia, nor in the neighborhood were the slaves satisfied. The man I belonged to did not give us enough to eat. My feet were frostbitten on my way North, but I would rather have died on the way than to go back.

It would not do to stop at all about our work,—if the people should try to get a little rest, there would be a cracking spell amongst them. I have had to go through a great deal of affliction; I have been compelled to work when I was sick. I used to have rheumatism, and could not always do so much work as those who were well,—then I would sometimes be whipped. I have never seen a runaway that wanted to go back,—I have never heard of one.

I knew a very smart young man—he was a fellow-servant of mine, who had recently professed religion—who was tied up by a quick-tempered overseer, and whipped terribly. He died not long after, and the people there believed it was because of the whipping. Some of the slaves told the owner, but he did not discharge the overseer. He will have to meet it at the day of judgment.

I had grown up quite large, before I thought any thing about liberty. The fear of being sold South had more influence in inducing me to leave than any other thing. Master used to say, that if we didn't suit him, he would put us in his pocket quick—meaning he would sell us. He never gave me a great coat in his life,—he said he knew he ought to do it, but that he couldn't get ahead far enough.

His son had a child by a colored woman, and he would have sold it—his own grandchild—if the other folks hadn't opposed it.

I have found good friends in Canada, but have been able to do no work on account of my frozen feet,—I lost two toes from my right foot. My determination is to go to work as soon as I am able. I have been about among the colored people in St. Catharines considerably, and have found them industrious and frugal. No person has offered me any liquor since I have been here: I have seen no colored person use it. I have been trying to learn to read since I came here, and I know a great many fugitives who are trying to learn.

HARRIET TUBMAN

I grew up like a neglected weed,—ignorant of liberty, having no experience of it. Then I was not happy or contented: every time I saw a white man I was afraid of being carried away. I had two sisters carried away in a chain-gang,—one of them left two children. We were always uneasy. Now I've been free, I know what a dreadful condition slavery is. I have seen hundreds of escaped slaves, but I never saw one who was willing to go back and be a slave. I have no opportunity to see my friends in my native land. We would rather stay in our native land, if we could be as free there as we are here. I think slavery is the next thing to hell. If a person would send another into bondage, he would, it appears to me, be bad enough to send him into hell, if he could.

MRS. — —

[The lady who gave the following narrative wished to withhold her name, for private reasons. She is well known at St. Catharines as a very intelligent and respectable person.]

I was held as a slave in — — without even legal right according to the slave laws. When I was ten years old, a young man was punishing me—I resisted: I was in consequence called "a rebellious wretch," and put out of the family. At the place where I was hired, it happened on communion Sunday in March, that the dogs got hold of a pig, and bit a piece off its ear. In consequence of this misfortune to the pig, a boy of sixteen years, or thereabouts, was whipped in the barn; and a man-slave was tied up to a tree, with his arms extended, and whipped. I was peeping and saw the man whipped. The blood ran as they whipped him. His wife had to take care of him and dress his wounds. It affected me so that I cried and said I wouldn't stay at the place,—then the same man—the man of the house—whipped me. At twelve o'clock that night, I ran away to my owners. He came to the folks where I was, and requested them to send me back, lest the others should follow my example. I went back and stayed two weeks,—when I had got within a mile of home, my master got on his horse, and trotted along behind me, to let folks see that he had got the runaway.

After my escape from slavery, I married a free colored man. We were comfortably settled in the States, and were broken up by the fugitive slave law,—compelled to leave our home and friends, and to go at later than middle life into a foreign country among strangers.

I look upon slavery as the worst evil that ever was. My life has been taken from me in a measure by it. If any are disposed to apologize for slavery, it would be well for them to try it awhile.

REV. ALEXANDER HEMSLEY

[The famous decision of Judge Hornblower, of New Jersey, some years ago, in a case of a fugitive, will doubtless be recollected by many readers. The narrative subjoined was given by the individual more immediately interested in that decision. Mr. Hemsley is confined to his bed a great part of the time by dropsy. He is a very intelligent man, and his face wears, notwithstanding his many trials and his sickness, a remarkable expression of cheerfulness and good-will. His dwelling is clean and nice, and he is well nursed and cared for by Mrs. Hemsley, a sensible, painstaking woman, the very impersonation of neatness. As it does not appear in the narrative, it may properly be stated here, that Mr. Hemsley has lost two children by death, since his removal to St. Catharines; their sickness, alluded to in the narrative, extending through three consecutive years. If any capitalist is looking about him for an opportunity to invest, I think he might profitably employ two hundred dollars in lifting the mortgage from Hemsley's house and garden. Rev. Hiram Wilson of St. C. who has managed to keep himself free from the care of riches, by giving to the needy, as fast as he earned it, every thing which he might have called his own, will be happy, without doubt, to attend to the business without fee or commission. Apropos, of Mr. Wilson,—we know "there is that scattereth, and yet increaseth." But in Mr. W.'s case, it requires but little financial skill to perceive, that while "scattering" to relieve the sick and suffering,—the fugitive and the oppressed,—to an extent sometimes fully up to the means in his hands, any "increase" must come from those who may feel disposed to let their means assist his abundant opportunities of benevolent action. But to the narrative.]

I was in bondage in Queen Anne County, Maryland from birth until twenty-three years of age. My name in slavery was Nathan Mead. My master was a professor of religion, and used to instruct me in a hypocritical way in the duties of religion. I used to go to church on Sunday to hear him talk, and experience the contrary on Monday. On the Sabbath he used to catechize us, and tell us if we were good honest boys, and obedient to our master, we should enjoy the life that now is, and that which is to come.

My idea of freedom during my youth was, that it was a state of liberty for the mind,—that there was a freedom of thought, which I could not enjoy unless I were free,—that is, if I thought of any thing beneficial for me, I should have liberty to execute it. My escape was not owing to any sudden impulse or fear of present punishment, but from a natural wish to be free: and had it not been for near and dear friends, I should not have remained in slavery so long. I had an uncle who was a preacher. He had a good many boys. I confided to him that I wanted to leave, and would like to have his boys accompany me. He said he would not dare to tell his boys, for if we were to undertake it, and get caught, it would ruin us all. The fear of being caught was then, I think, a greater restraint than it is now. Now there is a different spirit in the slaves, and if they undertake to escape, it is with a feeling of victory or death,—they determine not to be taken alive, if possible to prevent it even by bloodshed.

I was accustomed to leave home every Saturday night to visit friends seven miles inland, and to return on Sunday night. One Sunday night when I had got back from my visit, I took leave of my friends, they not knowing what I intended, as I had often told them on the Saturday nights, in the same way, that I never expected to see them again. After I bade them farewell, I started for New Jersey, where, I had been told, people were free, and nobody would disturb me. I went six miles, and then ambushed. On Monday night, I went thirty-three miles, and found a good old Quaker—one [we omit the name, but it will be published one day]—with whom I stayed three weeks. At the expiration of which time, I went to Philadelphia. I made no tarry there, but went straight over into New Jersey. After a stay of two months at Cooper's Creek, I went to Evesham, where I resided eight or nine years, being hired and getting my money. No

one disturbed me all this time. I heard that I had been pursued by
the son of my master, but that not hearing from me he went back. I
then received favorable offers to go to Northampton, and I removed
there, taking with me my wife whom I had married in Evesham, and
my three children. At Northampton I remained unmolested until
October, 1836. Then some four or five southerners, neither of whom
had any legal claim upon me, having found out that I had escaped
from bondage, went to the executor of my old master's estate (my
master having been dead six or seven years) and bought me
running,—that is, they paid some small sum for a title to me, so as to
make a spec. out of poor me. To make sure of the matter, they came
about my house, pretending to be gunning,—meanwhile looking after
my children, and appraising their value in case they could get them.
This I know, for they promised a lawyer my oldest son, if he would
gain the case.* They hung round my house from Wednesday to
Saturday morning, when, while it was yet dark, they surrounded my
house. It was my usual way to open the door, put my shoes on, and
go off to work. Just as I opened the door that morning, an officer of
the town followed the door right in, put his hand on me, and said,
"You are my prisoner!" I asked him "what he meant by that?" He
said he had received a writ to bring me before the court of common
pleas. I told him "I have no master, but I will go with you." I sat
down to put on my shoes,—then the five southerners flung
themselves upon me and put me in irons. Then one of them
pretended to be a great friend to me. "Now," said he, "if you have
any friends, tell me who they are, and I'll go for them." I showed
him the house where my employer lived, and told him to step up
there, and ask him to come to me immediately. He came, and
commenced reproving the constable for being in so low business as to
be arresting slaves for slave-hunters. "Poor business!" said he. I told
him I was afraid they were going to smuggle me off, without taking
me before the judge. The constable then, at his request, pledged his
honor, to take me safe to the court at Mount Holly. They put me in
a carriage, handcuffed, between two armed men of the party. One of
these had been a boy with whom I had played in my young days in
Maryland. He was there to swear to my identity. On the way, he

---

*Mrs. H. was from Caroline Co., Md. Her parents were made free "by word of
mouth,"—but as her mother had no free papers,—it was feared that the daughter might be
enslaved. She was enabled to avoid the danger by emigration.

tried to "soft soap" me, so as to get some evidence to convict me, when we got before the judge. But I made strange of him and of every thing he said,—I wouldn't know him nor any of his blarney. At Mount Holly, the judge told me, that it was alleged that I had escaped from the service of Mr. Isaac Baggs of Maryland,—and that, if that were proved I might be sure that I would be sent back. The judge being a Virginia born man, brought up in New Jersey, was found, like the handle of a jug, all on one side, and that side against me. The friends employed counsel for me, and by the efforts of my counsel, the trial was put off to Monday. On Monday, the case was called, and the other side had an adjournment of a week, in order to get an additional witness. I was imprisoned during the week. A brother of the former witness was then brought forward—one whom I had known when a boy. The two brothers, who were both mean fellows, as they appeared against me to get money, swore to my identity, and that they knew me to have been the slave of Isaac Baggs. My counsel were David Paul Brown, John R. Slack, George Campbell, and Elias B. Cannon. The trial was not concluded until the lapse of three weeks. Then the judge decided, that my wife was a free-woman and might remain with her children,—"but as for you, Alexander or Nathan, the case is clear that you were the slave of Isaac Baggs, and you must go back."

Then Mr. John R. Slack went up to the judge, and laid the writ of *habeas corpus* before him. The judge looked it over in quick time—his color came and went tremendously. He answered in a low tone of voice, "I think you might have told me that you had that before." The lawyer answered, "We thought it would be time enough, after seeing how far your Honor would go." A good old friend—one Thomas Shipleigh—had ridden forty miles to get that writ. On the next day the sheriff took me before Judge Hornblower; two of my counsel went also, and one of the other party. My oppressor planned to take me out of New Jersey on the route, as if we left the State, Judge Heywood's certificate would take effect. Our party, however, were wide awake, and kept within N. J., but they prepared bull-dogs (pistols) in case any attempt were made at carrying me off. When we arrived at the court, Mr. Brainard Clark, my claimant's lawyer, in the course of his argument, stated what great expense the claimants had been to for jail fees, &c., "even seventy dollars." Judge H. answered, "If it had been seven times seventy, it would create no sympathy in me for them,—we can't expect to pass away human liberty for a mere trifle,"—or words to that effect. It was concluded that I should be given into the custody of the sheriff until February term,—then to be brought before the supreme court at Trenton.

I remained in jail until the February term, about three months, as comfortable as a man could be, imprisoned, and with the awful doom of slavery hanging over his head. The case was then taken up by Hon. Theodore Frelinghuysen. The other side could not meet Frelinghuysen's argument. In about three weeks the court declared me a free man. I was then let out of jail; but as I had become so well known, my friends were afraid that my claimants would waylay and smuggle me, and thought I had better leave for the North, which I did. I travelled some two hundred miles, most of the way on foot into Otsego county, N. Y., where I gave out through fatigue. I was sick when I got there. Here I was joined by my wife and children. I remained here until navigation opened,—we were forty miles from the canal at Utica. Then, from visions of the night, I concluded that I was on dangerous ground, and I removed with my family to Farmington. Years before I had had visions of the road I was to travel, and if I had obeyed the visions, the trouble would not have occurred. I had dreamed of being pursued, and that they had caught me, and so it turned out. From Farmington, I went on directly to Rochester, where I remained but one night. My health was good, with the exception of my eyes, which were dim of sight and inflamed, owing to the change from imprisonment to exposure to pelting storms of rain and snow. I felt that my persecutors who brought this trouble on me were actuated by a demonlike principle. We embarked from Rochester, on board a British boat, The Traveller, for Toronto.

When I reached English territory, I had a comfort in the law,—that my shackles were struck off, and that a man was a man by law. I had been in comfortable circumstances, but all my little property was *lawed* away. I was among strangers, poverty-stricken, and in a cold country. I had been used to farming, and so could not find in the city such assistance as I needed: in a few days, I left for St. Catharines, where I have ever since remained.

My master did not use to do much at buying and selling, but there was a great deal of it in his neighborhood. The unwillingness to separate of husbands and wives, parents and children was so great, that to part them seemed to me a sin higher than the heavens,—it was dreadful to hear their outcries, as they were forced into the wagons of the drivers. Some among them have their minds so brutalized by the action of slavery, that they do not feel so acutely as others, the pangs of separation. But there are many who feel a separation from their offspring as acutely as human beings can possibly feel.

Masters sometimes show respect toward some particular persons among their slaves. I was never an eye-witness to a punishment where a man seemed to inflict it in any spirit of kindness or mercy. I have heard of a merciful disposition at such times, but never witnessed it; as a general thing they would manifest malignant, tyrannical feelings. I have seen a woman who was in state of pregnancy, tied up and punished with a keen raw hide.

Contrasting my condition here with what it was in New Jersey, I say, that for years after I came here, my mind was continually reverting to my native land. For some ten years, I was in hopes that something might happen, whereby I might safely return to my old home in New Jersey. I watched the newspapers and they told the story. I found that there would be a risk in going back,—and that was confirmed by many of my fellow men falling into the same catastrophe that I did,—and the same things happen now.

When I reached St. Catharines I was enfeebled in health. I had come to a small inferior place; there were pines growing all about here where you now see brick houses. I rented a house, and with another man took five acres of cleared land, and got along with it very well. We did not get enough from this to support us; but I got work at half a dollar or seventy-five cents a day and board myself. We were then making both ends meet. I then made up my mind that salt and potatoes in Canada, were better than pound-cake and chickens in a state of suspense and anxiety in the United States. Now I am a regular Britisher. My American blood has been scourged out of me; I have lost my American tastes; I am an enemy to tyranny. I would as lief meet serpents as some people I know of in the States. If I were to meet them, my fighting propensities would come up. To meet one here, I would not mind it; there I would be afraid of the ghost of a white man after he was dead. I am no scholar, but if some one would refine it, I could give a history of slavery, and show how tyranny operates upon the mind of the slaves. I have dreamed of being back on my master's farm, and of dodging away from my master; he endeavoring to get between me and the land I was aiming for. Then I would awake in a complete perspiration, and troubled in mind. Oh, it was awful! When you go back home, remember poor Joseph in Egypt.

I am now about sixty years of age, and have been lying sick about nine months. I have here a house and a quarter acre of land. I have had a deal of sickness in my family, and it has kept me comparatively poor: it would take two hundred dollars to clear my estate from incumbrances. Had it not been for sickness, it would have been paid for long ago.

I have served the people in the provinces as a minister in the Methodist persuasion for some twenty years. My pay has been little, for our people all start poor, and have to struggle to support themselves. My mind has ever been to trust the Lord. I have never prayed for wealth nor honor, but only to guide his church and do his will.

JOHN SEWARD

The man that owned me, was not fit to own a dog. I had been wanting to get away for the last twenty years. I grieved over my condition, and groaned over it. A few months ago I succeeded in escaping. After I got among abolitionists, I was almost scared; they used me so well, I was afraid of a trick. I had been used so ill before that I did not know what to make of it to be used decently.

JAMES SEWARD

Brother of the Foregoing

Where I came from, it would make your flesh creep, and your hair stand on end, to know what they do to the slaves.

I had a niece, who was married and had two children; one at her breast. The estate being in debt, I was imprisoned. Before I went to jail, my niece was hired out; then her owner concluded to sell her. She was taken away from her children, handcuffed, and put into the jail where I was. Her irons were taken off; she was in great grief, crying all the time, "Oh, my children! my poor children!" till it appeared to me, she would kill herself for grief. She was sold and carried away, leaving her children behind. I have been in Canada but a short time.

MRS. JAMES SEWARD

The slaves want to get away bad enough. They are not contented with their situation.

I am from the eastern shore of Maryland. I never belonged but to one master; he was very bad indeed. I was never sent to school, nor allowed to go to church. They were afraid we would have more sense than they. I have a father there, three sisters, and a brother. My father is quite an old man, and he is used very badly. Many a time he has been kept at work a whole long summer day without sufficient food. A sister of mine has been punished by his taking away her clothes and locking them up, because she used to run when master whipped her. He kept her at work with only what she could pick up to tie on her for decency. He took away her child which had just begun to walk, and gave it to another woman,—but she went and got it afterward. He had a large farm eight miles from home. Four servants were kept at the house. My master could not manage to whip my sister when she was strong. He waited until she was confined, and the second week after her confinement he said, "Now I can handle you, now you are weak." She ran from him, however, and had to go through water, and was sick in consequence.

I was beaten at one time over the head by my master, until the blood ran from my mouth and nose: then he tied me up in the garret, with my hands over my head,—then he brought me down and put me in a little cupboard, where I had to sit cramped up, part of the evening, all night, and until between four and five o'clock, next day, without any food. The cupboard was near a fire, and I thought I should suffocate.

My brother was whipped on one occasion until his back was raw as a piece of beef, and before it got well, master whipped him again. His back was an awful sight.

We were all afraid of master: when I saw him coming, my heart would jump up into my mouth, as if I had seen a serpent.

I have been wanting to come away for eight years back. I waited for Jim Seward to get ready. Jim had promised to take me away and marry me. Our master would allow no marriages on the farm. When Jim had got ready, he let me know,—he brought to me two suits of clothes—men's clothes— which he had bought on purpose for me. I put on both suits to keep me warm. We eluded pursuit and reached Canada in safety.

MR. – – BOHM

I escaped from slavery in Norfolk, Va.

I think that the institution of slavery is of no utility whatever to the colored race. Slavery is the worst kind of robbery.

JAMES M. WILLIAMS

I came from bondage in Norfolk, Va. Slavery is horrible! horrible! horrible!

JOHN ATKINSON

I escaped from Norfolk, Va. A man who has been in slavery knows, and no one else can know, the yearnings to be free, and the fear of making the attempt. It is like trying to get religion, and not seeing the way to escape condemnation.

MRS. ELLIS

It is more than a year ago, that I left slavery in Delaware, having been thirty-two years a slave. I was treated tolerably well, compared with others. I was brought up in ignorance. I felt put down—oppressed in spirit. I did a great deal of heavy out-door work,—such as driving team, hauling manure, etc. I have been whipped with a wagon whip and with hickories,—have been kicked and hit with fists. I have a bunch on my head from a blow my master gave me, and I shall carry it to my grave. I have had four children—two died there, and two I brought with me.

I thought I had paid my master for raising me, and I wanted some time of my own: and when he threatened to sell me, and keep my children, I left him. I got off without much trouble. I suffered a great deal from wet and cold, on the first part of the way—afterwards, I was helped on by kind white men.

Rents and provisions are dear here, and it takes all I can earn to support myself and children. I could have one of my children well brought up and taken care of, by some friends in Massachusetts, which would much relieve me,—but I cannot have my child go there on account of the laws, which would not protect her. This is a hardship: but had I to struggle much harder than at present, I would prefer it to being a slave. Now, I can lie down at night in peace,—there I had no peace even at night, on account of my master's conduct.

Slavery is a wicked institution. I think if the whites were to free the slaves, they would incur no danger. I think the colored people would go to work without any trouble.

DAN JOSIAH LOCKHART

I belonged in Frederick county, Va. I was sold at five years of age; and when I first saw my mother to know her, I had a wife and child. My business was to clean knives, forks, candlesticks, etc., until my mistress died, say when I was twelve or thirteen. My master remained a widower some time—say eighteen months,—when he married the daughter of a farmer, upon which he quit merchandise, and went on a small farm. The hands in a rainy day worked in the shop with tools. I was made overseer. The management was pretty much left to me. I would carry my gun down into a hollow, and have a book,—the children had taught me to read. Every thing worked pretty comfortably with me.

One of the women called me a liar. I punished her. My master took me to the granary to whip me,—he told me to take off my coat. Said I, "master, whip me with my coat on!" I prayed hard for him to whip me with my coat on. He did finally whip me with my coat on, and slightly at that. He was an Irishman. He said he would whip me till I was as striped as a *zaybra*.

I was harder on the servants than he wanted I should be. At another time he undertook to whip me, and I told him I would leave him if he did. I had my mind on my wife, Maria. She was sold to a man in Winchester, eight miles. This was too far,—so I wanted to be sold. He said if he sold me, he would sell me where I would never see her. At this time I was studying divinity, having met with a change of heart. I took my books and started off in daytime. I went on five miles,—then I met Mr.— —, who asked me where I was going. I told him I was sold. He persuaded me back. I was thinking of trying to be free. Mr. — — said he would buy me. I told him, "I will do the best I can for you." He slapped his hand on his pocket and said, "I've got the money in my pocket for you." He then rode forward to see my master. The bargain was made there, and money paid to — —, a Methodist preacher. Mr. — — took me, and southern traders who came for me were too late. I lived with my new master three years and two months. Then he whipped my wife and children,—(I had now ten children by Maria). I could not stand this abuse of them, and so I made up my mind to leave. I told my wife so. She said she was afraid they would catch me and bring me back and—you know what then.

It was in the year 1847, that I made my escape. My master had gone to Philadelphia. I told my mistress that my father was sick, and she gave me permission to go and see him. Between two and three o'clock next morning, Sunday, I got up and dressed myself to leave. One of my little children came to me when I had stepped out. Said I, "Jane, where are you going?" "Daddy, I'm looking for you." My feelings were very tender at the time. I took her up in my arms, and carried her and laid her back in the bed with her mother and the other little child, Julia. I sat down and waited till they were all asleep; I then got up, looked at the mother and the two little children,—said "Farewell!" and started on my journey.

The night previous I had got some meat and bread, and had taken my master's saddle-bags, cramming both ends full of provisions. By daybreak I was out of the neighborhood of the folks that knew me. . . . .

When I reached the Potomac River, the ferry-boat had left the shore for the last time. I sung out "Ferry, ahoy!" They put about and came for me. I got in and seated myself with a colored man and a white man. I inquired the damage for crossing? Ferryman said "Fippenny bit." I gave him a ten cent piece, and told him may be I'd be passing again, and he could make it right next time. The colored man asked me, "Are you a free man?" It staggered me at first to think that a colored man should ask me that question. The white man reproved him. "What the d—l do you ask that question for? do you think a man dressed like him can be a runaway?" I got across safely. . . . . [Some highly interesting portions of Lockhart's narrative are omitted from prudential considerations.]

I got employment in Pittsburg, but my mind being uneasy, I wrote to a friend to tell my wife that I was there, and assuring her of my continued affection. My old master got hold of this letter, and so pursued me with two officers, K— — and J— —, with a bill of sale specifying the sum paid for me. They secured themselves in Crawson's Hotel, Pittsburg,—set their trap, baited their hook, put out a reward of one hundred and fifty dollars for my arrest. One very smart gentleman came down to Diamond Square,—I was there looking at a busy knife-grinder with a crowd around him: the smart gentleman, knowing by the description who I was, selected me from the crowd, under the pretence that he wished me to carry a trunk—told me he would give me a quarter of a dollar for it. I went to the place where he directed me, expecting to find the trunk,— went to the Monongahela House,—he conducted me up stairs: going down the hall, to a lady, sweeping, he says; "Where is the 160th room?" "Yes, that middle door." "Sure enough," said he,—then to me, "Open the door, and bring out my trunk." However, he opened the door,—when lo! up jumped the old man! He gave me a pat on the shoulder,—"Hallo, Dan! don't you want to go back and see your wife and children?" I said nothing,—I couldn't say any thing. Then came up K. and J. to me,—"Dan, you've got the best master in Virginia,—come, go back with me." The old man then left the room and went away. I began to feel like speaking—had a watch in my pocket,—I put my hand to it, to see if it was safe, and K. said, "Dan, you needn't do that,—we knew you'd fight, but we've come prepared to take you—don't want to hurt you." This was on a Friday, between eleven and twelve o'clock, A.M. Said I, "Gentlemen,"—this was the first time I had spoken, and I called no name,—"let me go; you have no business with me here." This was all out in the hall; they had irons in the room, but they couldn't get me in there. We were now engaged very smartly for a time, each man for himself. The noise reached the people in the house, and some of the servants came up to see what was the trouble; I called them,—"Come to me;" some of them were colored, but being alarmed, they did not interfere. I spoke out,—"You go to John — —, and tell him that I am in trouble here; that I am in kidnappers' hands." In a short time, the landlord came up stairs. Says he to the officers, "This man has got to go down, or there'll be bloodshed here,—it will ruin my house to have the word go abroad that there are kidnappers here." By this time John — —, Peter — —, Hadley — —, and old Uncle Sammy — —, had marshalled a troop; they came and surrounded Crawson's Hotel, started in, and came up the stairs. I was hollowing "murder!" and "fire!" being in the hands of K. and J. I said to the colored men,—"I thought I had friends in Pittsburg." They answered,—"Mr. Lockhart, you have friends,—we did not know you were here until just now." John — — and Peter — — took hold of me, and told K — — to let go. He answered,—"*You* let go—if you don't I'll shoot you." Peter said,— "Shoot, and make a sure shot, if you don't the next is mine." Then Peter knocked J— — down, and from that they got me out of the hands of the Philistines.

My friends conducted me to a house not far from Crawson's, and told me to lie down. I was fatigued, but not hurt. Peter — — said,—"We are going to get K. and J. in where your master is,—he is safe." They were arrested and tried for breaking the peace of the city, so it was told me. Some new act had been passed, and the judge wanted some time to see how it differed from the former law. On Monday afternoon he decided that there was no violence on the part of the whites, but that the colored men had been seen to knock down some persons; that my master had a right to take me; and that K— — and J— — had acted in discharge of their duty as officers. I was told on Tuesday morning how the law was, and that I could be carried back if I remained in the United States. I then started off for Canada by the underground railroad. . . . .

My work is as hard here as it was in slavery. The hardest thing in slavery is not the work,—it is the abuse of a man, and, in my case, of a man's wife and children. They were not punished severely,—but I did not want her whipped at all—I don't want any man to meddle with my wife,—I bothered her enough, and didn't want anybody else to trouble her at all. It is ignorance that keeps the slaves there. I was told before I left Virginia,—have heard it as common talk, that the wild geese were so numerous in Canada, and so bad, that they would scratch a man's eyes out; that corn wouldn't grow there, nor any thing else but *rice;* that every thing they had there was imported.

I attended a church for colored people in Virginia, and had good privileges in religion. The children showed me to read and write.

MRS. NANCY HOWARD

I was born in Anne Arundel county, Maryland,—was brought up in Baltimore. After my escape, I lived in Lynn, Mass., seven years, but I left there through fear of being carried back, owing to the fugitive slave law. I have lived in St. Catharines less than a year.

The way I got away was,—my mistress was sick, and went into the country for her health. I went to stay with her cousin. After a month, my mistress was sent back to the city to her cousin's, and I waited on her. My daughter had been off three years. A friend said to me,—"Now is your chance to get off." At last I concluded to go,—the friend supplying me with money. I was asked no questions on the way north.

My idea of slavery is, that it is one of the blackest, the wickedest things that ever were in the world. When you tell them the truth, they whip you to make you lie. I have taken more lashes for this, than for any other thing, because I would not lie.

One day I set the table, and forgot to put on the carving-fork—the knife was there. I went to the table to put on a plate. My master said,—"Where is the fork?" I told him "I forgot it." He says,—"You d—d black b—, I'll forget you!"—at the same time hitting me on the head with the carving-knife. The blood spurted out,—you can see. [Here the woman removed her turban and showed a circular cicatrice denuded of hair, about an inch in diameter, on the top of her head.] My mistress took me into the kitchen and put on camphor, but she could not stop the bleeding. A doctor was sent for. He came, but asked no questions. I was frequently punished with raw hides,—was hit with tongs and poker and any thing. I used when I went out, to look up at the sky, and say, "Blessed Lord, oh, do take me out of this!" It seemed to me I could not bear another lick. I can't forget it. I sometimes dream that I am pursued, and when I wake, I am scared almost to death.

Slaveholders ought to be prayed for. I find it harder to get work here, than I did in Massachusetts. It is a sin on the slaveholders that I had to leave and come here. It has brought me lower to the ground. I think the slaveholders don't read the Scriptures the right way,—they don't know their danger.

My master bragged one day to his friend, that I would not lie. He said, "I came nigh laying that d—d b—'s side open, and she stuck to it she was telling the truth, and it turned out she was." We ain't no more than the brutes, at the South. I used to think they would speak better to a dog or cow. Then they would say, "Get out of the way,"—they wouldn't put the other to it.

One Sunday my master promised me and my boy, that he hoped God would damn him, if he did not tie us up and whip us the next morning. I went into a corner and prayed to God, to allow me to take all the whipping, but to spare my boy. By and by, my mistress ran for me; she said "your master is dying!" I blew the horn to call people to us. My master lay on the floor—he never spoke afterwards, but he lived a week. He seemed to have his senses—he would make signs with his head. He would allow no one to pray with him. I prayed for him all the time he was sick. To the last, when they asked him to have prayers, he would shake his head.

GEORGE JOHNSON

I arrived in St. Catharines about two hours ago. [1855, 4,17.]

I was raised near Harper's Ferry, I was used as well as the people about there are used. My master used to pray in his family with the house servants, morning and evening. I attended these services until I was eighteen, when I was put out on the farm, and lived in a cabin. We were well supplied with food. We went to work at sunrise, and quit work between sundown and dark. Some were sold from my master's farm, and many from the neighborhood. If a man did any thing out of the way, he was in more danger of being sold than of being whipped. The slaves were always afraid of being sold South. The Southern masters were believed to be much worse than those about us. I had a great wish for liberty when I was a boy. I always had it in my head to clear. But I had a wife and children. However, my wife died last year of cholera, and then I determined not to remain in that country.

When my old master died, I fell to his son. I had no difficulty with him, but was influenced merely by a love of liberty. I felt disagreeably about leaving my friends,—but I knew I might have to leave them by going South. There was a fellow-servant of mine named Thomas. My master gave him a letter one day, to carry to a soul-driver. Thomas got a man to read it, who told him he was sold. Thomas then got a free man to carry the letter. They hand-cuffed— —, the free man, and put him in jail. Thomas, when he saw them take the free man, dodged into the bush. He came to us. We made up a purse, and sent him on his way. Next day, the man who had carried the letter, sent for his friends and got out. The master denied to us that he intended to sell Thomas. He did not get the money for him. Thomas afterward wrote a letter from Toronto to his friend.

I prepared myself by getting cakes, etc., and on a Saturday night in March, I and two comrades started off together. They were younger than I. . . . . We travelled by night and slept by day until we reached Pittsburg. When we had got through the town, I left the two boys, and told them not to leave while I went back to a grocery for food. When I returned, they were gone,—I do not know their fate. I stopped in the neighborhood two nights, trying to find them—I did not dare to inquire for them. The second night, I made up my mind to ask after them, but my heart failed me. I am of opinion that they got to Canada, as they knew the route. At length I was obliged to come off without them.

I think that slavery is not the best condition for the blacks. Whipping and slashing are bad enough, but selling children from their mothers and husbands from their wives is worse. At one time I wanted to marry a young woman, not on the same farm. I was then sent to Alabama, to one of my masters's sons for two years. When the girl died, I was sent for to come back. I liked the work, the tending of cotton, better than the work on the farm in Virginia,—but there was so much whipping in Alabama, that I was glad to get back. One man there, on another farm, was tied up and received five hundred and fifty lashes for striking the overseer. His back was awfully cut up. His wife took care of him. Two months after, I saw him lying on his face, unable to turn over or help himself. The master seemed ashamed of this, and told the man that if he got well, he might go where he liked. My master told me he said so, and the man told me so himself. Whether he ever got well, I do not know: the time when I saw him, was just before I went back to Virginia. *

ISAAC WILLIAMS

My master's farm is in Virginia. When my first master died, his widow married a man who got into debt and was put into prison. The woman gave up her rights to get him out. Then we were sold. Every man came to be sold for her lifetime,—then to revert to the heirs. The heirs bought in all they could—among them my two sisters. They were sent straight to a slave-pen at Richmond. Where they went I know not: that was the last I heard of them; we could not help it,—they went off crying. My purchaser bought also the interest of the heirs in me, and I remained with him ten years—until my escape, near the close of 1854.

Before I was sold I was hired out to work: at one time to a man on the Rappahannock. Three of his men got away—went as far as Bluff Point. Then they were overtaken, tied to his buggy by the overseer,

---

*Mr. Johnson had already engaged work when I saw him.

who whipped up, and they had to run home. One, our employer and his overseer whipped, taking turns about it, until they cut him through to his caul, and he died under the lash. The employer, it was said, caused the man's heart to be taken out and carried over the river, so as not to be haunted by his spirit. He was arrested, and heavily fined. The other two runaways were sold south. Then I worked for another person, being hired out to him. Directly after I went to him, I went to a haystack to feed cattle: accidentally I set fire to the haystack which was consumed,— for which I received three hundred lashes with hickory sticks. The overseer gave me the blows and Jo — — counted them. His feeding was herrings and a peck of meal a week—never enough—if one wanted more he had to steal it.

My last master's allowance was a peck and a half of corn meal a week, and a small slice of meat for each dinner. If any thing more was got it had to be obtained at night. He had but one overseer, and that for but one year. He was a sharp man—whipped me with a cowhide. I've seen him whip women and children like oxen. My master owned a yellow girl, who, he feared, would run away. I was his head man and had to help do it. He tied her across the fence, naked, and whipped her severely with a paddle bored with holes, and with a switch. Then he shaved the hair off of one side of her head, and daubed cow-filth on the shaved part, to disgrace her—keep her down. I tried hard to avoid the lash, but every year he would get up with me for a whipping in some way. I could not avoid it,—he would catch me on something, do how I would. The last time he whipped me, was for stealing corn for bread for Christmas. George — — was with me. He tied our wrists together about a tree, and then whipped us with a carriage whip—that was six years ago. He whipped till he wore the lash off; then he tied a knot in the end, and gave me a blow which laid me up limping three weeks,—the blood ran down into my shoes. After that he used to whip the others. George and others would have their shirts sticking to their backs in the blood. I have seen him strip my wife and whip her with a cobbing board or cowhide. . . .

One Sunday he sent me into the woods to look for hogs. I could not find them, and I told him so on my return. Said he, "They are killed and eaten, and you know the going of them." I told him the truth that I did not know of it. He then seized me by the collar, and told me to cross my wrists. I did so,—but when he laid a rope across to bind them, I jerked them apart. He then undertook to trip me forward with his foot, and as I straightened back, to avoid it, it threw him. He kept his hold on my collar and called for help. The servants came pouring out,—they seized me, and he tied my wrists together with leading lines, eleven yards long, wrapping them about my wrists as long as there was a piece to wrap. Then he led me to the meathouse and said, "Go in there—I'll lay examples on you for all the rest, to go by—fighting your master!" Whilst one was making a cobbing board, and another was gone to cut hickory switches, and he was looking up more leading lines, I got a knife from my pocket, opened it with my teeth, and holding it in my mouth, cut through the lines which bound me. Then I took a gambrel, and broke open the door. I had made up my mind, knowing that he would come wellnigh killing me, to hit with the gambrel any one who came to seize me. When I burst the door open, no one was there,—but master was coming. I sprung for the flats: he hailed me to come back. I stopped and told him that I had worked night and day to try to please him, and I would never come back any more. I stayed away nine days—then he sent me word, that we would not whip me, if I would come back. I went back, and he did not whip me afterward. But he used to whip my wife to spite me, and tell her, "you must make Isaac a good boy." This is true, God knows.

At one time, one of the hands named Matthew was cutting wheat. His blade being dull, our master gave him so many minutes to grind it. But Matthew did not get the blade done in the time allowed. Trouble grew out of this. Matthew was whipped, and kept chained by the leg in one of the buildings. One day when master was at church, I showed Matthew how to get away. He went away with the chain and lock on his leg. The neighbor's people got it off. He then took to the bush. After two or three weeks, my master sent me to look for him, promising not to whip him if I could get him in. I did not see him, but I saw Matthew's sisters, and told them master's promise not to whip. On a Saturday night, soon after, he came in. He was chained and locked in the house until Sunday. Then he was given in charge to Wallace (a colored man employed in the kitchen) to take care of him. On Monday, he was whipped. Then master got me to persuade Matthew not to run away. He wouldn't tell Matthew he was afraid of his running, but would tell him he *couldn't* get away,—that times were so straight with the telegraph and railway, that he couldn't get away. And that's what keeps the poor fellows there: that, and knowing that some do set out, and get brought back, and knowing what is done with them. So Matthew stayed on the farm. This occurred last summer, [1854].

In the fall, I was making money to come away, by selling fish which I caught in the creek, and by other means, when a woman on Mr. − −'s farm came to see me about some one that she feared would leave. As we talked, she said, "You wouldn't go away from your wife and children?" I said, "What's the reason I wouldn't? to stay here with half enough to eat, and to see my wife persecuted for nothing when I can do her no good. I'll go either north or south, where I can get enough to eat; and if ever I get away from that wife, I'll never have another in slavery, to be served in that way." Then she told her master, and he let on to my master, that I was making money to go away.

By and by I saw Mr. E− −, who had a little farm in the neighborhood,−then I said to one of the men, "There's going to be something done with me to-day, either whip me or sell me, one or the other." Awhile after, as I was fanning out some corn in the granary, three white men came to the door−my master, Mr. E− −, and a neighboring overseer. My master came walking to me, taking handcuffs out of his pocket,−"Come, Isaac," says he, "it's time for you to be corrected now; you've been doing wrong this year or two." Said I, "What's the matter now, master − −?" He answered, "I'm not going to whip you; I've made up my mind to sell you. I would not take two thousand dollars for you on my farm if I could keep you. I understand that you are getting ready to go off." He had then put his handcuffs on me: "Well, Sir, it is agreed to go as freely as water runs from the spring,"−meaning that I would go with him without resistance or trouble. "I have done all I could for you, night and day, even carting wood on Sunday morning,−and this is what I get for it." "Ah, Sir," said he, "you are willing to go, but 't will be none the better for you." "Well, master − −, there's good and bad men all over the world, and I'm as likely to meet with a good man as to meet with a bad one." "Well, Sir, if there's not less of that racket, I'll give you a good brushing over." I was going over to the house then, from the granary. I answered, "Well, master − −, you may do as you please, I am your nigger now, but not long." Then I met my wife, coming crying, asking,−"What's the matter?" I told her, "Eliza, no more than what I told you,—just what I expected was going to be done." His word was, "Take her away, and if she don't hush, take her to the granary, and give her a good whipping." She was crying, you see. He took me to his bedroom, and chained me by one leg to his bedpost, and kept me there, handcuffs on, all night. He slept in the bed. Next morning, he took me in a wagon and carried me to Fredericksburg, and sold me into a slave-pen to George Ayler, for ten hundred and fifty dollars. Here I met with Henry Banks. He entered the slave-pen after I had been there three days. He had run away since May, but was taken in Washington, D. C.

On a Thursday evening, came a trader from the south, named Dr. — —. He looked at Henry, and at a man named George Strawden, and at me, but did not purchase, the price being too high. I dreamed that night that he took us three. Next morning I told Henry, "That man is coming to take you, and George, and me, just as sure as the world; so Henry, let's you and me make a bargain to try and get away; for I'm never deceived in a dream,—if I dreamed master was going to whip me, he would surely whip somebody next day." That's as good a sign in the south as ever was.

About breakfast time, Dr. — — came and stripped us stark naked to examine us. They frequently do, whether buying women or men. He says, "Well, boys, I'm satisfied with you all, if you are willing to go with me, without putting me to any trouble." He had his handcuffs and spancels (ancle-beads, they call them for a nickname) with him. I said to him, "Yes, we are willing to go with you, and will go without any trouble,—I came without any trouble, and will *go* without any trouble,"—but he did not know my meaning. "I have no farm to keep you on myself," said he, "I live in Tennessee,—I am going on to Georgia, and will take fifteen hundred dollars apiece for you—I'll get as good places for you as I can—'t is not so bad there as you have heard it is." I said, "Oh, yes, Master — —, I know you'll do the best you can; I'm willing to go." "Well, get up all your clothes against the cars come from the Creek, and then we'll go to Richmond." "I suppose, Master — —, we'll have time to get 'em,—how long will it be before the cars come along?" "About three quarters of an hour, boy." Then he went to George Ayler to give him a check on the Richmond Bank for $3,400 for the three men. Henry and I then got up our clothes,—I put on two shirts, three pairs of pantaloons, two vests, a thick coat, and a summer coat in the pocket,—Henry did the same with his; so we had no bundles to carry. We were afraid to let George know, for fear he would betray us.

Dr. — — left the gate open, being deceived by our apparent readiness to go with him. We told George, "Stop a minute, we are going to get some water." Then we walked through Fredericksburg—having left the city we crossed the bridge to Falmouth, turned to the left, and made for the bush. Then we heard the cars from the creek, as they were running to Fredericksburg. On looking round, we saw a number of men coming after us on horseback. The way we cleared them was, we went into the bush, turned short to the right, leaving them the straightforward road,—we then moved on toward the very county from which I was sold. We were out three weeks, during the last of which we made a cave by digging into a cliff, at the head of the creek. The southern men who saw the cave (as we heard afterward when we were in jail) said they never saw so complete a place to hide in.

All this time I had visited my wife every day, either when the white folks were occupied, or before day. One Saturday night we hunted about for something to eat, without finding any thing until midnight. It then came into my head about the man who had persuaded my master to sell me,—so we went to him and got a dozen chickens, which we took to our cave. This made us late,—it was sunrise when we reached our cave, and then H— —, who was standing in the woods, looking for my brother Horace, saw me, and saw us going into our den. Then he went off and got N— —, with a double-barrelled gun, and T— — with a hickory club; and himself returned with a six-barrelled revolver.

Then I heard N— — asking, "Who is in here?" I looked up, and there was the gun within two feet of my head, up to his face and cocked. "Surrender, or I'll blow your brains out!" I looked out, but saw no way of escape, but by going across the creek,—N— — was on one side with his gun, H— — on the other with his revolver, and T— — over the entrance with his hickory stick. I said to Henry, "What are we to do? I started for death, and death we must try to go through. I want to see the man that bought us, no more." N— — hailed me by name, for he had now seen my face, "Surrender, for if you come out, I'll blow your brains out." "Then," said I, "You will have to do it." Then I came out, bringing my broadaxe weighing seven and a half pounds in my hand,—he just stood aside and gave me a chance to come out by the muzzle of his gun. We sprung for the creek, I and my partner. In the middle it was over my depth, but I reached the other side, still holding on to the axe. While I was struggling to get up the bank, N— — fired, and shot the broad axe out of my hand, putting twenty-nine shot into my right arm and hand, and seven into my right thigh. I ran until I got through a piece of marsh, and upon a beach near some woods.

I was standing looking at my arm; and on looking around for Henry saw him in the sedge. By this time H— — had crossed the creek too. I called to Henry to come on, and as he rose from the hedge, N— — shot him. He fell; then he got up, ran a little distance, and fell again. Then he rose up, presently fell a third time, but again recovered himself and came to me.

Finding ourselves wounded and bleeding, so that we could do nothing further toward escape, we gave up. They tied our hands behind us with a leather strap, which was very painful, as my wounded wrist swelled very much. I begged them to loosen it but they would not. They took us to jail in — — county. Dr. H. there counted ninety shot in Henry's back, legs, and arms. We stayed in the jail, a month lacking three days,—two weeks in a sort of dungeon in the cellar: then, Henry being sick with fever, from the effects of the shooting, they put us up stairs, one story higher. We were kept on water and *collots* (outside leaves of cabbage half cooked). I begged the Lord, would I ever get out, and if 't was so that I was to be caught after I got out, not to let me get out. In my dream I saw myself prying out, and heard a man speaking to me and saying, "As long as there's breath there's hope." His voice awoke me. I told Henry, and we got up, and went to the place where I had dreamed of trying, but we could not open it. This was after three weeks. Then the agent of Dr. — — came to examine us. He found we were shot so badly, that he would not take us to Richmond, unless he first heard from Dr. — —, as there was said to be some dispute between Dr. — — and Ayler about the money. On a Thursday, three days before the month of November was out, we expected Dr. — —. But he did not happen to come.

I had been trying several days at one of the windows, but despaired of getting out there,—so I took a stove leg and a piece of a fender, and tried at another window facing the jailer's house. Then *conscience* said to me, "Go and try that window that you left, and see if you can't get out." I looked at Henry to see if he was talking, but he said he had not spoken. I then returned to the first window, and pried off a short plank by the window to see how it was built. The jail was of brick, and the window frame was secured in its place by an iron clamp, spiked. On removing the plank I found behind it a short piece of iron spliced on. This I pried off with the stove leg; then I replaced the plank.

At night, just after dark, I went to work at the window. Henry was too sick to work, but when I needed his help, he would come and aid me. With the piece of iron I had taken from the wall, I got a purchase against the clamp. We took the bedstead to pieces, and using the short or long pieces as was convenient, we started the frame off on one side, splitting the sill at the bottom, where the grates were let in, and bending all the cross bars. Where the sill split off, it left a place so wide, that by removing the bricks underneath the window, we enlarged it sufficiently to get through. I stretched out of the opening full length, and let go, falling to the ground. Henry followed me, I assisting him down.

We walked eight miles that night, to my master's farm, and hid ourselves in the neighborhood, until Saturday night. Then I went out for something to eat. On my return, I saw as many as fifteen men hunting for me, some on horse, some on foot, with four hounds. I squatted close behind a thick cedar bush: the hounds came around me, and I gave them portions of the food I had collected, to keep them quiet, until the white men were out of sight,—then I scared away the hounds. I then rejoined Henry at our tent. If the runaways knew enough they could keep clear of the hounds by rubbing the soles of their shoes with red onion or spruce pine.

It now came on to rain, so that we were obliged to dig a den in the ground, expecting to stay there until spring, as we thought it would be too cold to travel in the winter, and that in the warm season we might live on fruits by the way. About this time, a neighboring farmer had two mules killed by a boar. His overseer, H— —, the same who found me before, told him that Henry and I had done it,—then S— — D— — and others sent to Fredericksburg for men and hounds to drive night and day, and take us, dead or alive, with orders to shoot us down at the very first sight. This we learned from some of our good friends,—and we then determined to leave. Here I come to speak of Kit Nichols, a slave on another farm. Kit had been beaten, and had run away,—he laid down in a wet ditch to avoid his pursuers. I met Kit in the woods. He was anxious to go with us, and we all three started on Monday night, the 1st day of December, 1854.

We walked eighteen miles the first night, to . . ., kept on through the towns of – – and – –, up to M– –. At M– –, I met a colored man, and asked him for food, as I had been fasting a long time. He directed us to a place where he said we could get food. Then he went away, and soon we saw him returning with three white men. Kit and Henry dodged, and I went on and met the white men face to face. Kit and Henry heard them say there were "three boys going to Warrenton." They passed on to the place where the colored man had sent us. We travelled on towards Warrenton, until we struck the railroad, and then footed it to Alexandria. On the way we went up to a house, where was a white man and his wife,—we asked him to sell us some bread. Said he, "Have you got a pass?" Said I, "I have no pass, but we want some bread, and we will pay you for it." He went on, "You can't travel without a pass." We told him we were hungry,—he kept on talking about a "pass." Finding we could get no bread we left him, and he then set his dog on us.

On the Virginia side of the bridge, we bought cigars and a few cakes. We lighted our cigars, and I walked on, swinging a little cane. We passed through Washington city. It now rained. We wandered about all night in the rain in Maryland. Just at daybreak we heard cars, and walked for the railroad. Before reaching it, we went into the bush, and with some matches which I had kept dry in my hat, made a fire and dried our clothes. We remained in the bush all day, watching and sleeping, and at night went on to the railroad. On our way, we met two white men, who asked us, "Where are you going?" I told them, "home." "Where?" "In Baltimore." "Where have you been?" "Chopping wood for John Brown'" They asked, "Are you free?" "Yes." "Where are your papers?" "At home, in Baltimore." They went into a shanty to arm themselves. While they were doing this, we ran as fast as we could.

We reached Baltimore just at light, and laid down in a small piece of bush in the corporation. We watched as the trains came in through the day to see where the depot was, as we wished to get on the track for Philadelphia. At night we walked boldly past the depot, but we were bothered by the forking of the roads, and came out at the river. Then we tried back,—by and by we saw a long train moving out from the city. We followed it, and went on to Havre de Grace,—but we did not cross the bridge—we could not cross over as we had wished. We moved in another direction. We concealed ourselves the next day, and again travelled all night. In the morning, we met with a friend, a colored man, who guided us about ten miles, and then directed us to a place where we had abundance of food given us, the first we had tasted since Thursday, although it was now Saturday night. We met with no more trouble. We reached Canada the morning after Christmas, at 3 o'clock.

It is the wickedest thing a man can do to hold a slave—the most unconscionable sin a man can do. If there were any chance to fight for the slaves' freedom, I'd go and stand up at the south and fight as readily as I would now go out of doors. I believe it would be just, and a righteous cause. I feel great pity for the poor creatures there, who long for a way, yet can see no way out. They think if Great Britain were to get into a war with America, it would be the means of freeing them. They would slip round and get on the English side.

If slavery were abolished, I would rather live in a southern State,—I would work for some one, but I should want to have a piece of land of my own.

CHRISTOPHER NICHOLS

I made my escape from slavery in Virginia; don't know my age,—suppose some forty odd. I belonged to but one man until after I was married. I tried to do my work. The lash was used in season and out of season. The whip was cracking from Monday morning to Saturday night. We were up before day—when the rooster crowed, the horn blowed. By the time one could see his hand before him, he was at work, and we were kept at work until late. If a man ran away after he had been whipped, the rest of us were put on half allowance till he came back, and the runaway must make up his lost time by working Sundays.

If I were to sit here until to-morrow morning, I couldn't tell you half as bad as I have been used since I can remember.

One Sunday, when I was about nineteen years old, the white children were playing in the stack-yard. The boys (slaves) had hooked a sheep, and these children found the hide in the straw. Master had all the slaves brought up Sunday evening. The overseer came home half drunk—worse than if sober. They whipped one hard; I and another thought of running,—but I was innocent, and thought they wouldn't whip me. I went up and pulled off my jacket,—they stripped me and whipped me until I fainted. Then they carried me to the kitchen and sent for the doctor. I was out of my head two or three days; the master told the boys I was playing 'possum. They never found out who took the sheep. They whipped four—the rest dodged.

At about twenty-one or twenty-two, I went to live with a man who had married my master's daughter. The first word he ever said to me was, "Where's the key to the corn-house?" "I don't know, Sir." Said he, "Has the horse been fed?" "Yes, Sir." "Has he had enough?" "I don't know, Sir." "Do you think you are talking to a poor man, or to a nigger, like yourself?" He then seized a stake from the fence, and said if I talked so to him any more, he would "lay me sprawling."

After he found that by my old master's will, I belonged to him, he began to beat me. He came down to the mill one day,—I tended a mill—I was picking,—I had stopped to fix the spindle; he thought me asleep, and hit me one or two blows. Then he went out and cut some hickory sticks. He came to the door and called me. I came to him with the pick in my hand. "Lay that down." I did so. While he was looking for a place to tie me up, I went by him and ran into the woods. At night I went back for my clothes; then, with two more boys, I started for the free States. We did not know where they were, but went to try to find them. We crossed the Potomac and hunted round and round and round. Some one showed us the way to Washington; but we missed of it, and wandered all night; then we found ourselves where we set out. In a week's time, we got to Washington—then to Scatterway, and were caught. They took us to Marlborough jail, and we were kept there two days and nights. Then the masters took us out handcuffed together. On the next morning, we went to Alexandria and were put in jail. Then the traders came from Washington to examine us. One of the boys was sold to go south. Jarvis and I were chained together, and our hands were together. On our way back we encountered Mr. S— —, M— —'s father, who seized a large club and hit Jarvis over the head with it, drawing blood terribly. Young M— — stopped him. Then they took us to Mr. S— —'s house, and chained us to different trees, where we stayed all day. Young M— — came to me and slung my leg up into the tree so that I fell on my back. Said I, "Master M— —, you hurt me." Said he, "I want to hurt you, because you give meal to my boys."

By and by Mr. M— — W— — came and took me home, chained to a horse. My master I saw coming with a cobbing-board full of auger holes, and somebody was cutting switches. Said he, "How are you? how are you? this country is too hot for you, isn't it? You were making for the north where it's cool." Then he told Mr. W— — to take me to the barn, in the late afternoon, and said he would get it out of me. He used the cobbing-board until he burst it to pieces, then a boy came with an arm full of switches. The boy was going, but he stopped the boy to see it done, so that he might tell the others. Then he began to whip me, and he whipped, and he whipped, and he whipped, and he whipped; I was in hopes the switches would break up, but it seemed as if one would last all the evening. When he had done whipping it was dark, and I was hardly able to get to the house. His wife sent me down a piece of mutton suet to grease my back. My shirt was as if it had been dipped in a barrel of blood. The next day, I had to go and stand before the drum of the wheat machine, and tend the machine all day. At night I was compelled to stack straw. I could not get along with my master at all. He was all the time hitting or whipping me—I was "a bad example for the boys," he said, "but he'd get it out of me yet." One day he found some wheat in the mill, which I was going to grind for the boys. Then he took me to the carriage-house and tied me to the carriage wheel, and whipped me as badly as when I had run away. After the whipping, he made a boy take spirits of turpentine and rub on my back. Next day, every one who saw me—the white people who came to the mill—said it was a shame to use anybody in that way. This was in the summer of 1854.

I always had it in my mind, that if I could get to a free State, I should be better off than where I was. But I had been told by N— — W— — that I could not get away: there were guards at every corner of the street in Washington, etc.

My master used to allow us one piece of meat a day, and a peck and a half of corn meal a week.

He whipped a woman before I came away, Wm. Dunkan's wife, who had a young child. He laid her on a bench, and threw her clothes up over her head, and made a boy and a woman hold her. He whipped her with a cobbing-board until she fainted,—she was so bad that they sent for Dr. W— —; but he was so angry at what my master had done, that he would not go. A week or two after, I saw the woman about again.

Another case on the same farm was that of Mary Montgomery, who had a small child at her breast. She had been sick for two or three days, but went out to get some ice for her master. The foreman told her to go back to the house, as she was too sick to work. She went back, and then master drove her out to go again for ice. Then she took to the woods, and he has not seen her since. It was said, that she got to the North, but nobody knew. Her child was taken care of by another woman, who tried to bring it up by hand, but it died.

My master used me so, that I was determined to start off, live or die. I made up my mind that I would rather die than be taken. I took no pistol—no knife—nothing but a stick to walk with. I came away with Isaac Williams and Henry Banks. When I found that Isaac was going, I determined to start, as I thought it would be a poor chance for me, if he got off before I did.

I left a wife and three children, and three grandchildren,—I never expect to see them again in this world—never.

I have seen parents and children, husbands and wives, separated by sale.

It seems not right for slavery to be. I do not think it does any good to the colored men. I feel no inclination to go back—I don't want to cross the line. All the time I was in slavery, I lived in dead dread and fear. If I slept it was in dread—and in the morning it was dread—dread, night and day. It seems to me I must have been dead by this time, if I had not got away. My master was killing me as fast as he could when I got away.

HENRY BANKS

I was born in Stafford Co., in 1835. I was brought up on a farm. I did not go to school. I learned to read of my brother-in-law, but I cannot write. There was a Sunday school, but not for colored children.

One of the earliest things I remember is my being sold to Mr. N— —, a farmer in the neighborhood. My mother and brothers and sisters were sold at the same time to N— —. I lived with N— — until about fifteen years old. When I was eight years old, I was put to work regularly on the farm, ploughing, hoeing corn, and doing farm work generally. I have belonged to several owners, but I have no recollection of any one of them ever coming to my cabin to inquire into my wants, nor to ask whether any thing was necessary for my comfort or convenience,—nor whether I was well used by the overseer or foreman. If I were sick, the overseer attended to me,—if he thought it needful, he would give me medicine,—if he thought it a hard case, he would send for a doctor. I had the doctor once, but the owner did not come to see me. This was nothing strange,—it was so with all, so far as I have heard. N— —'s overseer whipped me often—stripped me, and tied me up when he did it, and generally drew blood,—sometimes he would not be so severe as at others, but I have frequently had to pull my shirt from my back with a good deal of misery, on account of its sticking in the blood where I had been lashed. Let daybreak catch me in the house, instead of currying the horses, that was as good for a flogging as any thing else,—if caught standing at the plough, instead of moving, that was good for fifty lashes more or less,—the least of any thing would provoke it. I was whipped once because the overseer said I looked mad: "Come here, you d—d selfish son of a b—h, I'll please you by the time I've done with you." Then he whipped me, so that I couldn't hollow. I always tried to do the work faithfully that was assigned me,—not because I felt it a duty, but because I was afraid not to do it: I did not feel it right, however, to be compelled to work for other folks.

N— — broke up,—sold the farm and all his people. We were scattered, but not very far apart—some six or seven miles. I was sold to R— — S— —, in Spotsylvania county, across the R appahannock. I was the only one of the family that S— — bought. I lived with him about a year and a half. He had a colored slave foreman, who had to do as he was commanded, and I hardly had so much consideration as from a white overseer. S— — did not clothe nor feed his hands well. We were worked very late at night and were at it again before day. Sundays differed little from other days. Sometimes he would give us Sunday or part of a Sunday; but if he were in the least angry, we had to work all day. I did not hear a sermon preached during the time I lived with S– –, there was no meeting for us to go to. I would sometimes hear of there being meetings about there, but I had no chance to go. At this place there was no colored minister–there were no Christian people on that place. I never heard any religious songs while I was there. It was work, work, and nothing else; that's all they asked of me,–and if we did not do it, we were whipped. Nobody was excused–we were all used one way–all kept at it. I left him on account of work. It was in harvest–harvesting wheat. I was cradling–I couldn't make the cradle cut well. S– – said, "You can make that cradle cut better if you choose to,–but you don't choose to." I told him "I had tried to make it do the best I knew how." Then he said to the men, "Come here and take hold of this d–d nigger, I'll make it all right with him." Then they took me to the barn, stripped me stark naked, and then he tied my hands together and my feet together, and swung me up so I could move neither way. While he was tying me up, I told him, "I will do all I know how to do." He said "'twas a d–d lie,–I didn't do it,–but he knew I could do it,–and when he was done with me, he'd show that I would do it." Then he commenced whipping me with a cowhide, made keen at the end; he put on the blows forward and backward–every blow bringing the blood. He must have whipped me a solid half hour. Before he took me down, he said, "Now will you go and do the business?" I told him then, that "I had told him before that I would willingly do all that I knew how." He said, "I'll try you with this–if I tie you up again, I'll give you five hundred." Then he took me down. I was then unable to do any work. He told me to go to work, but I could not even stand. He then had me carried by the hands into the shade of a tree, where I laid just as I could,–I could not lie any way long. The men brought buckets of water and threw on me,–I knew what it was for–they thought I was dying. I did no more work for S– –. I ran away that same night into the woods.

I ran away in order that master might sell me running,–I didn't care much whose hands I fell into, if I got out of his. He put out advertisements for me, as I was told, of twenty-five dollars reward, for bringing me home not injured. I had heard tell of a free country–but I did not know where it was, nor how to get there. I stayed in the woods three months; I then thought I would start for a free country somewhere. I got as far as the city of Washington; there I went aboard a vessel which the captain told me was going to

Boston. But it was not. He asked me for free papers—I told him I had none. Then he suspected me, and said I could not ship without them. He said, if I were a slave, he would make a free man of me,—that he had a habit of doing so,—but he lied. I believed him, however—I trusted him, and told him my case, how my owner treated me, and all,—he said he thought it was very wrong. Then, after he had got it all out of me, he went into the city, and told me to stay aboard till he came back; to get what I wanted to eat, and cook it, but not let myself be seen, because I might be taken up. He was gone a short time, and then he came back, and asked me to go with him to his house, to bring some provisions down for his vessel. I went with him up the street—there were several persons standing on a corner. The captain said, "Come this way; there's a constable—don't let him see you!" Then the constable came along behind us. The captain led me into an office and said, "Here's a runaway I've took up." There was some questioning, and I was put in jail.

In one week's time, R— — S— — came and shook hands with me through the grates. He asked, "What made me run away?" I told him, "I wouldn't have run away if he hadn't whipped me" "Do you want to go home?" "I'll go back if you won't whip me any more." He made no promise, but took me home. Directly he sold me to George Ayler. I escaped from Ayler's slave-pen in company with Isaac Williams. . . . .

In the den we were; three white men came upon us. We took across the creek. I was in the den when they fired at Isaac. I then jumped for the creek. I was shot by one of the white men. I caught the shot from my legs to my shoulders—all over my back. About a hundred shot holes were counted in my back,—they were ducking shot, and are mostly in me now. I suffer from them now in my right arm, if I do any work.

I do not think it was intended for any man to be a slave. I never thought so, from a little boy. The slaves are not contented and happy. They can't be: I never knew one to be so where I was.

JOHN W. LINDSEY

[Mr. Lindsey reached St. Catharines in an entirely destitute condition. He is now reputed to be worth from eight to ten thousand dollars, acquired by industry and economy.]

I was born free. At the age of seven, I was kidnapped by S— — G— —, and carried to West Tennessee. When I was about twenty-five years old, I went to a man who had been Postmaster General, and asked him if he would do any thing toward restoring my freedom, as I had been kidnapped wrongfully, and was unlawfully detained by Mr. — —. He answered, that "Mr. G— — had settled all that," and advised me to "Go home and be a good boy." Finding that I was to get no assistance from any quarter, and that justice was refused me, I resolved to free myself. I was whiter then than I am now, for it was twenty-one years ago, and I worked under cover at blacksmithing. A person across the street could not tell whether I were a white or a colored man. Whether I was pursued or not I am unable to say. I walked by day and rested at night.

I passed people working in the fields, and once I heard one ask another, "Do you think that is a white man?" I took no notice of this, and walked on. At one time I met a man on horseback who stopped and talked with me. I spoke so familiarly of this great man and of that great man, and talked in so important a way, that he did not dare ask me if I were a slave! At one place, I was somewhat afraid of pursuit, and there seemed to be some suspicions entertained in regard to me. I walked away from the town on the bank of the river and prayed to the Lord for deliverance. Just then a steamboat came along—she was bound for Pittsburg. I got a passage on board. The cook, who was a very black man, asked me "if I was free?" I told him that I had heard of a man in Maryland who got rich by minding his own business, and that he would find it for his own interest to attend to his own affairs. However, I found little difficulty in reaching the frontier and crossing the line.

I have travelled in Maryland, Virginia, Kentucky, and Tennessee. If a man says slavery is a good institution, he might as well say there is no God—only a devil. Slavery is like the bottomless pit. You hear people say to the negro, "Why don't you accomplish something?" You see the colored men, their faces scarred and wrinkled, and almost deprived of intelligence in some cases,— their manliness crushed out; stooping, awkward in gait,—kept in entire ignorance. Now, to ask them why they don't do some great thing, is like tying a man or weakening him by medicine, and then saying, "Why don't you go and do that piece of work, or plant that field with wheat and corn?" Slavery is mean. The slaveholders want their slaves for pocket money. The slaves are their right hand to do their work.

HENRY ATKINSON

I belonged in Norfolk, Va., from birth until thirty-four years of age. I never saw my owner, but when I was a little boy. I was hired out by the year by an agent of my owner. Sometimes I was well cared for, sometimes not, according to the man's disposition that employed me. There was one man who was a kind hearted man, who hired me nine years of the time. He treated me well, giving me enough to eat, drink, and wear, and a quarter of a dollar every Saturday night to support my wife. She lived in the city, being a slave: I could not see her when I wished always,—sometimes I was not permitted to see her. The way we were married was, a few words were read out of a book; no license was granted, as to free people. During all these nine years, my mind was continually running upon this,—how am I to get out of this bondage?—for, as well as I was used, I felt that I was under a hard bondage. I studied upon it long. I have lain awake more than half the night, many a time, studying on that one thing—should I ever be able to get clear? But I could not see my way out.

At one time I was hired out to a man whose treatment of me was very bad. Many times I would be sick and could scarcely hold up my head: this man would do nothing for me on the plea that it belonged to the agent to do it,—the agent would say it was not his duty, but my employer's,—and so I suffered from neglect. If neither of them would help me, I had nowhere to go for relief. He would allow me no money: if I wanted a few cents for myself or my wife I had to work nights to earn them.

I had no chance to learn to read or write. The agent never came near me to see if I were well used or abused by the people who hired me. All I ever saw of him was when the year was up and he came to get his money. Excepting the nine years' time I have spoken of before, I was put up in the ring and let to the highest bidder,—I was hired out, did the work, and others got the money,—that was mean and hard too.

In regard to religious instruction, I was allowed to go to church on Sunday, to a white clergyman—no colored preacher being allowed in Norfolk. We call some colored men, ministers, but they read nothing from the Bible—they exhort a little sometimes,—but 't isn't preaching. The white clergymen don't preach the whole gospel there. Since I have been here, I have heard the passage about the fast that the Lord hath chosen, to loose the bands of wickedness, to undo the heavy burdens, to let the oppressed go free, and that ye break every yoke. I never heard that down South. If a colored man were to say it, he'd have the handcuffs put on quick,—if a white man were to say it, he'd have to leave, because they'd say he was "putting too much into the niggers heads." I've seen white children driven away from among the colored, when they said something the old folks did not like, because it was "putting something into the nigger's head."

I was a member of the First Baptist church. I heard the white minister preach, and I thought within myself, I will seek a better world above,—here I am in bondage, and if there is a better world above where I shall not be pulled and hauled about and tormented as I am in this, I will seek it.

The person I termed my owner was a woman who removed to England, and lived in London. When I was about twenty years old, I heard of her death, and that she had made a will leaving all her slaves, fifteen in number, free; and that the property and money which had belonged to her, was to be divided amongst us. I was told so by a white person—a lawyer. But she had one son living in Calcutta. He was written to, to find out who were the heirs to these people and this property. He returned word that he had no heirs for the people and property, and that he did not want them,—but that he wished them to do what his mother requested—liberate the slaves, give them the property, and let them go where they pleased. My employer told me and my fellow-servants—all relatives of mine—that we should have our time,—but still we were hired out. He kept feeding us with the tale that we should have our time, and still kept hiring us out. This was done to keep us from running away.

By and by, to blind us, the agent told us that my mistress' son was dead, and that we had fallen to his nearest relations, Mr. W— —, of

Philadelphia, and Mr. M— —, of Washington: but they were no more his relations than that lamp. Mr. W. and Mr. M. came to Norfolk, and actually divided us as equally as they could. The family consisted of two sisters with seven children each, and an uncle. In the division, I was taken from my mother's family, and put with my aunt's, and with them fell to Mr. M. We still remained in Norfolk, but it grieved me so that I knew not what to do to think that I was so robbed. For my mistress, when I was a little boy, sat at the table with me, and she put her hand on my head and said, "My poor little servant, you shall never serve any one after I am dead, but shall have enough to live on the rest of your days." To remember this, and that she had died and left it in her will as she had said, and then to be cheated out of it, grieved me so, that I knew not how to bear it. I was hired out a short time, but expected every day to be carried up to Washington.

At last, I found an opportunity to escape, after studying upon it a long time. But it went hard to leave my wife; it was like taking my heart's blood: but I could not help it—I expected to be taken away where I should never see her again, and so I concluded that it would be right to leave her. [Here Atkinson's eyes filled with tears.] I never expect to see her again in this world—nor our child.

I reached Canada about a year ago. Liberty I find to be sweet indeed.

I think slavery is the worst and meanest thing to be thought of. It appears to me that God cannot receive into the kingdom of heaven, those who deal in slaves. God made all men—He is no respecter of persons—and it is impossible that he should, on account of my color, intend that I should be the slave of a man, because he is of a brighter skin than I am.

WILLIAM GROSE

I was held as a slave at Harper's Ferry, Va. When I was twenty-five years old, my two brothers who were twelve miles out, were sent for to the ferry, so as to catch us all three together, which they did. We were then taken to Baltimore to be sold down south. The reason was, that I had a free wife in Virginia, and they were afraid we would get away through her means. My wife and two children were then keeping boarders; I was well used, and we were doing well. All at once, on Sunday morning, a man came to my house before I was up, and called me to go to his store to help put up some goods. My wife suspected it was a trap: but I started to go. When I came in sight of him, my heart failed me; I sent him word I could not come. On inquiry in a certain quarter, I was told that I was sold, and was advised to make my escape into Pennsylvania. I then went to my owner's, twelve miles, and remained there three days, they telling me I was not sold. The two brothers were all this time in jail, but I did not then know it. I was sent to the mill to get some offal,—then two men came in, grabbed me and handcuffed me, and took me off. How I felt that day I cannot tell. I had never been more than twenty miles from home, and now I was taken away from my mother and wife and children. About four miles from the mill, I met my wife in the road coming to bring me some clean clothes. She met me as I was on horseback, handcuffed. She thought I was on the farm, and was surprised to see me. They let me get down to walk and talk with her until we came to the jail: then they put me in, and kept her outside. She had then eight miles to go on foot, to get clothes ready for me to take along. I was so crazy, I don't know what my wife said. I was beside myself to think of going south. I was as afraid of traders as I would be of a bear. This was Tuesday.

The man who had bought us came early Wednesday morning, but the jailer would not let us out, he hoping to make a bargain with somebody else, and induce our owners to withdraw the bond from the man that had us. Upon this, the trader and jailer got into a quarrel, and the trader produced a pistol, which the jailer and his brother took away from him. After some time, the jailer let us out. We were handcuffed together: I was in the middle, a hand of each brother fastened to mine. We walked thus to Harper's Ferry: there my wife met me with some clothes. She said but little; she was in grief and crying. The two men with us told her they would get us a good home. We went by the cars to Baltimore—remained fifteen days in jail. Then we were separated, myself and one brother going to New Orleans, and the other remained in B. Him I have not seen since, but have heard that he was taken to Georgia. There were about seventy of us, men, women, and children shipped to New Orleans. Nothing especial occurred except on one occasion, when, after some thick weather, the ship came near an English island: the captain then hurried us all below and closed the hatches. After passing the island, we had liberty to come up again.

We waited on our owners awhile in New Orleans, and after four months, my brother and I were sold together as house servants in the city, to an old widower, who would not have a white face about him. He had a colored woman for a wife—she being a slave. He had had several wives whom he had set free when he got tired of them. This woman came for us to the yard,—then we went before him. He sent for a woman, who came in, and said he to me, "That is your wife." I was scared half to death, for I had one wife whom I liked, and didn't want another,—but I said nothing. He assigned one to my brother in the same way. There was no ceremony about it—he said "Cynthia is your wife, and Ellen is John's." As we were not acclimated, he sent us into Alabama to a watering-place, where we remained three months till late in the fall—then we went back to him. I was hired out one month in a gambling saloon, where I had two meals a day and slept on a table; then for nine months to an American family, where I got along very well; then to a man who had been mate of a steamboat, and whom I could not please. After I had been in New Orleans a year, my wife came on and was employed in the same place, (in the American family).

One oppression there was, my wife did not dare let it be known she was from Virginia, through fear of being sold. When my master found out that I had a free-woman for a wife there, he was angry about it, and began to grumble. Then she went to a lawyer to get a certificate by which she could remain there. He would get one for a hundred dollars, which was more than she was able to pay: so she did not get the certificate, but promised to take one by and by. His hoping to get the money kept him from troubling her,—and before the time came for her taking it, she left for a distant place. He was mad about it, and told me that if she ever came there again, he'd put her to so much trouble that she would wish she had paid the hundred dollars and got the certificate. This did not disturb me, as I knew she would not come back any more.

After my wife was gone, I felt very uneasy. At length, I picked up spunk, and said I would start. All this time, I dreamed on nights that I was getting clear. This put the notion into my head to start—a dream that I had reached a free soil and was perfectly safe. Sometimes I felt as if I would get clear, and again as if I would not. I had many doubts. I said to myself—I recollect it well,—I can't die but once; if they catch me, they can but kill me: I'll defend myself as far as I can. I armed myself with an old razor, and made a start alone, telling no one, not even my brother. All the way along, I felt a dread—a heavy load on me all the way. I would look up at the telegraph wire, and dread that the news was going on ahead of me. At one time I was on a canal-boat—it did not seem to go fast enough for me, and I felt very much cast down about it; at last I came to a place where the telegraph wire was broken, and I felt as if the heavy load was rolled off me. I intended to stay in my native country,—but I saw so many mean-looking men, that I did not dare to stay. I found a friend who helped me on the way to Canada, which I reached in 1851.

I served twenty-five years in slavery, and about five I have been free. I feel now like a man, while before I felt more as though I were but a brute. When in the United States, if a white man spoke to me, I would feel frightened, whether I were in the right or wrong; but now it is quite a different thing,—if a white man speaks to me, I can look him right in the eyes—if he were to insult me, I could give him an answer. I have the rights and privileges of any other man. I am now living with my wife and children, and doing very well. When I lie down at night, I do not feel afraid of oversleeping, so that my employer might jump on me if he pleased. I am a true British subject, and I have a vote every year as much as any other man. I often used to wonder in the United States, when I saw carriages going round for voters, why they never asked me to vote. But I have since found out the reason,—I know they were using my vote instead of my using it—now I use it myself. Now I feel like a man, and I wish to God that all my fellow-creatures could feel the same freedom that I feel. I am not prejudiced against all the white race in the United States,—it is only the portion that sustain the cursed laws of slavery.

Here's something I want to say to the colored people in the United States: You think you are free there, but you are very much mistaken: if you wish to be free men, I hope you will all come to Canada as soon as possible. There is plenty of land here, and schools to educate your children. I have no education myself, but I don't intend to let my children come up as I did. I have but two, and instead of making servants out of them, I'll give them a good education, which I could not do in the southern portion of the

United States. True, they were not slaves there, but I could not have given them any education.

I have been through both Upper and Lower Canada, and I have found the colored people keeping stores, farming, etc., and doing well. I have made more money since I came here, than I made in the United States. I know several colored people who have become wealthy by industry—owning horses and carriages,—one who was a fellow-servant of mine, now owns two span of horses, and two as fine carriages as there are on the bank. As a general thing, the colored people are more sober and industrious than in the States: there they feel when they have money, that they cannot make what use they would like of it, they are so kept down, so looked down upon. Here they have something to do with their money, and put it to a good purpose.

I am employed in the Clifton House, at the Falls.

DAVID WEST

I came from King and Queen county, Va., where I left a wife and four children. I was treated well—I paid my master two hundred dollars a year, and acted honorably all through the time I remained there. My master died, and I heard that I was to be sold, which would separate me from my family, and knowing no law which would defend me, I concluded to come away.

When my master died, I made his coffin and buried him. I am a carpenter, and well known in King and Queen county. I did not believe that slavery was right, but as I was born there, and had a family there, I tried to content myself to remain, and should probably have done so, but for the dread of being sold south. My mistress told me that I was not to be sold, and my master's brother told me the same,—but I had seen him carry away my father, sister, and aunt to Alabama to be sold: my father being then sixty years old. When he returned, I asked him "what he had done with my father?"—all he said was, *"Sir?"* and that was all the answer he made me. Of course I could not believe him, when he said I was not to be sold: for he had fooled my father with the story that he was going to remove to Alabama himself. Gentlemen in the neighborhood told me I was going to be sold.

When I left, I told my purpose to no one. I studied a plan by which I might get away, and I succeeded.

I am now in Canada doing well at my trade, and I expect to do yet better. My only trouble is about my wife and family. I never should have come away but for being forced away.

A Baptist preacher told me once, when I was working for him, that there was no country in the world equal to Virginia. My answer was, "Yes, I believe it is the greatest country in the world: for one third of the people are doing nothing, and the other two thirds are working to support them." He then spoke of something else.

My family are perpetually on my mind. I should be perfectly happy if I could have my wife and the four children. If my wife had known it, and had said half a word, I should have stayed to the moment of being sold.

I look upon slavery as a disgrace, and as breaking the laws of God: that no man can keep the laws of God and hold to slavery. I believe my own master was as good a man as there is in the whole South: I loved him in health, and I loved him in death,—but I can read the Bible, and I do not see any thing there by which he could be justified in holding slaves: and I know not where he has gone to.

It is a common remark that they have a right to hold the slaves, because they were given them by their fathers,—justifying their own sins by those of their fathers: would it excuse them for stealing or drinking, to say that their fathers were thieves and drunkards?

I was taught, secretly, to read, but never taught to write: I feel that I have been wrongfully deprived of the knowledge of writing. I could have done better for myself every way had I known how to write.

I was led to religious knowledge, by hearing old colored people talk, and by the preaching I had heard. I was constrained to seek repentance, was converted, and joined the Pokaroan church, [Baptist]. I used to partake of the sacrament after the whites had had their communion. We could have no night meetings without fear of the patrols, who would lash those they could catch during or after service.

I wish well to the members of that church; and, although my name is now taken off the records with scorn, I have done nothing wrong, nor have I offended my Maker by the course I have pursued. I hope to meet them in heaven with the hundred and forty and four thousand whom John saw in Mount Sion (or the New Jerusalem), where we all shall meet and no more to part.

We shall never be able to meet in that city holding that which does not belong to us.

I want to ask the southern people if their own consciences do not tell them it is wrong to hold slaves, knowing that it is against the laws of God?

I have seen the slaves to be underfed and half clothed, and the masters would say they were well taken care of. I have known this of three or four counties. I have known a slave to be sick, and to be neglected until he was about to die, and then a great stir would be made,—and if he died, they would say, "The best nigger is dead," although when living, it would seem as if he could do nothing to please them. I have seen separations of families every year for many years.

The slaveholders so far as I know are generally mean people. I have been cheated by a rich slaveholder out of half a bushel of corn in buying half a barrel. I knew it and he knew it; but he knew I would not dare say any thing about it,—the law was such that he could have me whipped, if I were to contradict him. He was worth ten thousand dollars, and I was not worth ten cents: I believe that trade was just as much right as it is to hold slaves. I told some white people of this before I left, and they cried out "shame!"

I believe that if the slaveholders were to say, "Here, boys, you are free; you may go to work for me at so much a day,"—if 't was done all over the South, there would be no trouble: 't would be no great credit to set them free, for 't is no more than their duty.

I have known slaves to be hungry, but when their master asked them if they had enough, they would, through fear, say "Yes." So if asked if they wish to be free, they will say "No." I knew a case where there was a division of between fifty and sixty slaves among heirs, one of whom intended to set free her part. So wishing to consult them, she asked of such and such ones, if they would like to be free, and they all said "No:"—for if they had said yes, and had then fallen to the other heirs, they would be sold,—and so they said "No," against their own consciences. But there will be a time when all will be judged. The Lord, He made us out of the dust of the earth, and He is the greatest Judge of the earth, yet even He does not compel us to serve Him: but among men, who are so frail, the stronger takes the weaker by force, and binds them slaves, and murders them.

These views I have not got since I left the South; they were in me all the time I was there. I have often tried to love my minister and brethren in Pokaroan church, but when I heard them say, "Do unto others as ye would that others should do unto you," and saw what they were doing to their own brethren in Christ, I thought with the disciples, "Who, then, can be saved?" I never knew in all my living in the South, a colored man to separate a family of whites by sale or in any way, but have often known this to be done by the whites.

HENRY JACKSON

I was born free at Chatham Four Corners, N. Y. State. I was sent to school and learned to read and write. My parents were free at the time of my birth, but had been slaves under the old laws of New York. At about the age of sixteen, my father bound me out to a mand named G— —, to remain till twenty-one, then to receive two haundred and fifty dollars. G— — went to California, where he remained over a year, and then came back for his wife and children and me to take us to that State. Then I went with him by railway and by water: the vessel was a steamer,—took us into some port, the name of which I do not know; there G— — and another man came on board, and asked me to go up into the town,—it was a middling-sized town. They took me to an auction room where were other colored people, and I was sold at auction to the highest bidder for four hundred and fifty dollars. I thought it a strange transaction, but I felt that I was in their power,—I was among strangers, had no friends there, knew it would be of no use to remonstrate, and so said nothing. A man by the name of W. K. S. bought me. I saw no papers passed,—there might have been. S. said, "You are in my hands now, and you must obey my orders." I answered him nothing,—did not say a word to him. As soon as I was sold, G— — left, and I have not seen him since. I was taken into S.'s family, and went to work for him and the family, doing house-work, errands, etc. I was treated kindly,—had enough of every thing,—his son gave me a little change occasionally. My mind was all the time occupied by the thought of my freedom, and I made up my mind to escape on the first opportunity. I said nothing to Mr. S. about my past life: he never said any thing about setting me free. Whether he knew it was illegal for G— — to sell me, I do not know. I had some fears in regard to running away—fears that something—I could not tell what— would be done with me. At last I started on foot for Philadelphia, which I reached in due time, without any trouble on the way, except being worn out with fatigue.

I did not travel about much while in slavery: but from my own experience of it, and from what I have seen, I pronounce it a very great curse.

I think G— —'s conduct is mean. I think it would be a good thing for him to be sold for a few years down South,—I think that by the time he had been there five years, he would be glad to set all the slaves free.

I think it necessary for all free people of color to be on their guard.

I had the privilege of going to church every Sunday. I belonged to the Methodist church before I went away, as did my father and mother. Mr. S. was a member of the same church with myself,—we heard the same preaching and sat at the same communion table. The colored people partook after the others had done. I have not seen S. since I came away, and have no desire to see him.

TORONTO

The population of this wealthy, enterprising, and beautiful city is estimated at forty-seven thousand, of whom about one thousand are colored persons. Of these no separate count is made in taking the census. The greater part of the colored people reside in the north-western section of the city. Their houses resemble those of the same class of persons in St. Catharines: but as they have not generally so extensive gardens, more time can be allotted to the beautifying and general care of their dwellings than in St. Catharines.

Many of the colored people own the houses in which they dwell, and some have acquired valuable estates. No distinction exists in Toronto, in regard to school privileges. One of the students in the Normal School was a fugitive slave, and colored youths are attending lectures in the University. There are three churches exclusively belonging to the colored people—a Baptist and two Methodist churches. They are excluded, however, from none of the churches, and in all of them a few of the African race may be found.

The colored people in Toronto are, on the whole, remarkably industrious. Their condition is such as to gratify the philanthropist, and to afford encouragement to the friends of emancipation everywhere. A portion of them sustain a lyceum or debating club (which is attended by both sexes) where debates are held, and original essays are read. A large majority of the adult colored people are refugees from the South. Several of these furnished their testimony in regard to the institution under whose fostering care they were reared. They gave their statements readily and with every appearance of truth. Their evidence is as reliable as any which can be obtained. No longer dreading the lash, they are free to utter their real sentiments, and to communicate their actual experiences. Some of the details would appear too shocking for credence, were it not admitted on all hands, that the only limit to the cruelty of a mean, ill-tempered, virtually irresponsible tyrant, is the capacity for suffering with which the victims of his malignity may be endowed.

Those who have been most cruelly treated and unjustly used, are most likely to undertake an escape. Those who have succeeded in the undertaking, therefore, may fairly be expected to give a very dark picture. Ought slavery then, as a whole, to be condemned by the evidence they present? We answer, that every slave is *liable* to the same maltreatment and abuse from which the fugitives in Canada have escaped; and that an institution which holds such liabilities over the heads of millions, and inflicts the most enormous evils on many thousands, might as well be set aside.

Again, in forming a judgment of slavery as to its merits and demerits, this testimony should receive at least as much weight as a class of anecdotes so readily chronicled, and so widely circulated, of individual slaves who have manifested great attachment to their masters, or refused to receive their freedom. The excellence of pious masters who exhort and pray with their slaves from the best of motives, is also deemed worthy of record; and if from such anecdotes, of slaves loving slavery, and of the kindness of some masters, inferences are drawn favorable to the continuance of slavery, facts of the opposite class, although it is a more ungrateful task to expose them, ought also to be fully stated, lest humanity and benevolence be lulled to sleep over evils which they should do their utmost to remove.

Let it not be understood, however, that in this work we intend to make a selection of the most atrocious cases of abuse. Any instances of kind, self-sacrificing masters, or humane, benevolent overseers, will be mentioned at greater length and in greater fulness than those of opposite character, to relieve, if possible, the canvas which truth is reluctantly obliged to crowd "with bitter and with black."

What is here incidentally said in regard to the narratives of the fugitives in Toronto, applies with equal force to all statements of fugitives in Canada West in this work.

CHARLES HENRY GREEN

I was a slave in Delaware from birth, until twenty-three years of age: am now twenty four. I never had any religious or other instruction from my master. I picked up a knowledge of reading, and some religious knowledge among people where I was hired out. I was well used—have been hit over the head with chunks of wood,—hit over the back with a pitchfork handle, but was never whipped with a cowskin.

Slavery is horrid. I think if, the slaves were set free, they would readily go to work for money.

JAMES W. SUMLER

Arrived in Canada, March 3, 1855. I came from Norfolk, Va.; was in bondage twenty-six years. I was not sent to school—never. My first master and mistress gave me no religious instruction at all, nor any other. I learned to read: the way was, I hid in a hayloft on Sunday, and got the younger white children to teach me. I bought the book with a ninepence that a man gave me for holding his horse.

My master was a Methodist. I used to get his horse ready, and hold him when master was going to meeting, but he never asked me to go. At twelve years, my first master died and I was hired out. I was put to work in a lumber-yard. I generally had enough to eat, but was sometimes short for clothes.

My second master and mistress never gave me any instruction about God, and Christ, and the Bible: they used to object to my going to meetings. It was nothing but come and go. They were Methodists. I was never punished very severely, but I have seen servants of the same family punished in various ways. I have seen them tied down, stripped bare, and struck with the paddle, bored with auger holes, until they couldn't walk straight. This was because they did not perform the tasks assigned them. I consider the tasks given them were such they *could not* perform them. I have seen them tied up and whipped until the blood ran down to the ground. I have seen a man—Elick Smith—so badly whipped with the cobble and cowhide, that he could not lie down any way. The use of brine after whipping is very common.

After I got to years of maturity, and saw the white people sitting in the shade, while I worked in the sun, I thought I would like to be my own man. The first that started me was, they sold my brother down south, and I have not seen him since. I thought my chance would come next, and so I put out.

A white man—a Baptist, used to preach to us. The white people took the communion in the morning, and we took it in the evening. The minister used to tell us not to be disorderly on taking the sacrament—I thought he was disorderly himself, for he kept slaves.

I left home at 2 P.M., and walked a very considerable distance. Then I saw fit to remain concealed nine months. Meanwhile I was advertised, and a reward of $200 was offered for me. On seeing this I felt somewhat troubled in mind,—at last I started, but I had to run back to my hiding-place. A second time I got very near a place where I would have been safe, but I was pursued, and had to put back. A third time I was successful.

I enjoy myself here more than I did in slavery. I believe that liberty is the true and proper state for the colored man, and for every man. I came here with nothing. I think I can make a living here, and am disposed to try. I left slavery with the expectation that I would have to work, and I am glad to get work.

I look upon slavery as wrong, and as a curse upon the masters. I do not believe that there is any religion in the masters. The slaves are not religious in consequence of slavery; they have often impediments in the way of their going to meetings. I believe that the slaveholders know that that they are guilty in holding slaves. If the slaves were all set at liberty, I think it would be better for the slaves and for the slaveholders too. The abolitionists have helped me a great deal.

PATRICK SNEAD

I belonged in Savannah, Georgia. I am as white as my master was, but I was born a slave. My first master dying, I fell to one of the sons, who died when I was about fifteen. He was a sporting character. He had always promised my mother to give me my freedom at some time,—as soon as I could take care of myself. I was sent to school a little while by mother, so that I could spell quite well,—but I have lost it all. My master gave me no religious instruction, but I was allowed to attend a Sunday School for colored children. I was put to the cooper's trade, which I learned in five years. While my master lived I was well used. But at length he was taken sick with consumption; I attended him, and took care of him. I said nothing to him about my freedom, not feeling any great interest in the matter at that time. I have good reason to believe that he was persuaded not to set me free. At length he departed this life.

After his death, the doctor's bill of three hundred dollars had to be satisfied out of the estate. Other property being deficient, I was given up, and was for one day the property of the physician. I was then sold to a wholesale merchant for five hundred dollars. The merchant employed me about the store four years; he found me smarter than many others, and I had to work hard, lifting heavy bales of goods. This lifting caused me to wear a truss some time before I left. In the easiest time of the year, the summer, my working hours were from 6 in the morning to 7 in the evening. In the fall and spring I worked from 6 in the morning until 12 at night, the bales of goods being opened in the night: in the winter from 6 to 6. I had plenty of food and good common clothing. The merchant's manner of address to me was generally pleasant: I had the privilege of going to church on Sundays, if I pleased.

He never on Saturday nights allowed me any money: I liked female society as well as he did, and wanted some spending money. I was not provoked to ask for it by seeing others have money, but I felt that I ought to be allowed something for my encouragement, after performing so much hard labor. His answer was, that he gave me enough to eat. I told him that he would have to sell me, "for to work in this way I shall not." He grinned and bore it.

About a year before this I had been attentive to a young free-woman who lived with her aunt. One evening, on leaving, the aunt cautioned me to tell Billy (a boy on the place) to fasten the gate after me, as the night before he had left it open. Accordingly, on coming out, I said, "Billy, be careful to fasten the gate, for you did not fasten it the night before." There was, as I afterwards learned, a white man concealed behind the tree close by,—he heard me, and fancied that what I said was meant to hit him in some way; for he meanwhile was, unbeknown to me, sustaining a peculiar relation to the very girl that I was visiting. The next day that man said he would buy me, if it cost him a thousand dollars, so that he could give me a hundred lashes. My master heard of this threat,—I heard of it, and believe I told my master. Some days after I met the man, told him what I had heard,—that it was a mistake,—that I did not know he was behind the tree, or that he had any thing to do with the person I was visiting, and that I would not be in his way any further. So it blew over.

After my talk with my master about the money, he, remembering the affair just mentioned, went to that party, and offered to sell me to him. Then the same man who had made the threat to buy me, asked me if I was willing to belong to him. I told him I would as lief belong to him as to anybody, if he would allow me a living chance. He told me that he would hire me out at my trade of coopering, and provide me with tools. He bought me—giving for me a woman and two children, and a hundred dollars. I went to work as he had promised. My task was eighteen barrels a week: I could make more than twice as many, so then I began to have money. My treatment was good.

I went on in this way four years; then my colored employer was going to Liberia, with a ship load of emigrants—free people of color. He bade me goodby, and shook my hands; at this I felt an anxious wish to go with him, and from that moment I felt what liberty was. I then told him, that I hoped one day to be my own man, and if so, that I wished to go to Liberia. He said, "I hope so, my son." He had baptized me, and was pastor of the church to which I belonged. After he left, I went on working nearly one year more, with his partner, who had bought him out.

During this time my desire for liberty grew stronger and stronger. I had spent my money as I went along. My master refused to buy me new tools after my old ones were worn out—said I dressed better than he, and must buy tools for myself. I thought this ought not to do, and I made up my mind, "it sha' n't do either." I had now come to a resolution, and I started for a land of liberty. I left in July, 1851, at 3 on a Monday morning. I reached Canada safely, and had no difficulty until two years had elapsed. Then I was employed in the summer of 1853 as a waiter in the Cataract House, on the American side of the Falls. Then a constable of Buffalo came in, on Sunday after dinner, and sent the barkeeper into the dining-room for me. I went into the hall, and met the constable,—I had my jacket in my hand, and was going to put it up. He stepped up to me. "Here, Watson," (this was the name I assumed on escaping,) "you waited on me, and I'll give you some change." His fingers were then in his pocket, and he dropped a quarter dollar on the floor. I told him, "I have not waited on you—you must be mistaken in the man, and I don't want another waiter's money." He approached,—I suspected, and stepped back toward the dining-room door. By that time he made a grab at me, caught me by the collar of my shirt and vest,—then four more constables, he had brought with him, sprung on me,—they dragged me to the street door—there was a jam—I hung on by the doorway. The head constable shackled my left hand. I had on a new silk cravat twice round my neck; he hung on to this, twisting it till my tongue lolled out of my mouth, but he could not start me through the door. By this time the waiters pushed through the crowd,—there were three hundred visitors there at the time,—and Smith and Grave, colored waiters, caught me by the hands,—then the others came on, and dragged me from the officers by main force. They dragged me over chairs and every thing, down to the ferry way. I got into the cars, and the waiters were lowering me down, when the constables came and stopped them, saying, "Stop that murderer!"— they called me a *murderer!* Then I was dragged down the steps by the waiters, and flung into the ferry boat. The boatmen rowed me to within fifty feet of the Canada shore—into Canada water—when the head boatman in the other boat gave the word to row back. They did accordingly,—but they could not land me at the usual place on account of the waiters. So they had to go down to Suspension Bridge; they landed me, opened a way through the crowd—shackled me, pushed me into a carriage, and away we went. The head constable then asked me "if I knew any person in Lockport." I told him "no." Then, "In Buffalo?" "No." "Well, then, " said he, "let's go to Buffalo—Lockport is too far." We reached Buffalo at ten o'clock at night, when I was put in jail. I told the jailer I wished he would be so good as to tell lawyer—to come round to the jail. Mr. — — came, and I engaged him for my lawyer. When the constables saw that, pretending to know no one in Buffalo, I had engaged one of the best lawyers in the place, they were astonished. I told them that "as scared as they thought I was, I wanted them to know that I had my senses about me." The court was not opened until nine days; the tenth day my trial commenced. The object was, to show some

evidence as if of murder, so that they could take me to *Baltimore.*
On the eleventh day the claimant was defeated, and I was cleared at
10, A.M. After I was cleared, and while I was yet in the court room,
a telegraphic despatch came from a Judge in Savannah, saying that I
was no murderer, but a fugitive slave. However, before a new warrant
could be got out, I was in a carriage and on my way. I crossed over
into Canada, and walked thirty miles to the Clifton House.

This broke up my summer's work at the Falls, and threw me back;
and as I had to pay money to my lawyer, I have hardly got over it
yet.

There is great difference in the modes of treating slaves on the
plantations, according to the character of the owners,—I have seen
enough of slave life to know this, and I have seen slaves in Savannah
used as badly as any on the plantation. I saw a man in Savannah, who
had been whipped severely, and thrust into a dark hole or dungeon in
a cellar. The maggots got in his flesh, and he was offensive to the
sense in consequence. When they turned him out, I saw the man, and
saw the maggots in his flesh. I knew a Methodist minister, on — —
Street, who had a colored woman for cook. Something which her
mistress told her to cook did not suit. The mistress complained to
the minister; he shut up the cook in a stable or barn and beat her,
having first tied something over her mouth.

At one time, I resided with the family in the jail-building. While
there, I used to see whipping, five or six a day, or more, with a large
cowskin. It is the most common thing in the world to have them
whipped in the jail,—that will be no news in Savannah,—not over
thirty-nine lashes in one day, by law. Sometimes slaves are whipped
in the guard-house.

I consider that the slaves in Savannah, where I was born and raised,
are poor ignorant creatures: they don't know their condition. It is
ignorance that keeps them there. If they knew what I know, they
could not be kept there a moment. Let a man escape, and have but a
month's freedom, and he will feel the greatest animosity against
slavery. I can't give slavery any name or description bad enough for
it.

CHARLES PEYTON LUCAS

My name in slavery was Peyton Lucas; I changed my name in running, to Charles Bentley.

I was raised in Leesburg, Loudon county, Va. My master never sent me to school, nor gave me any instruction from the Bible, excepting one passage of Scripture which he used to quote to me,—"He that knoweth his master's will, and doeth it not, shall be beaten with many stripes." He was a Baptist Minister—and after he had quoted the text, he would take me to the barn-yard and give me a practical explanation with raw hides. My mistress used to beat me over the head with a dairy key about as big as a child's fist.

I was kept mostly at the quarters until twelve or thirteen, wearing nothing in the summer but a coarse crocus shirt. Many a time have I taken it by the two ends, and pulled it round a post to break down the sticks. When I was taken to the house, my mistress used to find fault with me before him. "Oh, I can't stand this!" Then he would give me a kick or two in the house, then take me to the barn-yard, and finish it off with the cowskin. Both before and after, he would reason with me,—"now, you know better than to aggravate your mistress as you do, for you've often heard me read, "He that knoweth," etc. I used to hear him preach. While the whipping was going on and he was quoting Scripture, I thought of another way,—I yelled until the people and children climbed up and looked over the fence or peeped through, to see what was going on: so he gave it up. Then he gave me a note to carry to the overseer, and he followed after me. I went a short way, delivered the note and was off before he got there. He appeared to feel ashamed that I had circumvented him. Thus things went on for a year or two. My mother and myself came by the mistress,—my master thought more of *his* slaves than of her's.

One day my brother was playing with one of the boys of his side of the house. There was a dog there, which, when you said, "Help, Bull," would take hold of anybody. My brother said "Help, Bull," and the dog nipped the other boy. On the next morning, Saturday, the overseer, a good Baptist brother, told my master of the fray, whereupon he dismounted, (he was just starting for a place where he was to preach next day,) tied up the boy, and laid twenty-five lashes on his bare back with a cowskin: then he turned to the overseer,—my mother was there and heard him,—"Brother — —, take your satisfaction out of the dog, (meaning my brother,) and then let him down." Upon this, he mounted his horse and went off a preaching. At night, my brother went to the stable, took the halter from a very valuable horse, broke or divided it, leaving the pieces on the floor, and broke the doors, to make it appear that the horse had got loose; then he took the horse and ran away. Being a wagoner, and well acquainted, he was accosted by flour merchants on his way, about bringing flour on the morrow. He rode that horse forty miles before daylight. He got off clear. My master recovered his horse in Baltimore, after a great deal of trouble. He then stamped his foot in anger, and told us all to go. He had, some little time before this, sold my other brother, my sister, and her two children into Georgia.

At fifteen, I was hired out to the blacksmithing business. I served at it five years, and was then hired out as a journeyman, my Reverend master taking my wages. I worked out five or six years, and was well fed, well clothed, and well used. I enjoyed life then very well, and had many privileges: nor did I run away for either fear of my master, or of the man I lived with, nor in consequence of ill treatment.

My sister worked in the house where I lived. My master had come into the shop where I worked, bringing a stranger with him, and they had talked with my employer. On inquiry of her, she told me that the stranger had dined there, and that while she was clearing away the table, she heard master say, "I won't take less than fifteen hundred dollars; he is a first-rate blacksmith." We knew it meant me, as I was the only blacksmith on the place. This was in 1841.

In one week's time I started for the North with two companions; but it was cock-crowing before we reached the Potomac; so we went on a hill, and hid until the next (Sunday) night. Then we came down, and tied our provisions into bundles on our backs, and started for Potomac river,—whether to wade it, swim it, or get drowned, we knew not. We waded and swam, changing our ground as the water deepened. At last we reached the opposite bank in Maryland: we merely stopped to pour the water out of our boots, and then travelled on all wet, until morning: then we hid in the bushes. We travelled by night and concealed ourselves by day, for ten days and nights, suffering greatly from hunger and from rain, without shelter. One day in September, we sat on a mountain, exposed to a hot, broiling sun, and without food or drink. We could hear people at their work about us, but we did not dare ask for aid. For three days, we had neither food nor drink, excepting green corn. We sucked the juice for drink, and the corn itself was our only food. The effect of this was to weaken us very much.

One night we came to a farmer's spring-house,—I broke the lock and got a good pan of milk, but before I could find any thing else, the dogs began to bark, so that we had to hurry off. We quaffed the milk with a good relish and it did us a deal of service. We drank at times muddy water from horse tracks: on one occasion, we were run very severely by dogs and men, but we got away from them. One morning between two and four o'clock, we came to a white man tending a lime-kiln,—he was asleep. We knew nothing of the way; so we concluded to awaken him, and ask the way, and if he tried to stop us, or have us caught, that we would kill him and throw him into the kiln. We awoke him and told him that our harvesting was done, and we were hunting for work, as we had two days to work in. He did not believe it,—said we were runaways. I took out my pistol, cocked and capped it, and the others produced, one a bayonet, and the other a bowie knife. The man approached us, saying still we were runaways. Had he offered to touch us we would have killed him, but he proved to be the best friend we had ever had. He told us our way, and regretted that he had no food. Said he, "If you travel on, by day-light you will cross Mason and Dixon's line, and get among the Dutch. Keep away from the big road, walk near it, but not in it,—walk in the daytime, but keep in the woods." We followed his directions, and at ten o'clock, next morning, we reached a Dutchman's house. The man was out,—but the woman and girls set the table. We ate all they had in the house,—I ate till I was ashamed. The good woman told us to avoid Shippensburg, as six had been carried back from there just before. She told us, if anybody questioned us, to say that we were going to Horse Shoe Bottom camp meeting on the Susquehanna. We did accordingly, and soon struck the track of the underground railroad, which we followed into the northern free States.

At — —, I went to work on a building. One day a druggist came to me, and said an advertisement describing me was in the tavern,— "tawny colored man, tall, spare, and of a pleasing countenance when spoken to, and he works at blacksmithing. No scars recollected, except one on his neck. Any person who will return him to me, or lodge him in jail, so that I can get him, shall have a reward of five hundred dollars." My friends advised me to remove further. I worked in Geneva, N. Y., until the passage of the fugitive slave law, when my friends advised me to go to Canada, with which advice I complied, at a great sacrifice, on account of some property which I was trying to buy.

I feel that I am out of the lion's paw, and I feel that THERE IS NO CURSE ON GOD'S EARTH, EQUAL TO SLAVERY.

I think that emancipation ought to be so arranged, as that the sick and infirm should be taken care of by those who have had the benefit of their labor. Provision for education ought also to be made. It would take a generation to accomplish this: but the practical mode of emancipating ought to be planned by the South.

BENEDICT DUNCAN

I was a slave in Maryland, twenty-eight years. My father taught me my letters, and I had sometimes the privilege of going to the Sunday school, where I was further taught by a white teacher, and I read through a spelling-book. My father had a few other books and I had help from him in learning to read them. I received religious instruction in the Sunday school. My master and mistress belonged to the Presbyterian church, but never gave me any insight into their doctrines. I became a Methodist. My master had no overseer,—was boss himself. We considered him not so good as the generality of masters. Sometimes I did not get enough to eat, nor have clothes enough to make me comfortable. I could get straw enough, but I never had any bed,—wore the same clothes at night that I wore by day, the whole week. The other hands were not so well used,—the truth is, I was rather ahead of them. They used to get whipped with hickories or a club: I never had any severe punishment.

I left through fear of being sold, as my master's business was going down hill. I experienced no trouble in getting off. I walked one hundred and fifty miles of the way. I remained in the States four months and then came over here a short time since.

I had rather have a day free, than a week of life in slavery: I think slavery is the worst evil that ever was.

WILLIAM HOWARD

I was raised in Baltimore county, Md.—was a slave from birth, until twenty-seven years old. I had no master,—my mistress was a widow lady. She gave me no religious instruction, neither taught me to read nor write—didn't want I should know any such thing as that. She was kind to me, but I didn't hardly thank her for it. I hired my time, giving her seven dollars a month, although I could earn a great deal more. The reason she did this was, she was afraid I would come away: she never sold any of her servants. I married a free-woman, and had two children there. My mistress died, and I was told that the farm was to be sold. Upon this, I came away, and had no difficulty in doing so. My wife and children followed.

I stopped a while in the free States, but came here on account of my friends being here. I did not feel concerned as regards the fugitive slave law.

Slavery made the colored people where I lived, very unhappy. One thing was, they did not get enough to eat or to wear—some I knew did not. I have known that if some were not at work by daylight, they were tied up and received a hundred and fifty lashes with a raw hide, and then had brine put on their backs, and an iron yoke put on their necks afterward, for fear they would run away. Frequently they would have no bed to lie on. Sometimes when a young man and woman were attached to each other, the masters would interfere, and, may be, would sell one of the parties. I have known children to be dragged away from their parents, and wives from their husbands: that's no new thing to me. I knew one man who had children by his slave, a yellow girl, and then sold his own children.

My opinion is, that the yoke ought to be taken from every man, and that every one should be loosed. It looks quite strange to me when I look back into the country where I was born, and see the state of things there. If they would set the slaves free, they would go to work and make a living. If any people can make a living they can.

All they want is a little education, and something to start upon. I do not think the masters would incur any danger by setting the slaves free. I thought it honorable to carry to my mistress the money I earned: it seems to me now that she was not honorable in taking it, if I was in giving it.

I expected to work for a living, go where I would. I could not be stopped from working. Canada is the best place that ever I saw: I can make more money here than anywhere else I know of. The colored people, taken as a whole, are as industrious as any people you will find. They have a good deal of ambition to go forward, and take a good stand in the community. I know several who own houses and lands. They are a very temperate people.

ROBERT BELT

I came from Maryland,—I was in slavery about twenty-five years. I had heard that there was a notion of selling me. There was a mystery about it—some saying that I was born free. A white man told me that he thought I would be sold, as there was a dispute. In about one month after, I came away. In one place where I was concealed, I saw people from the neighborhood hunting for me. I travelled more than a hundred miles on foot, and suffered a great deal by getting sore feet, and from cold and want of food.

I got work soon after my arrival here, which was quite recent: since I have been here, I have prospered well. My calculation is, to own a house and a piece of land by and by.

I feel much better satisifed for myself since I have been free, than when I was a slave: but I feel grieved to think that my friends are in slavery. I wish they could come out here. My wife came on with me from an adjoining farm.

ELIJAH JENKINS

Last winter I came away from Norfolk, Va. I am thirty-six years of age.

My mistress, a young woman, died, and I fell to her mother, an old woman. Knowing that on her death I would have to be sold, I ran away, and did not meet with much difficulty in doing so.

We are told in Norfolk that they would set us free, but we couldn't get along without them to take care of us. But since I have got here, I find that colored people do get along without masters, better than those who are slaves.

I have no wish to go back, although I am sick. I intend to get work, as soon as I am well enough.

Since I grew up to be a man, slavery has never looked to me right. It seemed hard when I had earned any money to have to carry it to another man, when my wife needed it herself. I have left a wife and five small children. I had a good wife, and, if I could, would have her and the children here this minute. I never heard of a man running away from slavery to get rid of his wife.

JOHN A. HUNTER

I feel more like a man,—I feel that I am a man a great deal more than I did a year ago. A year ago I was in bondage.

I was raised in a city in Maryland, and was a slave from birth until twenty years of age. The slaves in cities are better treated than those on the farms and plantations. When I was young, while my first master lived, I was sent to a school for white children. My mistress's sister kept the school, and I was allowed to go to keep me out of the way. When I was about ten years old, my first master died. My mistress married again, and my new master said they ought not to have sent me to school—that I knew too much any how. So I was taken from school. I remained at home doing work for the family. At fourteen, my master wished to hire me out on a farm, but my mistress not giving her consent, I remained in the city.

I heard from a colored man that I was going to be sold; afterward from a white man, that I was sold, and that my master had the money in his pocket. . . . .I came away, and met no difficulty in reaching a land of freedom. I now attend the Normal School, to get an education if I can.

A great many slaves know nothing of Canada,—they don't know that there is such a country.

Whether the slaves as a body in the city are contented or not, I am unable to say. I know that I myself was discontented and unhappy in my servile condition. My impression of those slaves with whom I associated is, that they were dissatisfied. I have heard poor ignorant slaves, that did not know A from B, say that they did not believe the Lord ever intended they should be slaves, and that they did not see how it should be so.

I think that slavery is the greatest evil that ever existed.

I consider that the efforts of the abolitionists for the slaves are salutary.

SAM DAVIS

I was in bondage, in Virginia, from birth until thirty years of age. I have had no instruction at all. My mistress used me only tolerably well—she used the switch. At sixteen she began to hire me out at farming. I have worked on several different farms. Sometimes my employers would be good, sometimes bad: three bad masters to one good one.

I have seen a great deal of punishments. My brother and I were once set to breaking stone for a turnpike: he stopped work to straighten for a minute or two, when the overseer threw a stone and hit him on the ankle. My brother said, "If you have not any thing better to do than throw stones, you had better go home." For this he was tied up to a chestnut tree, stripped, and whipped with hickories until his back was raw. My brother's owner sued the man he was hired to, and a white man who happened to be a witness, swore that he counted a hundred lashes. The master recovered, I believe, two hundred dollars and the doctor's bill, but my brother received none of the money. I have been whipped by different persons I have been hired to: once with a cowhide, several times with hickories,—**not over thirty-nine lashes at one time.**

The man I was last hired to did not give me enough to eat, and used me hardly otherwise: I then thought I would leave for a better country. I travelled on three days and nights, suffering for want of food. When I was passing through Orangetown, in Pennsylvania, I went into a shop to get some cake. Two men followed me with muskets. They had followed me from a village I had passed through a little before. They took me, and were going to carry me before a magistrate,—they said to Chambersburg. I walked just before. By and by, watching my chance, I jumped a fence and ran. They were on horseback. I got into a piece of woods,—thence into a wheat field, where I lay all day; from 9, A.M. until dark. I could not sleep for fear. At night I travelled on, walking until day, when I came to a colored man's house among mountains. He gave me a good breakfast, for which I thank him, and then directed me on the route. I succeeded, after a while, in finding the underground railroad. I stopped awhile at one place sick, and was taken good care of. I did not stop to work in the States, but came on to Canada. I arrived here a few months ago.

I know that liberty is far preferable for every colored man, to slavery. I know many who are very anxious to be free, but they are afraid to start. Money is almost necessary to start with. When I set out, I had seven dollars: it cost me five to get over a river on my way. They knew I must cross, and they charged me as much as they thought I could pay.

I have had work enough to support myself since I have been here. I intend to work, and save all I can.

HAMILTON

This thriving city, by actual count in 1854, contained two hundred and seventy-four colored persons, namely,

St. Lawrence Ward		51
St. George's "		37
St. Patrick's "		12
St. Mary's " "		34
St. Andrew's "		140
Total,		274

The public schools of Hamilton contain about one thousand seven hundred pupils, of whom twenty-five are colored. Eight hundred scholars attend the Central School; and on the 12th of June, 1855, when the writer visited it, there were present but seven colored children, six of whom were girls.

It is much to be regretted that the colored people do not to a greater extent avail themselves of the advantages presented by the perfect equality of the English laws. Yet it is scarcely to be wondered at, when we consider that prejudice against them prevails to too great an extent in Hamilton. If the colored children were universally sent to school, prejudice would probably die out before many years: for those who attend the Central School, I have the best authority for saying, are as orderly and well behaved, and make as good progress in their studies, as the whites.

The commiseration felt for the colored population on account of their sufferings in the United States, seems to have been unduly modified by the disorderly conduct of a few among their number: still, the presence of "a moral and religious element to restrain and elevate" is preceptible in Hamilton. If the people can but "conquer their prejudices" much of good may be done. On the other hand, it is a question whether the colored people would not do well to give up their separate religious organizations, and separate schools, wherever they exist in Canada.

Many of the colored people in Hamilton are "well off;" are good mechanics, and good "subjects" in the English sense of that word.

REV. R. S. SORRICK

I was born in Maryland, Washington Co., two miles from the city. At a year old, I was sold with my parents, and lived in Hagerstown some years, and then sold back to my first master,—then he sold me to Mr. H. near Hagerstown. Then I was sold to Mr. M. I was then twenty-five years old. Mr. M. in 1841, put me in prison on the 16th of March for preaching the gospel to my colored brethren. I remained in the prison three months and eight days; then Mr. H. bought me back again. I must speak well of Mr. H., for he stood by me. I stopped with him more than a year after he redeemed me from the prison. Mr. H. remembered me in the prison.

It pleased the Lord to work a way through Mr. H., who believed I had a call to preach, to give me a chance for freedom, by offering me my liberty on condition I should earn and remit to him the sum of four hundred dollars. He gave me a pass and I went to Pennsylvania, in 1843, Oct. 11. Thence I remitted him a portion of the money. The balance I have never paid.

I came into Canada in 1845. Stopped at Toronto, where I found the colored people prompt, doing well, ready to help. I went to Oro, where I found some fifty persons settled; many comfortable and doing well, but many suffer a great deal from poverty. I showed them about agriculture, and instructed them as far as my limited learning would go. When I came away, many were poor, but they were not vicious: I never lived among a more teachable people. I never knew a fight among them or their children. The worst fault was, some tendency to slander each other: but they have been instructed by the missionaries to read and write.

On leaving Oro, I came on to the conference in Hamilton, where I have principally made it my home, since 1847,—although I have been absent a portion of the time in Canada East.

In regard to the colored people in Hamilton, I found them not in a very good condition, when I first came here, although some were wealthy. I never saw so much spirit consumed by the colored people as at that time, but most of those who were among the vicious, are dead and gone. Now the evil of drinking is comparatively slight, pretty much done away, and those who have come in within a few years, are generally well behaved and industrious. We have two respectable churches, in one of which I preach,—the A. M. Episcopal. My people come into this country with nothing, and they have to work for what they do get. One cannot expect a great deal at once from such people. Every thing is to be hoped for them,—but the main obstacle is a prejudice existing between colored and white.

Slavery is the worst system I have ever seen. Although I have been poor here, I can repeat, "give me liberty, or give me death." I have seen children at a month old taken from their mother's arms and sold. I have seen children sold from their parents and many separations of families, where the parties never could see each other again.

EDWARD PATTERSON

I was a slave in Maryland, till thirty-three years of age.

The prejudice in Canada is amongst the whites to the colored, and amongst the colored to the whites. The colored fancy that the whites are a little against them, and so they do not treat the whites as they would otherwise,—this brings back a prejudice from the whites. When the colored people here are insulted it is by the *ruffians* in Canada.

I was well used, as it is called in the South, but I don't think my usage was human. For, what is *good* treatment? Look at the dress,—two pairs of pantaloons and two shirts in the summer; in the fall, one pair of shoes, one pair of pantaloons, and one pair of stockings. If they want more, they must buy them themselves if they can. No more till summer. Look at the eating,—a bushel of corn meal a month, sixteen pounds hog meat a month, rye coffee sweetened with molasses, and milk if they have any; for a rarity, wheat bread and butter. This is what I called good treatment. Look at the bedding,—sometimes they have a bed, sometimes not. If they have one, it is filled with straw or hay, and they have one blanket, and must get along as they can. Those who have no beds must sleep how they can—in the ashes, before the fire, in the barn or stable, or anywhere they can get. Now look at the *privileges* where they are *well used,*—what is called *good* treatment. After eleven days and a half hard labor, the *kindest* masters give their slaves half a Saturday, and then the slave, through ignorance, goes to ask his master the privilege of going to see his neighbors and friends. He *may* allow this if he sees proper. All this is good usage to the slave.

Now I come to the great evil: it is,—recollect the human mind is progressive,—the raising up of a generation of people under gross ignorance, in the place of their being cultivated as they ought to be. Cut off from all proper human enjoyments, they are only instructed enough to do their master's will—the same instructions which is given to asses. If the slave happen to take to himself a woman, (marrying a wife would be too high phrase,) and there is any increase, his children are considered of no more consequence to him than the calf is to the cow. If the slaveholder becomes involved, or takes a dislike to any of these children, or to the woman, he takes them to a slave-market and puts them under the hammer. And all this in presence of the husband.

If any man has a wife and family, and has human feelings for them, can he call this humanity?

I was never sent to a day school—I went to a Sabbath school four Sundays. I have, however, picked up a knowledge of reading, writing, and ciphering.

WILLIAMSON PEASE

[A white man with blue eyes.]

My name in slavery was Williamson. I was born in Hardeman country, Tenn. I remained in slavery until January, 1854. I was a house-servant. At about six or seven years of age, the family I belonged to, removed to Haywood county, carrying my mother, her two sisters, and myself. I do not know who my father was, but have heard that he was a white man. My mother was called there a mulatto. I passed for a white man when among strangers. My master and mistress tried to teach me at home, but never sent me to school. I would get out of the way when they tried to teach me, being small and not knowing the good of learning. I have since learned to read and write.

In Haywood county I ploughed some, but when wanted, served in the house. While I lived with my first master, I was well used, and suffered nothing, except for want of education, which I now feel to be a great depriving.

When I was about eighteen years old, my master died, and I fell to his grandson, then, I believe, between twenty-two and twenty-three. All the property fell to him, my mistress having died some time before. My first master was an Englishman and had been a sailor.

Under this master I went on as before, and the change made no difference in my treatment or work. In about a year and a half, he sold out the place—the house and farm—and two children; and a woman he sold, or swapped off. Then he removed to Arkansas, to a place about fifteen miles east of Saline River, and about forty or forty-five miles from Gaines's Landing. Here he rented a plantation of cotton, I think of about one hundred and fifty acres. When we got there, we were put to picking out cotton in a field for the man who was moving off. I then drove the wagon, hauling rails, etc. When he had got the land partly prepared, but before the planting season, my master rented the place to another man. Then he sold all his slaves except me, at private sale to one man. Me he kept to go with him to California. I went there with him across the Isthmus to San Francisco, in 1850; from there to Merces River, in the southern mines. There my master and I worked in the mines about six weeks. We went out with a company, but had now left it. We got some gold, about eighty dollars' worth, but not enough to pay expenses. Then we went back to San Francisco. My master was sick before he got to the mines: his health continued rather bad, and he concluded to return. I told him I should stay in the mines until I got money enough to buy my freedom. He said I could do better in San Francisco. For that reason, I went back with him to that city. He went about with me to find a place. I was offered forty dollars a month as a waiter. Master said that would hardly pay my washing and clothing bill.

Before we left home, he had told me that I should be free after two years in the mines; and if we cleared enough over his expenses, he would give me five hundred dollars. After humbugging me about San Francisco, and even promising to make me out free papers, he urged me, on account of his sickness to go home with him. I told him if I went back, I would only be free myself, but my mother would still be a slave; while if I remained in San Francisco, I would be free, and might earn enough to buy her. He then told me that if I would go back, he would buy my mother back again, and so I would be sure that she would be just as well off, as if I were to buy her and set her free. I know now that it was foolish in me to go with him back, but I had been fooled and humbugged about so much that I did not know what to do. I was offered five dollars a day to drive a dray, but my master tried and discouraged me from every thing they would offer me. I have wished a great many times since, that I had stayed there: but at last he persuaded me so hard, saying that he only wanted me for company to take care of him, as he was sick, and might get worse, and none of the company who went out with him were going, that I concluded to return with him.

I worked my passage on board a sail vessel with him, bound to Panama,—but the wind being ahead, we were thirty days at sea, and then put into Acapulco, being short of provisions. There the passengers made a fuss in regard to their passage-money: some, among whom were my master and myself, took horses and rode across the country through the city of Mexico to Vera Cruz. My master was now perfectly well.

At Vera Cruz I was after him for my papers again. He said he would give them to me. I walked out to look at the town. On my return my master was snuffling as if he was crying, and he said that if he gave me my papers, and took me back through New Orleans, both him and me would be put in the penitentiary. After declining to give me the papers, he told me that if I would go back with him, and stay until he got married and settled, I could leave him if I wished, and he would give me thirty dollars to start with, to go where I liked. He said he would give me a bill of sale there in Vera Cruz, if I would not let anybody see it. I could not read, and supposed it would be some paper of no consequence, and I knew it would do no good if nobody else was to see it: so I concluded to go on with him on his promise that I was a free man, and that he would have no claim on me at all.

We embarked for New Orleans in a Spanish schooner, and reached port without any thing worthy of notice. We went on directly to

Monticello, near the place whence I came, where he had sold out. We stayed with his cousin, until he went to New Orleans and got a stock of goods, and opened a dry goods store, which I tended with him. Before he went for the goods, I spoke to him for my papers, and he said he would fix it in a day or two: but it was not done. This was in the spring; I remained with him until July. I did not say any thing more to him about the papers; I had got tired of fooling with him, and gave it up, not expecting to get them.

Just then a man who kept a billiard saloon was sick with rheumatism, and he hired me to tend the saloon, which I did seven months, boarding with him. Soon after I entered the saloon, my master got married, and about a month or six weeks before I left it, it was rumored that I was sold to his father-in-law. I went to him and asked him about it, but he denied it. Then his father-in-law came into the town from his plantation two miles out, and told me that he had bought me. After this, the saloon man proposed to buy me to keep his saloon, but I refused, and told him I would rather not: I had now made up my mind to leave on the first opportunity. I then went to my master again,—I took him away from the house about a hundred yards, and said to him, "There cannot be so much smoke without some fire, everybody has got it that you have sold me: your father-in-law has told me that he has bought me." Then he swore that it was a lie: that they were just trying to get me to run away. He told me to go to the man I was living with, and get my clothes, and come back and live with him; that he was going to Texas to open a grocery store, and put me in, and would give me one third of the clear profits. The saloon man wished me to remain, but my master and his father-in-law refused. My master told me I might have a balance of wages due, say fourteen dollars, and I afterwards got it. About the beginning of March, they told me to prepare to go to New Orleans next morning with the father-in-law, to wait on him; afterwards my master came out, and I told him that I knew I was going to New Orleans to be sold. He denied it, and offered to bet fifty dollars that I would come back. I rode over to see my mother, and told her how matters stood. She was very much hurt, but said it was my own fault,—meaning that I ought not to have returned from California. On my way back I met the father-in-law on horseback, bringing my clothes, but not my watch. I requested to go after it, but he would not let me, saying he would get me another. My watch was a good silver watch, which I did not carry, because the crystal was broken. I then rode with him to a place on Saline river called Long View; here we took a small boat, and sailed down to the Washita river, where we took a steamer for New Orleans. There were several slaves on board the boat.

One day, during the passage, a man who owned some of these slaves, came to me as I was alone, leaning against a stanchion, and putting his hand to his chin, he gave his head a twist, and said, "I hear bad news about you." Said I, "What is it?" Said he, "They tell me you are a slave." I told him I was. Then he said, "*You* a slave! you're as white as my daughter there;" he pointed to her,—all you've got to do when we get to a landing is to take your clothes and walk; you won't want no testimony nor nothing; just take your clothes and go."

Afterwards, a man who was on board came to me, and asked, "Have you been to California?" I told him I had. Then he asked me, "Don't you think you ought to be free?" I answered carelessly, "I don't know—maybe I ought." Then he took my hat off, felt of my hair, and looked at my head, and said, "Your hair is as straight as mine, and you've got as good a forehead as mine: by G–d, I know that you ought to be free, and if you were mine, I'll be d–d if I wouldn't set you free." I made no answer.

Soon after, a colored man came to me, and told me he had overheard the father-in-law trying to sell me to the man who had examined my head.

We went to a hotel in New Orleans for a day or two; then to a private boarding-house. He was trying all through the town to sell me, but could not. After he had tried a while, he came to me and told me that he wanted to sell me, and would get me a good place, and if I would go and help him to sell me, that he would make it profitable to me. I told him "very well,"—for I preferred to take my chances in New Orleans as a slave, rather than return to Arkansas as a slave. We went to three or four trading-houses; none would buy, saying I was too white for them. He took me to one house kept by a swarthy-looking man, and told him what a smart boy I was; that I could read and write, and had been to California, etc. Said the trader, "Can you read and write?" I told him "Yes." Then said he, "I don't want you in here,—I should have to chop your fingers off." Then we went to a cotton merchant whom he was owing, and offered me in payment. The cotton merchant objected, that I was too white, and knew too much, and might prove too smart for him. Finally, as the father-in-law was about leaving town, he came and asked me if I would go back with him. I told him that I did not want to go back,—that he had better leave me with the cotton merchant, or put me into some shop, or to learn a trade, until he could sell me. I suppose he expected to make a great trade out of me, but he got tripped up. I do not know what passed between the father-in-law and the merchant, but the latter told me he had bought me for nine hundred dollars, in part pay for a debt.

I went to the merchant's warehouse, and remained there four or five days: then my master told me that his family lived in a free State, and if he were to carry me there, it would be in my own will whether to stay or not,—that he had nothing for me to do, and would sell me to a good man who would use me well. He sold me to a man back in Arkansas, where I was employed in the house, and sometimes went round with him with guns to shoot squirrels off the corn. He had about a hundred slaves on this place, and he owned a part in two or three others. I stayed there from March, 1852, to January, 1854, when I was about twenty-one years old.

My master got rather against me,—he had no particular cause that I know of. He said, so I heard from others, that I thought I was white: that I was a good boy, but would have to be whipped to let me know that I was a "nigger;" for "niggers always should be whipped some, no matter how good they are, else they'll forget that they are niggers."

He told the blacksmith to be fooling with me in the shop some time, and get my measure for a pair of stiff-legs. These are, one iron ring around the ancle and one up on the thigh, joined together by an iron rod behind. When these are put on a man, he cannot bend his knees at all, and so cannot run away. I saw one pair of these on a man on this plantation. My master's plan was to whip me, as I have the best reasons to believe, then put on the stiff-legs, and chain me to work in the smith's shop. I then made preparations as quick as I could and left. I took my clothes and a few biscuit from the table at supper. I walked forty miles through the Arkansas Swamp to the Mississippi, along a muddy road, and at 2 o'clock the next day, got to Napoleon, on the Mississippi River. Nobody questioned me. . . . . .

I like living in Canada better than in the States. I had chills in

Arkansas, but have had first-rate health ever since I have been here. I am treated here as a man ought to be treated. I could not be pulled back into Arkansas,—I would have my head pulled off first.

Almost all the colored people that I know are doing well. It was so in London, where I stopped a while, and it is so here. There is some prejudice here among the low class of people, but it has not the effect here it has in the States, because here the colored man is regarded as a man, while in the States he is looked upon more as a brute.

I saw a great deal of oppression in Tennessee. People were kept from leaving the plantations on Sundays and evenings, when they might have gone as well as not. The excuse for this was that "the niggers would get whiskey, and then steal." Some of them were not more than half clothed.

In Arkansas, on the river, or on the farm where I lived last, the people were treated worse than brutes. Horses and mules have food by them all the time, but the slaves had four pounds of fat bacon a week, and a peck of corn meal,—not enough to last some men three days. On this account it is, that the slaves help themselves when they can get a chance. I don't see how any one can blame them for it. They are up at daybreak and work till dark and sometimes after dark, carrying cotton to the gin, and then have to prepare their food, or else at the first bell-ringing in the morning. Generally, in Arkansas, the men had good clothing so far as I saw, but there were some exceptions. Most I think of was, depriving them of the privilege of going off the place. It was worse imprisonment than the penitentiary. In the penitentiary, a man expects to get out in a few months, but on the plantations they do not expect to get out until they are dead. I never went to church while I was on that last farm: the people did not go. I heard my master say it was "perfect nonsense to have a preacher preaching to *niggers:* the driver was a good enough preacher for them." This driver was a colored man, as ignorant as the rest of the slaves, but he used to hold a sort of prayer-meeting on Sundays. He knew nothing at all of a book, and did not know enough to preach.

In Arkansas they whip men with a leather strap about three fingers wide at the handle, and tapering down to two fingers at the end. It is about three feet long, and has a very short handle. I was told that several who were buried while I was there, had strap marks on them.

I saw the overseer and the driver together give a man a terrible whipping in the night. The man had been promised fifty lashes, and ran to avoid them, but they caught him, and showed no mercy. They beat him over the head with the handle of the strap. They stripped him naked and drove four stakes in the ground to which they tied his hands and his feet. I saw it done—I was looking through the palings. Then they whipped him with the strap and then with a piece of white oak made limber. I saw his back, and it was all raw. The man was sent to work next day, but he gave out, and was laid up from August until some time in the fall—until the cotton had been picked over three times. I have often seen men with their clothes sticking to their backs in the blood. The women who do out-door work are used as bad as the men.

There was a great deal of excitement among the farmers there at one time about a woman on a plantation below, who had been whipped very badly and was then tied out naked all night in a swamp where the mosquitoes were very thick: there was a great deal said about it.

I think the slaves ought to be set free: I don't think they would cut their masters' throats,—if they would do that the time would be while they are oppressed. I believe if they were set free at once, they would go to work at once, except a few loafers,—for there are some loafers among the colored as well as among the white people.

HENRY WILLIAMSON

I came from the State of Maryland, where I was a slave from birth until thirty-three years of age, in a small town.

Around that part of the country, the slaves are better treated than in some other parts because they are so near the line. They are better used than they were a few years ago. I was taught to read but not to write. I used to tell my boss that I wouldn't stand such treatment as the people got on some farms. He used to laugh and say "you wouldn't, eh?" There was one Gen.— —had a slave, and it was town talk, that his overseer, by his order, dug a hole in the ground, and set a man in it as if he had been a post, and then cut him so badly with a whip that he died in about half an hour.

My father was sold about twelve years ago, and taken west. About two years ago, I came away because I wanted to be free. The circumstances were these. I had then been married about ten years. My wife's sister was sold at private sale to a trader to go south, and was carried away. Her father and mother were dissatisfied with this, and concluded to go to Canada. I concluded to start with them with my family. In all eighteen of us came away at one time. We were more troubled on the way from want of money than from any other cause.

Those who came out with me, are scattered in various parts of Canada. I have heard from them and they are doing well. We came like terrapins,—all we had on our backs. We took a house together when we came,—the house was bare of furniture: there was nothing in it at all. We had neither money nor food. It was in the fall: we gathered chips and made a fire. That is the way the principal part of our people come: poor, and destitute, and ignorant, their minds uncultivated, and so they are not fitted for business. In the face of these drawbacks, they have to do the best they can. I went to work on a railroad,—to which I was wholly unused, having been a waiter. I worked at it till I found something I could do better. I enjoy better health here than I ever did before in my life.

I heard when I was coming that Canada was a cold and dreary country; but it is as healthy a place as a man can find. The colored people tell me the climate agrees with them, and I do know it is so.

Some of our people are very jealous of the white people. If they approach them with the best intentions in the world, they are suspicious, and will not communicate any thing, even if it were to their own benefit. This is because they have been so much deceived and kept down by the white people. I have seen people who had run away, brought back tied, like sheep, in a wagon. Men have told me, that when making their escape, they have been accosted, invited into a house in a friendly way, and, next thing, some officer or their owner would be there. The lowest class of people do this to get money,—men who might get an honest living,—some having good education, and some good trades.

Others who owned servants used to find fault with my master and mistress for using us so well. They did use us well, and I would not have left them only for the love of liberty. I felt that I was better off than many that were slaves, but I felt that I had a right to be free.

In all places and among all kinds of men here are some loafing characters: so with my color. Some few of them get in with poor, low, white young men, and get into bad ways. But the better part are disposed to elevate themselves.

I am a member of the Methodist church, having had good religious instruction from Bible and catechism from my youth up.

I have heard that my master has set his older slaves free.

Contrasting what I feel now and what I was in the south, I feel as if a weight were off me. Nothing would induce me to go back,—nothing would carry me back. I would rather be wholly poor and be free, than to have all I could wish and be a slave. I am now in a good situation and doing well,—I am learning to write.

GALT

This is a busy, growing place, numbering about three thousand inhabitants: forty colored. An account of the colored population will be found in the testimonies which follow.

WILLIAM THOMPSON

I was born eighteen miles from Richmond. My master was my father and used me kindly, but gave me no instruction at school. I witnessed no barbarity myself, but have seen slaves handcuffed and kept in jail. I have heard their cries when they were punished. Slavery has no pleasances: it is cousin to hell. A slave cannot pray right: while on his kneess, he hears his master, "here, John!"—and he must leave his God and go to his master.

There are in Galt about forty colored people. As a general thing, they are more industrious, frugal, and temperate than the whites. There is but one colored person in this town who has been here longer than myself. There are six heads of families and one single man who own real estate.

I know the sentiments of the colored people here, and they have the greatest detestation of slavery. Freedom is sweet to them. They have tried the bitter and the sweet: nearly all the grown people have been slaves.

My master set his slaves free,—some three hundred of them. Some were sold again, by breaking of the will, or in some way. My brother George and I should have received some fifteen thousand dollars apiece, but for the same reason. I went to meeting on a Sunday after I had seen the gang chained, but the preaching did me no good.

I knew a man at the South who had six children by a colored slave. Then there was a fuss between him and his wife, and he sold all the children but the oldest slave daughter. Afterward, he had a child by this daughter, and sold mother and child before the birth. This was nearly forty years ago. Such things are done frequently in the South. One brother sells the other: I have seen that done. True, I have not seen any barbarities, as some have.

The colored children can all go to school here in Galt, and are generally sent to school. The black horse and the white are both ignorant: there is prejudice on both sides. When I came here, colored children were not received into the schools. I fought, and fought, and fought, and at last it got to the governor, and the law was declared that all had equal rights. Colored people were scarce in Canada twenty-six years ago. There were but five in Toronto.

HENRY GOWENS

I have had a wide experience of the evils of slavery, in my own person, and have an extensive knowledge of the horrors of slavery, in all their length and breadth, having witnessed them in Old Virginia, North Carolina, New Virginia, Tennessee, Alabama, and Mississippi. I belonged in the State of Virginia, and am, I suppose, about forty years old. Were I to write out all my experiences and what I have observed, (and I intend to do this, having commenced already) it would make quite a large volume. In Humphreys Co. on the Tennessee River, were one hundred and ten slaves; I witnessed their treatment with a heartache. In Alabama, I know how two plantations, of one hundred and fifty, and one hundred and thirty each, were managed, who were whipped and slashed under the kindest overseers they had,—and when they had a hard overseer, there was no peace at all. It was whip, whip, continually, old and young; nobody got too old to be clear of the lash. It seemed as if the whipping had to be done, whether the work was done or not. My own master was kind at first, but as he grew older, he grew more and more severe, getting overseers who were harder and harder.

About the first of Gen. Jackson's Presidency, my master employed an overseer, named Kimball, over one hundred and thirty slaves, in

Lauderdale Co., Alabama. This Kimball was one of the most cruel men I ever saw. When he commenced, all the field hands were called together on Sunday morning, up to the great house, and then Mr. Kimball, a well dressed gentleman in appearance, and a fine looking man, walked out in company with my master. The master said, "These are my hands, that I now give up to you; take charge of them and manage them to the best of your judgement." He gave the names of the foremen of the gangs, and pointed them out to Mr. K.: then the names of the men who had charge of the women in ploughing; then the name of the man who had charge of the women in grubbing: and so he went through all the different portions of work that were done on the plantation.

Then Mr. Kimball spoke to Donnison, one of the principal men, a field hand, and to each one severally, so that all could understand what his charges were. He told them what his rules were, and what should be law: "I give you a horn, Donnison, to blow two hours before day: and recollect, every one of you, every man, every woman, and every boy and girl who is able to work, is to be up within the hour after the horn blows: at the end of that hour, every one is to be found starting out of their doors, making ready for the field. If you have any morning bits," (these they are to provide for themselves in the best way they can, otherwise, they have nothing to eat until 12 o'clock; the calculation being, for the slaves, two meals a day,) "you can take them with you: but no time will be allowed to eat them until twelve. This is my law, and I give it not thinking that you will forget it. If *you* forget it, *I* will not, but will remember it by throwing the lash well on your hide." A most horrible man! "You recollect I don't whip any of you with a chemise on, nor with a jacket on your backs. I get at the naked skin. If I find any of you lagging back after the last horn blows, I shall whip you up to the spot where the work is to be done." My master gave Donnison a first-rate English watch to keep his time and blow the horn by. After Kimball had given his charge, my master spoke to all the people again: he said, "I want every one of you to remember that you are not to come to me with any complaints against the overseer, for I have nothing to do with you. If you have any complaints even among yourselves, you must go to the overseer; nor are you to go to your mistress at any time with any complaints against the overseer. If I know one of you to do it, either man or woman, I will give a note to the overseer, and he shall not hit on you less than a hundred lashes on your bare back."

On Monday morning, all were up to the mark. Tuesday morning, I was awakened by the noise of the lash, with cries and groans. From this time the lash was going every morning, and in the course of the day. I was a house-servant, and so was exempt from Kimball's orders, but my heart ached to see the suffering and punishment that our people had to undergo. Things went on so the whole year. The people were afraid to go to the master or mistress under the sufferings they endured from the torment and sting of the lash. In the course of about six months from the time Kimball took charge, some two or three ran away, he was so severe. That was a new thing to my master. He sent word by slaves that if they saw the runaways, to tell them if they would come home and go to work, they should not be whipped. Then they would come in. This running off happened occasionally all through the remaining part of the year.

In the picking cotton season, Mr. K. would punish the women in the severest manner, because they did not pick cotton fast enough. He would thrust their heads into a cotton basket. What I say now would scarcely be believed only among those who are in that neighborhood, because it looks too cruel for any one to do or to believe, if they had no experience of such things or had not seen the like,—they would not dare lift up their heads, as perhaps he would punish them twice as much. Then he would throw their clothes up over their heads and the basket, and flog them as hard as he could with a rugged lash, cutting their flesh terribly, till the blood ran to their heels. Sometimes they would from the torment lift their heads, when he would perhaps give them a third more than he otherwise would; and this without reference to any particular condition they might be in at the time. The men he would generally place across a log, tie their hands together, and their feet together, and put a rail through under the log with the ends between their feet and hands; and in this condition, which is itself painful, he would apply the lash. Sometimes, to cramp down the mind of the husband, he would compel him to assist in the punishment of his wife. Who will tell of the good of slavery? I would rather be a brute in the field, than to endure what my people have to endure, what they have endured in many parts of the slave-holding States.

There was one religious old woman, Aunt Dinah,—very pious: all believed she was, even my master. She used to take care of the infants at the quarters while the mothers were out at work. At noon, the mothers would come home to nurse their children, unless they were too far off—then the infants were carried to them. Aunt Dinah, knowing how cruelly the women were treated, at last, when the master was absent, picked up courage to go to the mistress and complain of the dealings of the overseer. My mistress belonged to the Presbyterian Church; Aunt Dinah to the Baptist. The mistress then began to my master about the cruelty on the place, without disclosing how she got her information. I do not think the master would have interfered, were it not that the mistress also told him of the overseer's intimacy with some of the female slaves. She being a well-bred lady, the master had to take some notice of the management. He told the overseer to change his mode of punishing the women; to slip their clothes down from their shoulders, and punish them on their backs. No interference was ever made except in this one instance.

The overseer had one child by a slave woman. I left the child there a slave. At the expiration of a year Kimball left. Three months after, or thereabouts, he was hanged in Raleigh, N. C., for the murder of his step-father. The slaves were rejoiced at his being hung, and thought he ought to have been hung before he came there to be overseer.

I effected my escape about sixteen years ago. I was questioned twice about papers, but got through it without much difficulty. I escaped from Alabama. I shall give the particulars more in detail when I publish the whole history of my life to the people of the United States and Canada.

The colored people can do as well in Canada as they could in the United States under any circumstances. Even in the free States they are accounted as nothing, or next to nothing. But in Canada, all are really free and equal. Color is not recognized in the laws of the land. During all the time I have lived in Canada, no white person has suffered any inconvenience, or had cause to complain, because I was placed on an equality with him. They come here destitute of any advantages—but they are getting along in a respectable, upright way, and there is plenty of work for them. If the colored people had come into Canada with a knowledge of reading, writing, and arithmetic, there would now be no difference between them and white people, in respect to property or business. They would have been just as skilful, just as far advanced in art and science as the whites. But they have to contend with the ignorance which slavery has brought upon them. Still they are doing well,—and no one could expect them to do any better.

Every thinking, every candid man that knows me, knows that I would not utter any thing that is not true.

How much longer, in the name of God, shall my people remain in their state of degradation under the American republic?

MRS. HENRY GOWENS

My name in the South was Martha Martin. When I came to the North I took the name of Martha Bentley—Bentley being my mother's name before she was married. My father was my master, Mr.— —, who died in 1843. He lived in Georgia, but removed with one set of farm hands to Mississippi. He had one other child by my mother, but it died young. He liberated all the children he had by my mother, and one other slave woman, with one exception—that was a daughter whom he had educated and put to the milliner's trade. After she had learned the trade, he went to the place where she was, with money to establish her in business. But he found she had two children by a white man. This so enraged him, that he carried her and her two children back to his farm, and put her to work in the field, and there, he said, she was to die. The father of the two children came on, and offered two thousand dollars for the woman and the children, as he wished to marry her. But her father would neither let him have her nor his children. Afterwards he offered three thousand dollars,—then five other grown-up slaves, for Minerva and the two children; but my master told him he would not, but if he ever set foot on the farm again, he would blow his brains out. So, I suppose, they are slaves yet, and will be: for their mistress never was disposed to sell; she would rather keep them and punish them, on account of his having so many wives. But he had told her beforehand, and said she need not find fault with it: all his wives were equally well used. Keep on the right side of him, and he was very kind: every slave would be well treated. He did not mind if they stole from him, but if they stole from another man, he would whip them. He was Scotch Irish.

My mother had been set free on the eastern shore of Maryland, in this way. My mother's mistress promised my mother's mother (who was at the time free) that on her death she would set my mother free. When she died, she left her to wait on her niece until the niece died, she being very low,—then her free papers were to be given her. That was in the white woman's will. The niece died in two or three weeks, and then they talked of selling my mother to the traders, because they had got so little work out of her. Then they all—the whole family—ran away into New Jersey. My master bought them running, and kidnapped my mother and her cousin's family, although he knew the circumstances, and that they were entitled to their freedom.

When I was twelve years old, my father took me to Cincinnati. He charged me to marry neither a white man nor a black man: if I should, he would take me back south, and put me on the farm. There he paid one year's tuition in advance, and money for shoes,—we had clothes enough. Two others went with me,—one a half brother, the other a half sister. But I was cheated out of my education: for the guardian in Cincinnati kept the money, but did not send me to school, excepting one year: whereas I was to have gone three. When my father heard of this, he started on to see to it, but fell sick and died before he got there. He was a large, heavy man, and had been liable to sudden fits of illness. When these came on, he would be frightened very much, and would send for some of the pious slaves to come in and pray for him. He was a very wealthy man, and always said he would leave me in comfortable circumstances. But the money which he sent us at different times was kept from us, and it may be that he died without a will.

I remained in the northern States a few years, and then came to Canada. I have five smart children, and send all to school but the two youngest. I mean they shall have a good education; what little knowledge I have, has just made me hungry for more.

My mother was in expectation of being set free, but did not get her free papers. She was religiously inclined, and being afraid of sinning, and thinking she might be left a slave after all, she married a colored man against my father's consent. For this reason, she remains a slave to this day, as I suppose, but I have not heard from her for thirteen years.

I remember enough of slavery and have heard and seen enough of it to know that it is unfavorable to virtue. I have known many owners to have two or three colored women for wives, and when they got a white wife, keep all. If the slave woman would not comply she would be whipped, or else sold to the lowest, meanest fellow he could find. Some of the masters have their slave children's hair shaved off, so that people not notice that they favor them. I have known cases of this kind close by me in Mississippi.

LONDON

This city contains twelve thousand inhabitants, three hundred and fifty of whom are colored persons. Some of the latter are among the most intelligent and respectable citizens; but others do not improve their time and opportunities as they ought. "The tyrant who held their persons in the chains of slavery, stifled their souls also in the rude grasp of ignorance and vice."

The common schools are open to all, without distinction of color. The Union School has an average daily attendance of 184. On the 21st of June, 1855, when the writer visited it, there were present 174 pupils of both sexes, of whom 13 were colored. In the St. George School, which has on some fortunate days, an attendance of 190, but 4 colored children were present.

The principal reason for this neglect of common school advantages by the colored people, is the prejudice of the whites. Many of the whites object to having their children sit in the same forms with the colored pupils; and some of the lower classes will not send their children to schools where the blacks are admitted. Under these circumstances, it is unpleasant to the colored children to attend the public schools—especially if any of the teachers happen to be victims of the very prejudice which they should induce others to overcome.

An interesting scene was presented in the school very recently organized by Rev. M. M. Dillon, (late Rector of Dominica,) and Mr. Ballantine, lay-assistant, under the patronage of the English "Colonial Church and School Society." Here were one hundred and seventy-five pupils of both sexes in attendance, fifty of whom were colored. The writer entered the school-room at the hour of recess. The children were neat and cleanly—not one of them wore the appearance of dejection; all were playing in the inclosure or amusing themselves in the room, in the most perfect good-humor. There was no separation into cliques,—black was playing with white, and white with black.

Rev. Mr. Dillon's mission is to minister to the spiritual wants of the refugees, and to establish schools of a high order, which shall afford religious and secular instruction especially to the children of fugitive slaves; the schools, however, to be free to all who may see fit to profit by their advantages. Both the Rev. Mr. Dillon and Mr. Ballantine are devoted friends of the negro race. They have very capable assistants in two young colored ladies from the West Indies.

At a signal, the scholars arranged themselves in lines on the floor, and then filed to the parts of the room allotted for recitations. Something of the monitorial system was observable; and two or three colored pupil-teachers attended to the reading from the Scriptures, of as many classes, composed indiscriminately of whites and blacks.

The "Colonial Church and School Society" is a union and extension of the "Newfoundland School Society," organized more than thirty years ago, and of the "Colonial Church Society," which has existed about twenty years. It is composed of the highest dignitaries of Great Britain both in church and State. The object of the Society is "to send Clergymen, Catechists, and Schoolmasters to the Colonies of Great Britain, and to British residents in other parts of the world." "The religious instruction in all schools maintained wholly or in part by the Society, shall be in the Holy Scriptures, and (except in cases where the parents or guardians of the children formally object) in the formularies of the Church of England."

The accommodations for the Society's school in London are found to be insufficient, as the numbers in attendance are rapidly increasing. A new building is shortly to be erected, which will afford ample room for five hundred pupils. Five or six similar schools are to be organized forthwith in other parts of the province. This is a noble charity, and full of the most hopeful auguries for the colored population of Canada.

The condition of the colored people in and about London, may be gathered from the testimonies which follow, given by those who are able to draw from their own experience the contrast between slavery and liberty.

ABY B. JONES

I was formerly a field hand in Madison Co., Ky.,—remained there until thirty years of age. My treatment was not harsh,—nor was there any hard treatment in the neighborhood.

My brother was set free in this way: his master was a millwright, and told him if he would serve him so many years he would set him free. He did so,—meanwhile building a large merchant mill, and employing my brother in it. My brother was subsequently employed in this mill as a miller and received high wages, his employer thinking there never was such a man, from his trustworthiness and the general confidence he could repose in him. His good opportunities enabled him to advance nearly money enough to free myself and a younger brother,—the deficiency we borrowed, and afterward paid up. The sum paid for the two was seven hundred dollars; our master favoring us in the price.

I was never sent to any school. Since I have been free I have learned to read and write.

Yet, although I was nominally free, and had free papers, I did not consider myself free in the eye of the law: the freedom was limited. The papers said I was to have as much liberty as was allowed to a free man of color. I saw at once that I was not really free; that there was a distinction made. I wished then to emigrate to some place where I could be really a FREE MAN.

I heard that in Canada colored men were free; therefore I came here, and am only sorry to say that I did not come years before I did.

When I came here I was not worth one cent. I neither begged nor received a farthing of money. I went to work at once, and, by the blessing of the Lord, I was prospered, and have placed my family beyond the reach of want.

I am satisfied, that any colored man coming to Canada, can, in a few years, accumulate property to give himself and family a living.

Slavery is, I believe, the most abominable system that ever men were subjected to. Although my treament was not severe, I never could form a good opinion of slavery. I believe it ruinous to the mind of man, in that it keeps the key of knowledge from him: it is stupefying to man. I believe that all men should be made free at once.

The future prospects of the colored people of Canada are very favorable. All that is required of them is, to use industry in common with white people. The colored children and white children are educated together in this place, and I see as fair an advancement in one as in the other.

The colored people usually attend divine service: some in the same societies as the whites; others maintain separate churches. But I do not think it advisable to have separate churches. In this place the door is open into all the churches of the denominations that the colored people profess, therefore I think those lines of distinction drawn by the colored people themselves will soon be put down. I speak of London.

I think there is as much morality and temperance among the colored people as among any others.

The amount required for supplying the wants of fugitives is so small, that it is hardly worth talking about. It can be silently raised in the towns by contribution, without any stirring appeals to the public. Where there is work to be done and money to pay for it, pecuniary assistance does more hurt than good.

[Mr. Jones, whose testimony is given above, resides on Gray St. in a brick dwelling-house, as good or better than the average of houses in London. In front is a garden of choice flowers, and it has a well-ordered kitchen garden in the rear. The estate, deducting the incumbrance of ground-rent, is worth about four thousand dollars. Mr. J. owns other property in various parts of the city,—a brick building, in the business quarter, comprising two stores which rents for between seven hundred and eight hundred dollars per annum,—and several building lots in the immediate vicinity of the freight depot of the Great Western Railway. Mr. J. is of unmixed African blood.]

ALFRED T. JONES

I keep an apothecary shop in Ridout street. I belonged in Madison Co., Ky. I have made an arrangement with my master to purchase my freedom for $350. This was in 1833, when I was twenty-three years old. But before the business was completed, I learned that my master was negotiating with another party to sell me for $400. Upon this, I wrote for myself a pass—it was not spelled correctly, but nobody there supposed that a slave could write at all. I had to exhibit it but once on my way.

I stopped a month at St. Catharines, then came to London, and have remained here ever since.

The people from the old country, being many of them unaccustomed to colored people, have some strange ideas respecting us: a sort of "second-hand prejudice," as Ward calls it. The majority of the people of color who come over here are not such as give a very good idea of what the people of color really are. They are not refined and educated. But as some years are passed since the colored men began to come in, there is an improvement perceptible.

There are colored people employed in this city in almost all the mechanic arts; also in grocery and provision stores, etc. Many are succeeding well, are buying houses, speculating in lands, and some are living on the interest of their money.

I expect to go to England shortly on a suit at law involving my title to a large property on Dundas street, valued at $45,000. The case has been through chancery in the provincial court, and I have now appealed to the House of Lords. I am winding up my business preparatory to leaving.

NELSON MOSS

I have lived in a slave State all my life until seven years ago. I am now forty-five. I lived three years in Pennsylvania, in which State I suffered more from prejudice than in Virginia, and there is a great deal here in London, but not so much as in Pennsylvania. I got along well, having energy to attend to business properly. I carry on the boot and shoe business. I was never sent to school in my life, and it is a loss to me not to know how to keep accounts; but I am able to employ another to do it for me.

I did not leave Pennsylvania so much on account of the prejudice, as on that of the fugitive slave bill. I did not like to live in a country which was governed by a partial law. I made considerable sacrifice in breaking up.

The laws here are impartial. We have access to the public schools here, and can have our children educated with the white children. If the children grow up together, prejudice will not be formed.

There are a large majority who are industrious; a few are wealthy; a good many are well off. There are not many who are dissolute and abandoned—not so many in proportion as of the whites, taking every thing into consideration. If there are some who are not so industrious as they should be, it is easily accounted for. Solomon says, "Train up a child in the way he should go, and when he is old, he will not depart from it." It's a bad rule that don't work both ways: they have been trained in a way they should not go. Accustomed to be driven when they work, it is no wonder that they don't work so smartly as they would otherwise. But in the face of this, I know many colored men who came here fugitive slaves, who came here without any thing to help themselves with, not even money for a night's lodging, and who had nothing given to them, who now have a house and land of their own. It is not necessary to give a fugitive money—it may make him lazy and dependent. All he needs to have given him is work.

Nearly all the grown colored people have been slaves. Of course, they are not capable of instructing their children well themselves,—but, under the free schools, I am of opinion that we are progressing.

FRANCIS HENDERSON

I escaped from slavery in Washington City, D.C., in 1841, aged nineteen. I was not sent to school when a boy, and had no educational advantages at all. My master's family were Church of England people themselves and wished me to attend there. I do not know my age, but suppose thirty-three.

I worked on a plantation from about ten years old till my escape. They raised wheat, corn, tobacco, and vegetables,—about forty slaves on the place. My father was a mulatto, my mother dark; they had thirteen children, of whom I was the only son. On that plantation the mulattoes were more despised than the whole blood blacks. I often wished from the fact of my condition that I had been darker. My sisters suffered from the same cause. I could frequently hear the mistress say to them, "you yellow hussy! you yellow wench!" etc. The language to me generally was, "go do so and so." But if a hoe-handle were broken or any thing went wrong, it would be every sort of a wicked expression—so bad I do not like to say what—very profane and coarse.

Our houses were but log huts—the tops partly open—ground floor,—rain would come through. My aunt was quite an old woman, and had been sick several years: in rains I have seen her moving about from one part of the house to the other, and rolling her bedclothes about to try to keep dry,—every thing would be dirty and muddy. I lived in the house with my aunt. My bed and bedstead consisted of a board wide enough to sleep on—one end on a stool, the other placed near the fire. My pillow consisted of my jacket,—my covering was whatever I could get. My bedtick was the board itself. And this was the way the single men slept,—but we were comfortable in this way of sleeping, *being used to it.* I only remember having but one blanket from my owners up to the age of 19, when I ran away.

Our allowance was given weekly—a peck of sifted corn meal, a dozen and a half herrings, two and a half pounds of pork. Some of the boys would eat this up in three days,—then they had to steal, or they could not perform their daily tasks. They would visit the hog-pen, sheep-pen, and granaries. I do not remember one slave but who stole some things,—they were driven to it as a matter of necessity. I myself did this,—many a time have I, with others, run among the stumps in chase of a sheep, that we might have something to eat. If colored men steal, it is because they are brought up to it. In regard to cooking, sometimes many have to cook at one fire, and before all could get to the fire to bake hoe cakes, the overseer's horn would sound: then they must go at any rate. Many a time I have gone along eating a piece of bread and meat, or herring broiled on the coals—I never sat down at a table to eat, except in harvest time, all the time I was a slave. In harvest time, the cooking is done at the great house, as the hands are wanted more in the field. This was more like people, and we liked it, for we sat down then at meals. In the summer we had one pair of linen trousers given us—nothing else; every fall, one pair of woollen pantaloons, one woollen jacket, and two cotton shirts.

My master had four sons in his family. They all left except one, who remained to be a driver. He would often come to the field and accuse the slaves of having taken so and so. If we denied it, he would whip the grown-up ones to make them own it. Many a time, when we didn't know he was anywhere round, he would be in the woods watching us,—first thing we would know, he would be sitting on the fence looking down upon us, and if any had been idle, the young master would visit him with blows. I have known him to kick my aunt, an old woman who had raised and nursed him, and I have seen him punish my sisters awfully with hickories from the woods.

The slaves are watched by the patrols, who ride about to try to catch them off the quarters, especially at the house of a free person of color. I have known the slaves to stretch clothes lines across the street high enough to let the horse pass, but not the rider: then the boys would run, and the patrols in full chase would be thrown off by running against the lines. The patrols are poor white men, who live by plundering and stealing, getting rewards for runaways, and setting up little shops on the public roads. They will take whatever the slaves steal, paying in money, whiskey, or whatever the slaves want. They take pigs, sheep, wheat, corn,—any thing that's raised they encourage the slaves to steal: these they take to market next day. It's all speculation—all a matter of self-interest, and when the slaves run away, these same traders catch them if they can, to get the reward. If the slave threatens to expose his traffic, he does not care—for the slave's word is good for nothing—it would not be taken. There are frequent quarrels between the slaves and the poor white men. About the city on Sundays, the slaves, many of them, being fond of dress, would appear nicely clad, which seemed to provoke the poor white men. I have had them curse and damn me on this account. They would say to me, "Where are you going? Who do you belong to?" I would tell them,—then, "Where did you get them clothes? I wish you belonged to me—I'd dress you up!" Then I have had them throw water on me. One time I had bought a new fur hat, and one of them threw a watermelon rind, and spoiled the hat. Sometimes I have seen them throw a slave's hat on the ground, and trample on it. He would pick it up, fix it as well as he could, put it on his head, and walk on. The slave had no redress, but would sometimes take a petty revenge on the man's horse or saddle, or something of that sort.

I knew a free man of color, who had a wife on a plantation. The patrols went to his house in the night time—he would not let them in; they broke in and beat him: nearly killed him. The next morning he went before the magistrates, bloody and dirty just as he was. All the redress he got was, that he had no right to resist a white man.

An old slaveholder married into the family, who introduced a new way of whipping,—he used to brag that he could pick a "nigger's" back as he would a chicken's. I went to live with him. There was one man that he used to whip every day, because he was a foolish, peevish man. He would cry when the master undertook to punish him. If a man had any spirit, and would say, "I am working–I am doing all I can do," he would let him alone,–but there was a good deal of flogging nevertheless.

Just before I came away, there were two holidays. When I came home to take my turn at the work, master wanted to tie me up for a whipping. Said he, "You yellow rascal, I hate you in my sight." I resisted him, and told him he should not whip me. He called his son–they both tried, and we had a good deal of pulling and hauling. They could not get me into the stable. The old man gave up first–then the young man had hold of me. I threw him against the barn, and ran to the woods. The young man followed on horseback with a gun. I borrowed a jacket, my clothes having been torn off in the scuffle, and made for Washington City, with the intention of putting myself in jail, that I might be sold. I did not hurry, as it was holiday. In about an hour or so, my father came for me and said I had done nothing. I told him I would return in the course of the day, and went in time for work next morning. I had recently joined the Methodist Church, and from the sermons I heard, I felt that God had made all men free and equal, and that I ought not to be a slave,–but even then, that I ought not to be abused. From this time I was not punished. I think my master became afraid of me; when he punished the children, I would go and stand by, and look at him,–he was afraid, and would stop.

I belonged to the Methodist Church in Washington. My master said, "You shan't go to that church–they'll put the devil in you." He meant that they would put me up to running off. Then many were leaving; it was two from here, three from there, etc.–perhaps forty or fifty a week. – – – – was about there then. I heard something of this: master would say "Why don't you work faster? I know why you don't; you're thinking of running off!" and so I was thinking, sure enough. Men would disappear all at once: a man who was working by me yesterday would be gone to-day,–how, I knew not. I really believed that they had some great flying machine to take them through the air. Every man was on the look-out for runaways. I began to feel uneasy, and wanted to run away too. I sought for information–all the boys had then gone from the place but just me. I happened to ask in the right quarter. But my owners found that I had left the plantation while they had gone to church. They took steps to sell me. On the next night I left the plantation. At length I turned my back on Washington, and had no difficulty in getting off. Sixteen persons came at the same time—all men—I was the youngest of the lot.

I enjoy freedom as all other hard-working men do. I was broken up in Rochester, N. Y. by the fugitive slave bill.

There is much prejudice here against us. I have always minded my own business and tried to deserve well. At one time, I stopped at a hotel and was going to register my name, but was informed that the hotel was "full." At another time, I visited a town on business, and entered my name on the register, as did the other passengers who stopped there. Afterward I saw that my name had been scratched off. I went to another hotel and was politely received by the landlady: but in the public room—the bar—were two or three persons, who as I sat there, talked a great deal about "niggers,"—aiming at me. But I paid no attention to it, knowing that "when whiskey is in, wit is out."

MRS. FRANCIS HENDERSON

I was born of a slave mother in Washington, D.C., and was raised in that city. I was to be set free at the age of thirty. When my old mistress died, I was sold for the balance of the time to an Irish woman. When I first went there, I was the only slave they had ever owned; they owned afterwards a man, a woman, and a male child. The man went out to get some one to buy him. He left word at the grocery: the grocer was not particular to report the one who would purchase him to the old man by himself, but let on before the folks. This provoked the Irishman and his wife, and as the old man was taking out ashes from an ash-hole, the master went down, and as the slave raised his head, the man struck him about the temple, with a long handled scrubbing-brush. The old man never spoke afterwards. I saw the blow struck. The old man died the next morning. An inquest was held. I was afraid, and told the jurymen I knew nothing about it. The white girl said the boss wasn't at home,—she swore a false oath, and tried to make it out that the old man fell and hit his head against the bake oven door. The man was bound over, not to put his hand on a servant any more. Mistress used to pinch pieces out of the boys' ears, and then heal them with burnt alum. She dared not do much to me, as my former owners were in the city, and would not suffer barbarity. Her husband was under bonds of two thousand dollars to treat me well. But she treated the others so badly that some of my friends told me I had better leave. – – – – was there then with some persons who were going to travel north with him, and I joined them and came away.

I like liberty, and if Washington were a free country, I would like to go back there,—my parents were there. There are so many congressmen there that the slaves are not treated so badly as in other parts.

JOHN HOLMES

My name in slavery was John Clopton. I belonged originally in Hanover Co., Va. My treatment was so bad, I hate to say any thing about it. Slaves were not allowed to open a book where I came from: they were allowed to go to meeting, if the master gave them a pass—some have that privilege, and some do not. My owners never gave me a hat in the world, nor hardly any clothes. When I got big enough, I worked nights to get me a hat and some clothes. There was one physician there, who I know as well as I know myself, who flogged one woman till the skin was off her back, and then whipped the skin off her feet. One neighbor of ours was worse than the evil one wanted him to be. He used to make a married man get out of his bed in the morning and he would go and get into it. What I have seen, I seldom say any thing about, because people would not believe it,—they would not believe people could be so hard-hearted. They whipped so much, I couldn't tell any particular reason for it.

The horn would sound at the time the cocks crowed. Then they all got up. When it blowed the second time all had to start for the field: if any remained after this, the overseer would go in and whip them. Daylight never caught us in the house. Then the overseer would get on his horse and ride to the field; and if any one came in after him, he would apply the lash—perhaps fifty, perhaps a hundred. I have seen the women jump for the field with their shoes and stockings in their hands, and a petticoat wrapped over their shoulders, to dress in the field the best way they could. The head magistrate of that county (L— — J— —) was about the hardest of any of 'em. When I came away, one of his men had maggots in his back. His brother E— — was not so hard,—he was killed in a duel. Another brother was very hard toward his wife, his slaves, and everybody else. His name was B— — J— —. He was so bad he couldn't live any longer—he killed himself by drinking a quart of brandy from a case-bottle—a case-bottle full. Next morning he was dead. This was before I came away, and I left in 1825. I don't know my age. They don't tell the slaves any thing about their age. There were but two that I know of, who used their people any way decent.

There was a young T— — P— — who had overseers who would kill his people with no more conscience than one would kill a snake. T— — P— — was so bad he wouldn't give his people Sunday. He had two or three farms. On a Saturday night his people would pack up, and travel Sunday to another farm, so as to be ready for work Monday morning. He had one overseer named L— —, who called himself a bull-dog, and said he could manage any "nigger." They allow eight ears of corn for a horse at noon. A young man was about feeding a horse; L— — says, "How many ears have you got?" "I didn't count them." L— — counted,—there were ten ears. Just for that L— — seized a flail, and struck the young man breaking two of his ribs—he hit him with the flail until he found the young man was dying—then he sent for the doctor. The doctor said, "What did you kill this man, and then send for me for?" I knew the young man and knew the overseer.

The first time I was shot, my young master, Dr. — — (who had married one of the girls) and I got into a skirmish. I was in the kitchen before anybody was up. He came in and wanted to know what I was doing in the house? Why didn't I go to work? He says, "If you don't go out and go to work, I'll give you a hundred lashes. Go, get your hoe, and come up to the house—I'll show where you can hill up a potato patch." I went, got my hoe and came back. Then he had been to the stable, and got leading lines, a whip, and his gun. He knew I would not let him whip me, because I had always fought like a tiger when they undertook it. The gun was to scare me, so as to make me take off my jacket. He left the whip and gun inside the door and said, "come in here." I had not seen then the lines, whip, or gun. He took up the lines, and came by me as if he was going out—when he got near the whip and gun he turned—"take off your shirt, I'll hit you a hundred lashes this morning." It was because I had not gone to work—that was all the quarrel we had had that morning. I turned round and faced him. "Pull off your shirt, you d— —d rascal." I said, "not to-day." The minute I said so, he snatched up his gun, pointed it at my breast and said, "I'll shoot you." I went towards him, opened my breast, and said, "shoot away." My temper was raised—I meant if he did not kill me, I would kill him. It seemed to daunt him. He said, "Stand your ground." I was approaching him. Said I, "I've got no ground to stand on." I was very near him,—he seized the whip, and struck at me, but I was near enough to prevent him from hitting. As he made a lick at me, I sprung for the door. He thought I was going to seize him, and dodged out of the way. I went out, took my hoe, and was walking away. I had got mad, and couldn't run. He called, "Stop, you d— —d rascal." I told him I would go away, and not come back while wind blew or water run. I had not got far, and looked around, when I saw him have the gun; I saw the flash, and was peppered all over with shot. I went off into the woods. The shot did not bother me much, except one in the ball of my thumb, which I got out some four or five years after. I stayed in the woods all summer. They used to hunt for me. I've seen them after me with dogs—dogs couldn't catch me. I used to watch when they started and follow behind them. I used something on my feet to keep dogs from taking a scent. At last they told all the neighbors if I would come home, they wouldn't whip me. I was a great hand to work and made a great deal of money for our folks. I used to tell them, if they whipped me, I wouldn't work. The only fault they could find with me was, I would not be whipped. The young master—this one I ran from—used to say, "a man must be whipped, else he wouldn't know he was a *nigger*." I finally went back.

I had a great many such scrapes with the overseers—two or three with the masters. At last they said, "better let him alone, he is a good hand to work." I would not be whipped. One day an overseer, who thought he was a better man than any of the others, came to me—I was a leader, and was pulling corn. He took me by the collar, and said I did not go fast enough—he would "tie me up to the persimmon tree, and hit me a hundred lashes;" he meant to do it, because the others had not made out to. I told him, "not to-day"—that's what I always used to tell them. He called two dogs, and they bit me in a great many places,—the marks of their teeth are all about my knees,—then he called several of the hands, but only one came up before I got away from overseer, dogs and all. I had to fling off the overseer, E— — E— —; he went to the ground. I took to the woods: I don't know how long I stayed out that time, but I have stayed in the woods all winter.

My young master had a bloodhound, very large and savage. He would let no one come near him. At night this dog was turned loose, and no negro could come round the house, nor along the road. He would not touch white people,—he was brought up so. At one time they were repairing a chimney,—several loose bricks were about the yard. One of the women and myself were sent through the yard. The dog was chained, and was enraged, because he could not get at us: the master was standing in the yard. The dog broke his collar: I saw him coming, and took up a half brick. I knew the dog would spring for my throat, and I took a position as for wrestling. When the dog sprung, I threw up my left arm: the dog just got hold, and I struck him on the side of his head with the brick—he fell stunned, but I did not kill him. Young master was laughing when he saw the dog springing about, and when he saw him coming; but when he saw the dog fall, he ran out and struck at me with his fist. I fended off, as I had pretty good use of my limbs then. He then tried to kick me, but I caught his foot every time. I told him, "You sha'n't strike me, and your dog sha'n't bite me, ne'er a one." He then ran for his gun, so ambitious, that his mother went to look, to see what he was going to shoot at. She got to the door as quick as he did: the gun was then pointed at me, but she seized it and pulled it out of his hands, and told me to be off quick. He was not of age when I came away. I never saw such a set of fellows as our folks were: one of them shot a dog, because he wouldn't come when he called him. This one was accidentally killed one Sunday morning, by a gun in the hands of the overseer. They were playing, and the gun went off at half cock, and blew his brains out.

A— — A— — was a great overseer, who never went on any plantation but what he whipped every man on it. He bragged of it, and was called a great negro-manager. There were two men and one woman, named Betty, on the place, who, like me, would not be whipped. They employed him to come on for overseer, because he could make a great crop any how, by managing the hands. When the new overseer comes, all hands are called up and given over to him. I would not go up at such times—once only I went into the yard.

A— — ordered all to meet him at the barn next morning, to get orders where to go. Every thing went on well till the middle of February, when we make plant-patches to put tobacco in. We would go to a wood and get brush, and burn it on the soil till bloodwarm, then plant it. All the women were raking dry leaves to put on the brush, to make it burn. The overseer first fell in with Betty—his word was, if any one did not work fast enough—"go to work! go to work!" He said this to Betty. Said she, "Where must I go?" "Go to work!" "I am working." He struck her with a stick he had in his hand—she struck him with the rake. They struck several blows. She got the stick and lost the rake: they fought then like two dogs. She was better with her fists, and beat him; but he was better at wrestling, and threw her down. He then called the men to help him, but all hid from him in the brush where we were working. We could see him, but he could not see us,—he was too busily engaged. They fought till they got out of breath, and then he started with her to go to the mistress; they never broke their hold. He got her over two or three fences; then came the doctor who had shot me, and J— — T— —, my mistress's son, and they took her to the barn, and whipped her almost to death: but she behaved worse afterwards.

Then the calculation was to whip us every one, because we did not help the overseer. He told us, the same afternoon to go to the barn to thresh oats: but the oldest son, who had the management of the whole estate, was not at home, which saved us that time; but it was to be done next day. While they were plotting it in the evening, one of the house girls overheard it. That night every one of us went away into the woods. (Among those woods I have seen, where there are large trees, the old corn hills and tobacco hills, where it used to be planted. At one time, I was hoeing in a field which we had just cleared of big pine-trees, and I found there two iron wedges and a hoe in the ground.) We stayed until they could not pitch a crop of corn. The head plougher and all,—all of 'em went away: they had only women and old men, and one young man who stayed behind, who was foolish. The overseer came to make a greater crop than they ever had, and he did not make any. They sent off the overseer to get us home. We went back, but after a while he came back too, and stayed the year out. He whipped the women, but he did not whip the men, for fear they would run away. He has cut many hickories and got chains made to put on me: but I was always looking out for him.

When I was young, before I got so watchful, I had blows and knocks. One morning I was sick: the rule was, to tell the overseer. I said I wasn't going all over the farm to look him up. First thing I knew, he was in, with some switches, cowhide, and a rope with a running noose. He put the noose over my head as I sat,—I cleared it, and he struck me with a knife which hit a button: I knocked the knife out of his hand,—we had a fight and I whipped him. I knew if I stayed, he would whip me. I ran for a swamp, and he after me; but I got there first, and went through the mud and water,—he stopped at that. I always started in time,—before the lash came, I was off.

One overseer we had was named E— — T— —; a stout, big, young man, who worked the people hard, night and day; all the time at our heels, "rush! make haste!" The weaker ones were called the "drop-short gang;" these were taking the lash all the time: he was always after them. He wanted I should blow the horn, but I wouldn't undertake it. The old head man used to blow it. He used to hide the horn sometimes, so that we need not get it to throw it away. One time I found it, and threw it in the river. The overseer wanted to know why the horn did not blow. The old man told him "somebody done hide it." The overseer threatened us with a hundred lashes, unless we would find it, but we told him we had nothing to do with it. T— — got another horn: I don't believe he blew it three times before it was gone,—it was in the river. We got up afterward without a horn. Several times, horns were got for the farm, but they could not keep them.

This overseer was very mistrustful and watchful, but he would get come up with sometimes. At threshing time, he accused me of stealing the wheat. At one time, he came down there, when he was sick to watch us. He had been taking medicine: he laid down on some straw,—it was damp, and he got worse. He called to me to take him up. I told him, "All I'll do for you will be, if you die, I'll close your eyes, and lay you out." Two others, a man and a woman went to him. Said I, "if you take him up, he'll get well, and you'll be the first ones he'll whip." They took him to the house: he was very sick there, crying, "let me pray! let me pray!" I could hear him at the barn. When he got out to the field again, I did not know he was there, till I heard the switch. I looked to see whom he was whipping. It was the very two who had carried him to the house. I said to them, "don't you remember what I told you? If you had let him stay there and die, you wouldn't have got that." It struck him so, he flung his switches down, and sat on the fence: he looked pale: he went back to the house, and we did not see him again for three days.

One morning I had a great scrape with him. He swore he would whip me at the risk of his life. That morning I did not get into the field until sunrise. All were at work but me: I had had something to attend to, and would not go. He said I should not strike a lick there, till he had whipped me. I told him, "you shall not, if everybody has to die between here and Kentucky. I'll die before I'll take a whipping." "You sha'n't do a stroke of work, before I whip you." The next word was, "master sha'n't whip me, mistress sha'n't whip me, nobody sha'n't whip me." He said, "I'll make all the hands catch you, and I'll whip you." "There ain't a man the sun shines upon, that shall whip me." The next thing he said was, "You ought to consider your mistress' interests." I told him, "let mistress consider her own interests, and let me consider mine,—let everybody consider their own interest." I was fixing then to come away, but he did not know it. "I will whip you any how. If you'll take off your shirt, I'll only give you a few licks,—I have sworn that I would whip you, and want to make my words good." I answered, "I have *said*, you should not whip me, and that's as good as if I had *sworn* to it." We were some five or ten yards apart. He said I should not work till I was whipped. I told him I was not doing myself any good,—that I wasn't working for myself anyhow, and didn't care whether I worked or not. I then turned for the woods,—when almost there he called me back,—not one of the hands would have dared to touch me. I always carried an open knife,—they never could catch me unprepared. I went back: said he, "I'll excuse you this time, but you mustn't do so any more." I answered, "I don't know what I am going to do."

The last year, we had to work backwards and forwards, from one farm to another—from my mistress' farm to her son's: two overseers,—we worked so till harvest time, when I came away. My master was mad with me all the time about the overseers. I was the leader on our farm—on the other farm, I followed their leader. There were fifteen cutting wheat in cradles, some were raking, some binding—master followed the cradles. The other leader and I cradled so fast, we kept ahead of the rest—so we would have time to stop a little. He was mad because he could not see us cut wheat—he said we did nothing, and were playing all the harvest. One forenoon a shower came up—all were busy to get the wheat out of the shower; master, to get occasion to whip me, came to me and said, "You shall run too." I did run; but that did not suit him: he came up and struck me three or four times. He then went and cut three or four long poles: he shook them at me, and said he would whip me a hundred lashes for the new and the old. All hands were now sent to the barn to shell corn,—that was where they were going to catch me. I took up my cradle and jacket; I spoke to Tom, and asked him if he knew he was to have one hundred lashes? He said, "Yes." "Are you going to the barn?" "Yes,—are you going?" "No: I'm going to the woods." "But you cannot stay in the woods always." Said I, "If you will go with me, I'll carry you into a free country." "Oh, you can't." I said, "I'll go, or die in the attempt a trying." Tom said, "I reckon you haven't sense enough to get away." I told him, "I'll walk as long as there's land, and if I come to the sea, I'll swim till I get drowned." I bade all the hands good-by—"I never expect you'll see me again: if they try to take me I'll fight till I die: but if it so happens that they master me, I'll never tell them where I came from." Then I went into the woods. I had some good clothes, and went round through the woods and got them. I waited till night, to see what they would do. I saw them going to the house where I had been for my clothes. I could hear them talking, telling the owner of the place, a poor white man, to catch me if I came there. I laid about the woods ten days, waiting for another man who had promised to come with me. I saw him, but he was afraid to come. I started without him. At sixty miles from home, I got work, and stayed until I got some clothes and a little money. Then I left for the North. I have two children in slavery. They were carried away from me when they were a few months old.

I have lived in Canada twenty-four years, and have made out pretty fair since I have been here. I came here expecting to work, but have not had to work so hard here as I did at the South. I know all the old settlers, but a great many have come lately, whom I am not acquainted with. Those that will work, do well—those that will not—not: it is the same here as everywhere. It is the best poor man's country that I know of—if a man comes without a shilling, he can get along well. There is no more idleness among colored than other people—there are idlers among all nations. I came here with money enough to buy a hundred acres of land. My money was stolen, but I did not get discouraged. I now own this house and land—ten acres here, and twelve in another place. I had a house and land which the railroad took, and I got a good price.

If I had had any knowledge how to calculate and scheme, as I should if I had learning, I should be worth ten thousand dollars. London has grown up since I came here. I had an opportunity to buy land in the heart of the city, but did not bother about it. Many of our people remain poor for want of education. It cannot be expected that men who have just got away from slavery should look far ahead: they are only looking for to-day and to-morrow. The colored people are mostly given to hard work: for the time we have been here, we have made great progress in this country. They have many good farms about Wilberforce. There is some prejudice, but not so much as there used to be. There is no separate school here. There are a Baptist and a Methodist church exclusively for colored people. Whether this is best, I cannot say. I used to persuade the colored people to go into the white folks' churches. They came near making me say I would never go to church any more: on coming out, the colored people were insulted: things were said then that would not be said now. Colored people attend at every church in London.

MRS. — — BROWN

I keep a boarding-house, and have now ten boarders, all fugitives, as nearly as I can recollect. One of them came last winter. They have all got employment.

JOHN D. MOORE

I lived in Pennsylvania and New Jersey some twenty years. I suffered a great deal there solely on account of my color. Many a time, when I have been travelling, and would come to a tavern tired and hungry, I would be told, "We have no accommodations for men of your color," and I would have to go on. Perhaps I might get a luncheon at a private house,—or at some place kept by a foreigner, who needed the colored man's money.

I have suffered a great many other ways on account of my color. Several times I wanted to go into business there, but was dissuaded by my white friends, who said I would be mobbed or burned out. I was discouraged in so many ways, that I came to Canada, to see if I could find a place where a colored man could have some privilege. I find it the reverse here from what it was in the States. There is prejudice here among the low class of people, but they have not got the power to carry it out here that they have in the States. The law here is stronger than the mob—it is not so there. If a man insults me here, he is glad to get out of the way for fear of the law; it was not so in the States where I lived. A ruffian there may insult or throw stones at a colored man, and he must get out of the way—I found no law on my side.

I can't complain—I am doing well here, and am satisfied with Canada. I have lived here eighteen months.

CHRISTOPHER HAMILTON

I was raised in St. Louis, Mo. I went to school a little, to a Sunday School, and learned to read, but was stopped—I suppose because I was learning too fast. My people came from Virginia. They were all free by right. My grandmother was an Indian woman. She put my mother with a man by the name of E— — G— —, to bring up. He moved to Kentucky, stopped a little while, then went to Missouri, thence to Jackson, Miss. While they were moving out, on their way to Kentucky, I was born on board a boat in Pittsburg. After we reached Jackson, my father, my mother, and all their sons and daughters, except myself and a sister who had two children, were sent to Mine Oburden—lead mines—they moved there with Dr. G— —, who kept them all for slaves. After he had stopped there awhile, he sold them to a man named S— — P— —. My sister, her two children, and myself, were sold by W— — G— —, to whom the Dr. had given us up for debt, to a man in St. Louis. W— — G— — was in debt to a man named H— —, and H— — was in debt to a Frenchman named B— —. We slipped along from one to another to pay debts. With B— — I remained from ten years old, till I left for the North. I have written kind letters to B— —, but got no reply. The people who were sold to S— — P— — all were finally removed with him to St. Louis, except one who died in the South.

I look on slavery as the greatest evil that ever existed. The preaching I used to hear was "Servants, be obedient to your masters." "He that knoweth his master's will, and doeth it not, shall be beaten with many stripes." I was well used by my master, and well treated, until he married a second time. He married a very mean woman. He was a very wealthy man, and when she married him, it raised her right up. Nothing could please her. I had been married two years, and she tried to persuade her husband to sell my wife down the river: she wanted to whip my wife, and my wife wouldn't let her. I did not wait to see whether he would sell her or not: but we came away,—got off very comfortably. I had only sixteen dollars when I started. When I got here, I found a brother of mine here,—he helped me about getting work, and I make out to live comfortably. I wouldn't go back for all St. Louis, poor as I am.

They have no good feeling there for colored people anyhow. All they care for is, to get all the work out of them they can. They whip them to death, starve them to death, and I saw one colored man burned to death,—McIntosh, who had killed a man.

I used to go to Sunday School in St. Louis, to Mr. Lovejoy—the man who was killed.

The colored people in London are generally saving; they do not waste their means; they are getting along as well as they can expect, as a general thing. I do not know of one who suffered so much here, as he would in slavery. There are some who are vicious and dissolute, and so there are of all nations. Take them in general, and they are getting along first-rate.

MRS. CHRISTOPHER HAMILTON

I left Mississippi about fourteen years ago. I was raised a house servant, and was well used,—but I saw and heard a great deal of the cruelty of slavery. I saw more than I wanted to—I never want to see so much again. The slaveholders say their slaves are better off than if they were free, and that they prefer slavery to freedom. I do not, and never saw one that wished to go back. It would be a hard trial to make me a slave again. I had rather live in Canada, on one potato a day, than to live in the South with all the wealth they have got. I am now my own mistress, and need not work when I am sick. I can do my own thinkings, without having any one to think for me,—to tell me when to come, what to do, and to sell me when they get ready. I wish I could have my relatives here. I might say a great deal more against slavery—nothing for it.

The people who raised me failed; they borrowed money and mortgaged me. I went to live with people whose ways did not suit me, and I thought it best to come to Canada, and live as I pleased.

ALEXANDER HAMILTON

I was brought up in St. Louis, Mo.,—was not very badly used, except that I was not taught to read nor write,—I was not used well enough to stay there. I have seen many very badly used, and many sent down the river to the south. It was a common thing to take off a drove for a cotton farm. I never heard that it was intended to sell me; but I knew it might be so, and I thought I would make hay while the sun shone. I left St. Louis in '34, at the age of about eighteen. We don't know our ages exactly.

I knew one man to cut off the fingers of his left hand with an axe, to prevent his being sold South. I knew of another who on hearing that he was sold shot himself: I saw physicians dissecting this man afterward. I knew of a woman who had several children by her master, who on being sold, ran down to the river and drowned herself: I saw the body after it was taken from the water.

I think that God made all men to be free and equal,—not one to be a slave. Other nations have abolished slavery, and there is no reason why the United States cannot do the same thing. We would many of us like to live in the United States were it not for slavery.

Many separations I have seen,—dragging husbands from wives, children from their mother, and sending them where they could not expect to see each other again.

I reached Canada in 1834. I had only a dollar and a half. I had no need to beg, for I found work at once. I have done well since I came here: have made a good living and something more. I own real estate in London,—three houses and several lots of land. It is a healthy country—Canada.

The colored people in London are all making a living: there is no beggar among them. Some of us would like to live in the South if slavery was done away with, and the laws were right. I am naturalized here, and have all the rights and privileges of a British subject.

Many have gone about, collecting money and clothes for fugitives, but I think that is not necessary now: they can get work.

A great many fugitives are coming into London, they are coming almost every day.

MRS. SARAH JACKSON

I belonged to a bachelor, who said I might come away with my three children if I chose. I always desired to come to a free State; and I could not bear the idea of my children's being slaves. He did not think I really would leave, although he said I might. There was some opposition from his relatives,—they told me they thought I was mighty foolish to come away from a good master. I thought I wasn't foolish, considering I had served all my days, and did not feel safe at night: not knowing whom I might belong to in the morning. It is a great heaviness on a person's mind to be a slave. It never looked right to see people taken and chained in a gang to be driven off. I never could bear to see my own color all fastened together to go to such a place as down the river. I used to go in the house and shut myself up. I did not know how long before it would be my own fate. I had just enough to pay my way here. I expect to work for a living, and I am trying to get a house. I am better here than I was at home,—I feel lighter,—the dread is gone. I have a sister and brother in slavery in Kentucky. I intend to send my children to school. I have been here about a week.

HENRY MOREHEAD

I came from Louisville, Ky., where I was born and bred a slave. The colored people have not sent their children to school in London, so generally as desirable, for this reason. The fugitives who come to this country for freedom from bondage, have been kept down in such a manner, that these privileges granted to them seem somewhat strange, and they have to take some time to consider whether they shall send their children to school with the white children or not. This free school is something so unusual to them, that they can't realize it, until they become naturalized to the country. Although they know they are free, they have a kind of timidness about them, so that they cannot mingle with the whites of this country, as they would if they had been born free. Yet the day, I believe is fast approaching, when the people of color will see that they stand in their own light by not sending their children to school. The time is now, when the colored men begin to see that it is the want of education which has kept them in bondage so long.

My owners used to object to my going to school, saying that I could learn rascality enough without it—that *"niggers"* going to school would only teach them rascality. I always felt injured when a slave and when free, at the use of that word. This dampened my feelings for getting learning, somewhat, but I went to a night school, at my own expense of course, to learn to spell and to read. My owners found it out, and set policemen to break the school up. This put an end to my schooling—that was all the schooling I ever had. I have looked at it, and have come to the conclusion, that it is best that colored people should teach their children to read and to write, in order that they may know the ways of the world.

I left slavery a little more than a year ago. I brought my wife and three children with me, and had not enough to bring us through. My owners did not know that we were coming. I left because they were about selling my wife and children to the South. I would rather have followed them to the grave, than to the Ohio River to see them go down. I knew it was death or victory—so I took them and started for Canada. I was pursued,—my owners watched for me in a free State, but, to their sad disappointment, I took another road. A hundred miles further on, I saw my advertisements again offering $500 for me and my family. I concluded that as money would do almost any thing, I ought to take better care,—and I took the underground railroad. I was longer on the road than I should have been without my burden: one child was nine months old, one two years old, and one four. The weather was cold, and my feet were frostbitten, as I gave my wife my socks to pull on over her shoes. With all the sufferings of the frost and the fatigues of travel, it was not so bad as the effects of slavery.

I am making out very well here—I have not been in the country long enough to accumulate any wealth, but I am getting along as well as the general run of people. It stands to reason, that a man must be doing something to pay a rent of five dollars a month, and support a family of four besides himself, as provisions are, and have been. To do this does not look much like starving.

AN OLD WOMAN

My name is — — — —, but you must not tell it, for I have children at the South, who would be eaten up if their masters knew. [The old lady detailed her history, but requested that no use should be made of it at the present time, excepting the part which follows.] . . . . . I am now eighty years old. Now I will tell you what I saw with my own eyes. I was called on to leave the room where was a dead body which they were going to strip for the grave. They said it would be a shame for me to remain. I said, "it is only a lifeless lump of clay, and I will stay and see with my own eyes what has been done, that I may say it is so, and that it is the truth." I remained and saw the man's body. It was a field hand, that had died under the lash. There were a few marks on the calves of his legs, a few on his breast where the whip had sometimes reached round. From his neck to the calves of his legs, the flesh was raw and bloody—completely cut up with two bull whips by the overseer and driver. It looked as sausage meat when you chop it. This man had children and grandchildren on the plantation. The man's fault was,—when they finish work Saturday night, they bring home the maul and wedges, and put under the bed, to have them ready Monday morning. On Monday morning, he forgot the wedge, and started back to get it. The overseer tackled him—he resisted; the overseer called the driver; between them both they staked him down, and whipped him, until he fainted. They got some water in a shoe, and revived him,—he fainted again and revived—the third time he fainted, and they could not bring him to—he died. The overseer ran away. . . . .

JOHN WARREN

I was born in Wilson Co., Tenn., lived there twelve and a half years, and was then carried to Mississippi, by my owners who settled in Marshall Co. Two of us, brothers, went down with the young man, to whom we fell on settlement of estate. Then he sold us to his brother who was a regular speculator, buying and selling all the time—kept from eighteen to twenty on the place. I went right to work on the cotton farm, under an overseer. The overseers changed every year I stayed there. There was pretty hard work and many kinds of it on the cotton plantations. The overseers were generally cruel, hard men, but some had more consideration than others. Four o'clock was rising time. We blew but one horn—when that sounded we all got up, fed the stock, hogs, horses, etc., and went to work. The farm contained 645 acres. We took a little breakfast with us, which we generally cooked over night: but at picking cotton time we had a cook to cook for us. Every man took his little bucket of breakfast to the field, where fifteen minutes was allowed for breakfast, sometimes with water, and sometimes without,—no coffee nor tea in the field. The provision was corn bread and pork—sometimes enough, and sometimes not. After breakfast we worked until one. The overseer generally stayed with the hoe-gang—women and children. He could see from one field to another. We had no drivers on our farm—plenty in the neighborhood. On the big farms they fared worse than we did.

The overseer walked to and fro behind to see that they did not cut out too much cotton with the hoe, and that they took up the grass; if they did not, he would whip generally with a long bull whip, sometimes with a bunch of six or eight black-gum switches, generally laying on hard. There are marks on me made soon after I went there. The only way I got shut of the whip was when I got stouter, to fight them and run away. I was always watching, and they hated to lose my time. Twenty-five acres of cotton and corn together were allowed to a hand, and if one goes, it makes it hard for them. Before I was twenty years old, I was tied up and received two hundred lashes. Generally, they give fifty, and then stop a little—then give fifty more. They sometimes tie round a tree, sometimes to four stakes, and sometimes gammon them. [*Gambrel* is meant here: the wrists are bound together—the arms made to embrace the lower limbs, and a gambrel is thrust through under the knees.] I have seen a man receive five hundred and fifty lashes for running away. The overseer and boss drank brandy, and went at him. They gave him brandy for devilment,—making fun with him: then they would leave him tied a while, and then go and put it on again. I have seen men on the next farm, whipped with a handsaw flatwise: the teeth would cut when the blow was put on. The saw was used after the bull whip.

I learned to spell and read some in Tennessee, among the children. The owners knew I could read. I bought a copy of the letters in writing of a white boy in Mississippi, for half a dollar. It was a good price, but I did not mind that. I kept that copy of the letters three years, and learned to write from it. I practised nights and Sundays. . . . I got so I could write, but I had nobody to show me, and did not know how to hold the pen. But I wrote three passes for myself. I wrote one to go to Memphis with. I left the farm on the night of the 3d July, 1854. I had beaten the overseer on the Sunday evening before: he undertook to whip me for going away Sunday. I knocked him over, bumped his head against the logs of the corn-crib, and went into the woods, where I staid all day Monday; Tuesday morning I left, and travelled to Memphis on foot, excepting the last four miles, which I rode. At Memphis, I threw away the first pass and took the second, which was a privilege to work out in Memphis a month: my calculation was to get on board a boat before a month was out. Then I had a third pass, which said I had hired my time for the rest of the year to work in the State or out of the State. I worked in Memphis three days, then went aboard a boat and showed my year's pass. The first trip, I went down the Mississippi and up White River to Jackson Port, in Arkansas: then back to Memphis. We were gone eight days, lacking an hour. Then I hired on a boat bound to Cincinnati. I saw the sign "Cincinnati," and went aboard: sailed that evening, and got safely to Cincinnati in five days. I stopped there two or three days, and then left for Canada. A man in Chatham hired me to come here to work. I get good wages.

I always hated slavery from the first. It never seemed right to work for nothing, driven in the rain, and so on. When I was small, I had heard of a free State where black people were free, and had no master nor mistress, and I wanted to go there. I have no disposition to go South again—I love liberty too well for that. I don't have to get up at four and work till nine; I don't have now to drive a wagon Sundays to haul cotton bales.

I believe that if the slaves were hired and paid for their labor, they'd all go to work, and they would do a great deal more work than they do now, for they would not be thinking all the time about running away, and fighting the overseers,—there would not be so much confusion. Sometimes, on a holiday, the boss hires them,—they go to work singing and hollowing, without an overseer, and they do the work better than when he is behind them. Now I don't study all day about running into the woods, nor dream of it nights, as I used to. There are no hounds here to be running after me. There is a man down there, who gets ten dollars for catching a runaway: if he has been gone longer, he gets more. A good "nigger dog" is worth four hundred dollars. I knew how to kill the scent of dogs when they came after me: I could do it with red pepper. Another way I have practised is, to dig into a grave where a man has been buried a long time, get the dust of the man, make it into a paste with water, and put it on the feet, knees, and elbows, or wherever I touched the bushes. The dog won't follow that.

I came here to work and expect to work. Time goes smoother with me than it did. One month there seemed longer than two do now.

A planter near us in Mississippi, bought a man from Kentucky out of a drove, who ran away, he was treated so mean. They followed him, got ahead as he was going back, caught him and brought him back. He fought hard not to be taken, gave them some bruises, but they took him. When they got him back, they gave him two hundred lashes every morning for seven mornings. The hands on the place told me so, the man told me so, and the master told my boss so, just like any other joke: he said "he was the d— —dest nigger on God's earth." They put a heavy log chain, which weighed twenty pounds around his body. In about a year they sold him to a speculator.

The white folks down south don't seem to sleep much, nights. They are watching for runaways, and to see if any other slave comes among theirs, or theirs go off among others. They listen and peep to see if any thing has been stolen, and to find if any thing is going on. "What is there in this barrel? Too many d— —d barrels in here,—I'll have 'm put out."

From those who had slaves we would steal whatever we could get to eat—chickens, turkeys, geese, etc.

The slaves have no particular rules, except in regard to marriage: they try to make it as near lawful as they can.

BENJAMIN MILLER

I came from St. Louis, Mo., about twenty years ago. I had the privilege of purchasing my freedom, and had paid of the $500 asked, all but $220: then I had good reasons to believe, from information which I received, that after all was paid, I was to be carried down the river and sold. I then made for the North. I was a slave, to be sure, but was doing business as boot and shoemaker. I learned the trade while I was paying $120 per annum for my time. If I had been sure of my free papers, I could have paid the $220, and would have been doing a good business there. My partner was a free man.

I have lived in and about London ever since I came out. My property here is worth about $1,800. It consists partly of a house and land. I have brought up a large family—have a wife and eight children living,—have buried ten—three in St. Louis, the remainder here.

I feel thankful that I can mention that I have given a part of my time to the spiritual interests of the people here without pay: having served them as pastor in the Methodist denomination some years.

I have travelled in all the principal places in Canada West, and, generally speaking, the colored people are doing well: thank God, uncommon well, considering the way they came. Men who at home know nothing but to come and go just as they are bid, here go into business, and do well, very well. They are temperate men, considering the way they are brought up.

We that begin here illiterate men, have to go against wind and tide. We have a learned, enterprising people to contend with; we have a colder climate than we have been used to, to contend with; we have our own ignorance and poverty to contend with. It takes a smart man to do all that: but many do it, all make a living, and some do lay up money. I asked one of our white 'squires, if he ever saw a colored man that was well, in this township, begging. He said, No.

QUEEN'S BUSH

This name was originally given to a large, unsurveyed tract of land, now comprising the townships of Peel and Wellesley, and the country extending thence to Lake Huron. While it was yet a wilderness, it was settled mainly by colored people, about the year 1846. The following, communicated by a resident of Galt, gives the main features of the settlement of the Queen's Bush. The testimonials following Jackson's, are from that part of the scarcely reclaimed wilderness now known as the township of Peel.

WILLIAM JACKSON

My father and myself went to the Queen's Bush in 1846. We went four and a half miles beyond the other farms, to Canestogo, where he cleared up and had a farm; for years scarcely any white people came in, but fugitive slaves came in, in great numbers, and cleared the land. Before it was surveyed, there were as many as fifty families. It was surveyed about two years after we went there. The colored people might have held their lands still, but they were afraid they would not be able to pay when pay-day came. Under these circumstances, many of them sold out cheap. They now consider that they were overreached—for many who bought out the colored people have not yet paid for the land, and some of the first settlers yet remain, who have not yet been required to pay all up.

Some colored people have come in from the free States, on account of the fugitive slave bill, and bought land. The farms are usually from fifty to one hundred acres. The timber is hard wood. The soil is productive, and it is a good wheat country.

A great many who sold out went to Mr. King's settlement, and to

Owen Sound. The health of the colored people was very good—there was hardly any sickness at all: indeed, the climate of Canada agrees with them as well as with the white people. It is healthy for all.

I have heard white people who lived at Queen's Bush say, that they never lived amongst a set of people that they had rather live with as to their habits of industry and general good conduct. I never knew of but one to be taken before a court, for any thing but debt, and I lived there seven years.

In regard to riding in coaches or cars, I never had any trouble in Canada. I have heard of some who have suffered from prejudice, but I never did. The amount of prejudice is small here, and what there is grows out of slavery: for some, when they first come, feel so free, that they go beyond good limits, and have not courtesy enough. But I find that they get over this after a while.

THOMAS L. WOOD KNOX

I was born free in the eastern part of Pennsylvania, but removed to Pittsburg. I should not have left the States only that I was not treated with respect. I would go to market with provisions off a farm I rented in New Brighton. When I got into Pittsburg, other farmers would drive in with their teams into the tavern yard, and get their breakfasts and go and sell out, before I could get any thing to eat: so that by the time I would get to market, the best of it would be over. The same thing would run through all the conduct of the whites. In the place where I went, they were opposed to my coming,—but after four years they were grieved to have me come away. But I could not stand it, and left for Canada. I have been in Canada eleven years—eight in the Queen's Bush. When I came here it was a complete wilderness: I took hold and cleared a farm. I would rather have remained in my native country, among my friends, could I have had such treatment as I felt that I deserved. But that was not to be, and I came into the wilderness.

Most of the colored people living here are doing as well, if not better, than one could reasonably expect. Most of the grown people among them are fugitive slaves. I know of but one, free-born, from Pennsylvania, and that is myself. The number here I cannot speak of with any certainty. Many have removed to Owen's Sound and other places: there may be now five hundred persons. All are equal here: I have been about here a great deal, but have seen no prejudice at all.

SOPHIA POOLEY

I was born in Fishkill, New York State, twelve miles from North River. My father's name was Oliver Burthen, my mother's Dinah. I am now more than ninety years old. I was stolen from my parents when I was seven years old, and brought to Canada; that was long before the American Revolution. There were hardly any white people in Canada then—nothing here but Indians and wild beasts. Many a deer I have helped catch on the lakes in a canoe: one year we took ninety. I was a woman grown when the first governor of Canada came from England: that was Gov. Simcoe.

My parents were slaves in New York State. My master's sons-in-law, Daniel Outwaters and Simon Knox, came into the garden where my sister and I were playing among the currant bushes, tied their handkerchiefs over our mouths, carried us to a vessel, put us in the hold, and sailed up the river. I know not how far nor how long—it was dark there all the time. Then we came by land. I remember when we came to Genesee,—there were Indian settlements there,— Onondagas, Senecas, and Oneidas. I guess I was the first colored girl brought into Canada. The white men sold us at Niagara to old Indian Brant, the king. I lived with old Brant about twelve or thirteen years as nigh as I can tell. Brant lived part of the time at Mohawk, part at Ancaster, part at Preston, then called Lower Block: the Upper Block was at Snyder's Mills. While I lived with old Brant we caught the deer. It was at Dundas at the outlet. We would let the hounds loose, and when we heard them bark we would run for the canoe—Peggy, and Mary, and Katy, Brant's daughters and I. Brant's sons, Joseph and Jacob, would wait on the shore to kill the deer when we fetched him in. I had a tomahawk, and would hit the deer on the head—then the squaws would take it by the horns and paddle ashore. The boys would bleed and skin the deer and take the meat to the house. Sometimes white people in the neighborhood, John Chisholm and

Bill Chisholm, would come and say 'twas their hounds, and they must have the meat. But we would not give it up.

Canada was then filling up with white people. And after Brant went to England, and kissed the queen's hand, he was made a colonel. Then there began to be laws in Canada. Brant was only half Indian: his mother was a squaw—I saw her when I came to this country. She was an old body; her hair was quite white. Brant was a good looking man—quite portly. He was as big as Jim Douglass who lived here in the bush, and weighed two hundred pounds. He lived in an Indian village—white men came among them and they inter-married. They had an English schoolmaster, an English preacher, and an English blacksmith. When Brant went among the English, he wore the English dress—when he was among the Indians, he wore the Indian dress,—broadcloth leggings, blanket, moccasins, fur cap. He had his ears slit with a long loop at the edge, and in these he hung long silver ornaments. He wore a silver half-moon on his breast with the king's name on it, and broad silver bracelets on his arms. He never would paint, but his people painted a great deal. Brant was always for making peace among his people; that was the reason of his going about so much. I used to talk Indian better than I could English. I have forgotten some of it—there are none to talk it with now.

Brant's third wife, my mistress, was a barbarous creature. She could talk English, but she would not. She would tell me in Indian to do things, and then hit me with any thing that came to hand, because I did not understand her. I have a scar on my head from a wound she gave me with a hatchet; and this long scar over my eye, is where she cut me with a knife. The skin dropped over my eye; a white woman bound it up. [The scars spoken of were quite perceptible, but the writer saw many worse looking cicatrices of wounds not inflicted by *Indian* savages, but by civilized (?) men.] Brant was very angry, when he came home, at what she had done, and punished her as if she had been a child. Said he, "you know I adopted her as one of the family, and now you are trying to put all the work on her."

I liked the Indians pretty well in their place; some of them were very savage,—some friendly. I have seen them have the war-dance—in a ring with only a cloth about them, and painted up. They did not look ridiculous—they looked savage,—enough to frighten anybody. One would take a bowl and rub the edge with a knotted stick: then they would raise their tomahawks and whoop. Brant had two colored men for slaves: one of them was the father of John Patten, who lives over yonder, the other called himself Simon Ganseville. There was but one other Indian that I knew, who owned a slave. I had no care to get my freedom.

At twelve years old, I was sold by Brant to an Englishman in Ancaster, for one hundred dollars,—his name was Samuel Hatt, and I lived with him seven years: then the white people said I was free, and put me up to running away. He did not stop me—he said he could not take the law into his own hands. Then I lived in what is now Waterloo. I married Robert Pooley, a black man. He ran away with a white woman: he is dead.

Brant died two years before the second war with the United States. His wife survived him until the year the stars fell. She was a pretty squaw: her father was an English colonel. She hid a crock of gold before she died, and I never heard of its being found. Brant was a freemason.

I was seven miles from Stoney Creek at the time of the battle—the cannonade made every thing shake well.

I am now unable to work, and am entirely dependent on others for subsistence: but I find plenty of people in the bush to help me a good deal.

JOHN FRANCIS

I was twenty-eight years old when I came into the Queen's Bush from Virginia. My usage down South was hard. I was sold three times: first, for debt; then I was traded off: the third time I sold myself to myself.

I came in ten years ago. Then there were few families. More kept coming,—colored people,—there were not many white. The land was not surveyed. We settled down where we saw fit. We knew nothing about price nor terms. After considerable many settlers had come in, we called a meeting, and sent a man to get a grant of the land if he could; or, if not that, to find the terms. The answer was, that we were on clergy reserves, and they could give no grant. Still we kept at work, clearing and planting. The land came into market about seven years ago, being surveyed and a price set on it.

Then came a land agent, to sell and take payments. He put up public notices, that the settlers who had made improvements were to come and pay the first instalment, or the land would be sold from under them. The payment was to be in ten annual instalments of 15s. 6d. currency, 5s. to the dollar. It was then hard times in Canada, and many could not meet the payment. The agent, as we now know, transcended his powers, for some people, white and colored, still hold their lands, not having made payments. The agent had a percentage for collecting. His course in driving people for money, ruined a great many poor people here in the bush. Fearing that the land would be sold, and they get nothing for their betterments, they sold out for very little and removed to other parts. The agent himself told me he would sell my land unless the instalment was paid. I sacrificed my two cows and a steer, to make the payment that I might hold the land. Others did not do that and yet hold. One man, fearing to lose all he had done, sold out for ten dollars, having cleared eight or ten acres—that property is now estimated at $15,000. Some borrowed money on mortgages, and some paid a heavy per cent. for money to meet that instalment: which was very hard on the poor settlers who had their hands full in trying to live, and clearing land so that they could live. But it was done: and it has kept many back by trying to meet that borrowed money, and others by their moving where they would have to begin again: that is what has scattered the colored people away from here. There are now about three hundred,—there were three times as many. Some went where they got grants of fifty acres for settling.

The young men growing up here have not so much knowledge as desirable, as there were no schools here when they were growing up. Now it is different, and many send their children. The teachers generally have not the feelings in regard to slavery that we have. It would be well to have the young taught, that they should improve themselves as a means of elevating their race. When my children get old enough to read, I intend to instruct them about slavery, and get books to show them what we have been through, and fit them for a good example.

My mother was sold away from me, when I was about eleven years old. In escaping, I sailed over two hundred miles on the sea in an open boat with my father, a day without eating, and ten days without drinking. One night we were near being lost in a storm. We put in to get water and were taken: but we made out to clear ourselves.

The colored people in the Queen's Bush, are doing pretty well—they have many drawbacks: as they can keep no books nor accounts, they are liable to be overreached—and are overreached sometimes.

JOHN LITTLE

[The hero of the following narrative is much respected, wherever he is known—in Canada West. And in that country of good farms, Mr. Little's is one of the best, and among the best managed.]

I have been bought and sold by several masters. I was born in N. C., Hertford Co., nigh Murfreesboro': I lived there more than twenty years. My first master, was just a reasonable man for a slaveholder. As slaveholders go, he used his people very well. He had but seven,—my mother and her six children; of the children, I was the oldest. I was never sent to school a day in my life, and never knew a letter until quite late in life. I was not allowed to go to meeting. My business on Sundays was looking after the mules and hogs, and amusing myself with running hares and fishing.

My master broke down, and I was taken by the sheriff, and sold at public auction in Murfreesboro'. I felt miserably bad to be separated from my mother and brothers and sisters. They too felt miserably about it, especially my poor old mother, who ran all about among the neighbors trying to persuade one and another to buy me; which none of them would promise to do, expecting the traders to give more. This she did on Sundays: week-days, she had to work on the farm.

Finally I was sold to a man in the same county, about ten miles from the first place. He abused me like a dog—worse than a dog,—not because I did any thing wrong, but because I was a "nigger." My blood boils to think about him, let me be where I will. It don't seem to me that even upon the Lord's day, and now I know that there is a hereafter, it would be a sin before God to shoot him, if he were here, he was so bad: he so abused me,—he, a wise man,—abused me because I was a fool,—not naturally, but made so by him and others under the slave laws. That is God's truth, that I was inhumanly abused.

At the time of this sale I was about twenty-three, but being a slave, I did not know my age; I did not know any thing. He came and said to me, "Well, boy, do you know who's bought you?" I answered, "I do not, sir." "Well," he said, "I've bought you: do you know me?" I told him "I did." "I have bought you, and I'll give you a pass (for there a colored man cannot go without a pass even from an auction,) to go to my farm; go down there, to the overseer, and he'll tell you what to do." I went on Sunday morning, the day after the sale, and delivered myself up. Said he, "Go down there to the quarters, with the rest of the *niggers,* and to-morrow I'll tell you what to do." When I got down there I found about seventy men, women, and children. They told me Mr. E— — was a hard man, and what I had better do to avoid the lash. They do that among themselves any time. It was in the winter time, and when the horn sounded for us to rise, we were allowed fifteen minutes to get to the overseer's house about a quarter of a mile off. I wish he were here now to hear me tell it, to see whether it's the truth,—I could look right in his face the whole time. Breakfast was not even talked about. We were dismissed from work at different hours, but never till after dark. Then we would go to our cabins, and get up our little fires, and cook, or half cook, our victuals. What we did not eat that night, we put into little old baskets that we made ourselves, and put it handy, so that when the horn sounded, we could take it and clear to the overseer's. This provision served us all the next day. We usually ate it at the time the horses ate. We were not allowed to eat during work, under penalty of fifty lashes. That was the law laid down by the master to the overseer. We had to plan and lay schemes of our own to get a bite. "A nigger could always find time to eat and smoke and shuffle about, and so he wouldn't allow it to us. He wouldn't have his work hindered by eating." I don't put the blame of cruelty on the overseer: I put it on the master who could prohibit it, if he would. No man ought to take the place of overseer,—I blame the scoundrel who takes the office; but if he does take it, he must obey orders.

After being there three weeks, I wanted to go back to see my mother who was broken-hearted at the loss of her children. It seemed as if the evil one had fixed it so,—for then two daughters were taken and carried off to Georgia. She had been sold before for the fellow's debts,—sold close by at private sale. I asked leave of my master Saturday night. I went to him, pulled off my hat, and asked him, if he would please give me a pass to go and see my mother, and I would come back Sunday evening. "No! I don't allow my niggers to run about Sundays, gawking about; I want you to-morrow to look after the mules and the horses along with the rest of the niggers." He was the greatest gentleman in that neighborhood. The white men all looked up to him. He was what is called a "nigger-breaker." If any one had a stubborn slave, that they couldn't bend just as they wanted to, they would hire him to S— — E— — for a year. I have known them to be sent from as much as fifty miles, to be broke, because he had so much cruelty: he was a hard-hearted, overbearing scoundrel: the cries and groans of a suffering person, even if ready to die, no more affected him, than they would one of my oxen in the field yonder. This I have seen and known, and partly endured in my own person.

His refusing the pass, naturally made me a little stubborn: I was a man as well as himself. I started and went without the pass, and returned on Sunday evening, after dark. Nothing was said until Monday morning,—then we went to the overseer, and were all told to go to the gin-house. As soon as I got there, the overseer and two colored men laid right hold of me, and tied me fast to an apple-tree with some of the baling-rope, and then sent for the master. He came,—"Well, Sir, I suppose you think you are a great gentlemen." I thought, as they had me tied, I would try to beg off as well as I could, knowing that sauciness would not make it any better for me. "I suppose," he went on, "you think you can come and go whenever you please." I told him "No: I wanted to see my mother very bad, and so I ran over there and came back as I told you." Said he, "I am your master, and you shall obey me, let my orders be what they may." I knew that as well as he, but I knew that it was devilishness, that he wouldn't give me a pass. He bade the overseer hit me five hundred lashes,—*five hundred lashes* he bade the overseer hit me! Men have received them down south, this morning since the sun rose. The overseer ordered two slaves to undress me, which they did: they turned my shirt over my head which blindfolded me. I could not see who put on the blows, but I knew. It was not the master,—he was too much of a gentlemen: but he had a plenty of dogs to set on. What I tell you now, I would tell at the judgment, if I were required. 'Tisn't he who has stood and looked on, that can tell you what slavery is,—'tis he who has endured. I was a slave long enough, and have tasted it all. I was black, but I had the feelings of a man as well as any man.

The master then marked on me with his cane where the overseer was to begin, and said, "Whip him from there down." Then the overseer went at it, the master counting aloud. He struck me a hundred lashes right off before he stopped. It hurt me horribly, but after the first hundred, sensation seemed to be beaten out of my flesh. After the first hundred, the master said, "Now, you cursed, infernal son of a b——, your running about will spoil all the rest of my niggers: I don't want them to be running about, and you shan't be running about." I answered, "Master, I didn't mean any harm; I wanted to go and see my mother, and to get a shirt I left over there." He then struck me over my head twice with his cane, and told me to "hold my jaw." I said no more; but he told the overseer, "put it on to him again like the very devil." I felt worse on account of the blows with the cane than for the overseer's whipping: that's what makes me feel so towards him now. It poisons my mind to think about him. I don't want to think about him. I was as much a man as my master. The overseer then went on with the bull whip. How many they put on, I don't know, but I know that from the small of my back to the calves of my legs, they took the skin clear off, as you would skin beef. That's what they gave me that day—the next day, I had to have some more. One of the slaves then washed me with salt and water to take out the soreness. This almost put me into a fit. It brought the pain all back—the abominable scoundrel knew it would. Then I was taken up to the blacksmith's shop to be fettered: that was the way S—— E—— broke "niggers." His name sounded around there as if he had been Satan himself: the colored people were as afraid of him as they would be of a lion out in these bushes.

Iron rings were put about my ankles, and a short chain to the rings. I was given in charge to two slaves. Some may deny that the slaveholders are so bad, but I know it's true, and God knows it's true. A stranger may go there, and they are not such fools as to put such punishment on a man before him. If he is going to do that, he will send him over the fields out of the way, and while they are enjoying themselves in the house, the slave is suffering under the whip. A regular slaveholder has got no conscience. A slaveholder knows the difference between a northerner and a southerner. If a man came from any other part, he never saw me in irons. G— — L— — might have seen me, or L— — K— —, or any other slaveholder might come and see it, and hold a council over it, and blackguard me for it: "Boy, what have you got that on you for? That shows a d— —d bad nigger: if you warn't a bad nigger you wouldn't have them on."

The two slaves took me in charge, with orders to kill me if I tried to escape. At night, my feet were made fast in the stocks, without removing the irons. The stocks were of wood with grooves for the ancles, over which laid an iron bar. I could lie on my back, but could not turn. The next morning, I was taken to the gin-house to receive fifty blows with the bucking-paddle. This was my master's order. I received three blows, and then fainted. When I came to, only one slave was with me, who took me to the field to work,—but I was in so bad state that I could not work that day, nor much for a week. After doing a hard day's work in the fetters which had now worn to the bone, for they would get wet with dew in the morning, and then sand would work in, I was placed in the stocks—my ankles sore, bleeding, and corrupted. I wished I could die, but could not.

At the end of three months, he found I was too stubborn for *him* to subdue. He took off the fetters from my ankles, put me in handcuffs, and sent me to Norfolk jail, to be shipped for New Orleans. But when I arrived, the time that niggers were allowed to be shipped to New Orleans was out, and the last boat for that spring had sailed. After two weeks, I had the measles. My master was written to, but neither came nor sent any answer. As the traders were coming there with slaves, the turnkey put me into the kitchen to avoid contagion. I soon got better,—the turnkey said, "You are well now, and must be lonesome,—I'll put you in with the rest in a day or two." I determined to escape if I could.

At night I took a shelf down and put it against the inclosure of the yard, and climbed to the top, which was armed with sharp spikes, fourteen inches long, and, risking my life, I got over the spikes. Just as I had done this, the nine o'clock bell rung the signal for the patrols. I fell on the outside and made for the river, where I found a skiff loaded with wood. I threw over half a cord in a hurry, and pushed off for the opposite shore, to go back into the neighborhood of my old place, hoping, by dodging in the bush, to tire out my master's patience, and induce him to sell me running. I knew nothing about the North then—I did not know but the northerners were as bad as the southerners. I supposed a white man would be my enemy, let me see him where I would. Some of the neighbors there would have bought me, but he refused to sell me in the neighborhood, being ashamed to sell there a slave whom he could not break. He gave up first, but I was the worse beaten. I was as big-hearted as he was: he did not like to give up, and I would not give in—I made up my mind that if he would find whips, I would find back.

Having lightened the skiff, I paddled across, and went back to North Carolina to my mother's door. I ran about there in the bush, and was dodging here and there in the woods two years. I ate their pigs and chickens—I did not spare them. I knew how to dress them, and did not suffer from want of food. This would not have taken place had my master complied with my reasonable request for a pass, after I had done my work well, without any fault being found with it. But when I found out by that, and by his cruel punishment, that he was a devil, I did not care what I did do. I meant he should kill me or sell me.

My master did not advertise me when he got the news of my escape, saying it was their loss, as I was placed in their charge. He sued, but was beaten. After this he advertised for me, offering fifty dollars for my capture, dead or alive. A free-born colored man, whom I had known, betrayed me. Some poor white fellows offered him *ten dollars* if he would find out where I was. He put them on my track. At ten one morning, they found me lying down asleep. I partially aroused, and heard one say, "Don't shoot: it may be somebody else lying down drunk." I arose with my face towards them: there were six young white men armed with guns. I wheeled, and ran; they cried out, "Stop, or I'll shoot you." One of them, a real youngster, hit me, firing first; the others fired, and said they shot their best, but did not hit. A bullet and a buckshot entered my right thigh; the shot came out, but the bullet went to the bone, and is there yet. It injured a sinew, so that my foot hurts me to this day, when I walk. I ran about a quarter of a mile, then my foot all at once gave out, and I fell. They came up with dirks, threatening me with instant death, if I even winked my eye towards molesting them. They took me in a cart, and put me into the county jail. All that night I lay wishing they had shot me dead. I did not want to face that hyena again. But he was as afraid of me as I was of him. He would not have me, he said, come on his farm again. He kept me in jail until a slave-driver came from Western Tennessee—he took me out to Tennessee, to hire out or sell—any thing to get rid of me. I was hired out to T— — R— —, in Jackson, Madison Co., two years. I did very well; the man who hired me was a pretty fair sort of a man for a slaveholder. During the two years I became satisfied with my condition, and, in about a year after, married a young woman, belonging to T— — N— —: she is living with me yet.

About nine months after our marriage, I was, on a sudden, without suspecting any thing, jerked right up and put in jail again to be sold. I was taken by a driver to Memphis, and put into the hands of a planter, who was to sell me when he got an opportunity. In about two weeks, when I had got rested, I started to go back to see my wife; but I got taken up on the course, and was put in jail. The people asked me where I was going. I told them the truth, "To Jackson." I've been into pretty much all the jails round there. It seems to me wonderful, when I have known men to be killed without doing so much, or going through so much as I have, that I should be spared. It is only by the mercy of God that I have escaped so many dangers. I have known men to be killed by less accidents,—but I was spared, although I have the marks of many wounds and bruises.

In jail they fettered my ankles again. There was a black man in the room with me, who was caught under the same circumstances as myself—going to see his wife, as a man has a right to do. I was very muscular and smart, but he was stouter than I. We broke through the top of the jail at night—the shingles cracking gave the alarm. My friend was scared, and did not dare fall: but I did not care what befell me, and I rolled off to the ground, without having time to use strips of bedclothes which we had prepared. I was chained, and could not spring to save myself: it was a hard fall, but I was not quite stunned. I should not have got off, but that my pursuers bothered each other. They first started for the roof, and finding we were outside, the jailer cried, "Go outside! don't let 'em come down! don't let 'em come down!" His wife, hearing this, thought we were coming down stairs, and secured the door. While they were breaking out, I crept on my hands and knees about two hundred yards, to a creek, which I crept over in the same way. Then I looked around, and saw the jailer on the top of the jail with a light, looking for me, not thinking I could get down chained. He called, "John! John! where are you? If you don't answer me, you son of a b—h, I'll kill you when I get you." A neighbor crossed over, and asked, "What is the matter?" He answered, "The d—d niggers are breaking out of jail." I heard this distinctly on the other side of the creek, where I sat listening, to hear what course they would take. As I crept, I had to spread my feet to keep my chain from rattling—a child could have taken me chained as I was. In a few minutes the whole village was in an uproar. I heard the jailer tell some one to go to a man that kept dogs, and "tell him to come in a minute—I want him to run a nigger." I then crept: I could *creep* faster than I could run. From what I had told my captors, they thought I had gone to Jackson, and so failed of finding my track.

I did not know where I was, nor which way to go. I found a road, and wandered long in that. When my hands and knees got cold with creeping, I would get up and shuffle along with my chain. At daybreak, as the Lord would have it, I came to a blacksmith's shop. No one was there. I went in and felt among the tools in the dark, and found a great new rasp. I took the rasp along with me, and crept on to find a bush, and wait for daylight. As soon as I could see to do it, I cut my feet loose. I would give fifty dollars if I had the irons here that I've been abused in, to show people who say they don't believe such things—who say that men are not so abused. I would like to show them the irons and the paddles and the whips and the stocks that I have worn on me and been punished with. I wouldn't take fifty dollars of the best British gold that ever was laid out to me, if I could have them here to show people how I suffered in the United States: and I should like to have them here who ordered the blows and fastened the irons, to see how they would look while I was telling of it.

At about 8 o'clock in the morning, my feet were free. I had had nothing to eat since noon the day before. I wandered through the woods all day, eating acorns, and trying to find the route for Jackson. I meant to get there: nothing would have stopped me but death. I was not going to have another man send me round the country just where he liked. That night I got the course for Jackson; and after walking an hour, I entered a barn-yard and found among the harness a bridle. I was barefooted and bareheaded—had nothing on but my shirt and pantaloons,—all else I had taken off to get through the roof of the jail. I then walked into the stable, and found what appeared to be a gentleman's riding-horse—and a better nag I never laid leg across. He took me in three hours further than he ever took anybody else in six, I think. When I got to Jackson, I turned the horse loose in the street: he wandered about a while, but the owner got him at last. When he sees that, he will know who borrowed his horse, and if he will send in his bill, I will settle it. I have plenty of land and plenty of money to pay off all debts, and if some of my old friends would come this way, I would pay off some other old scores—that are on my back.

At Jackson, I saw my wife: she had been bought by F— — T— —, a regular negro-trader—one of the biggest dogs in the bone-yard. He said he would buy me running if he could, but no one was to be told where I was, as he wished to buy me cheap. He wrote to my master that he had bought my wife, and that I was dodging about the place: that he didn't want me about among his "niggers,"—but that if he would sell me, he would catch me if he could,—if not, he would shoot me. The answer was, that my master would sell me for eight hundred dollars. T— — paid the money and took possession of me. He put me on his farm. He was overbearing—his overseer was more so. He was one of those who, when they get a "nigger," must whip him, right or wrong, just to let him know "that he *is* a 'nigger'." No fault was found with my work. He looked sharp to try to find some way to get at me. At last he found a way to do it—an excuse to whip me,—it was in this way: one day he heard me speak something to one of the hands; it was some of our nonsense, of no consequence whatever. But he was itching for an excuse to flog me, and now he had got one—for it was a rule that there should be no talk on work hours, except about the work. My master having heard that I was an old runaway, and had given trouble to my master, had cautioned the overseer not to bear down very hard upon me until I had got habituated to the place and the ways. The overseer went to the master and said it would never do to excuse that "nigger;" for if he talked the rest would stand and hear it; he should either whip me or take me off the place. Master told him, and was overheard to say it, that if I would not obey him, he might take me down and give me three hundred with the paddle. The overseer made up his mind to give me the punishment on the next evening. When I had got through work, I went home, tired and hungry—my wife met me at the door, laid her hand on my arm, "John, three hundred for you this evening with the paddle!" That news filled my stomach very quick,—it stopped my hunger, but made me feel thirsty for blood. I swore that I would not leave the quarters until I was killed, or had killed any man; master, overseer, or slave, who might come to take me. But as it happened, a gentleman from New Orleans came to see my master that night, and so the punishment was postponed. If this was done for a southerner, how could a northerner expect to see any punishment? That visit was what prevented my killing a man, and being killed for it that night: for I had a good sharp axe, and I know I should have used it. I waited some time for them to come,—but as they did not, my temper cooled down, and I concluded to take to the bush.

I had heard that if I could get into Ohio, and manage to stay there one year, I would, after that, be a free man. I intended to wait for my wife to get smart, she being sick at the time. I went into the woods, and once more took to living on chickens and geese, which I understood very well. In about two weeks I went for my wife. Another man had agreed to come with us: but he was weak enough to advise with a friend about it, and the friend turned traitor and told his master. They are just the same as white men. I have found out since I have been in Canada, that 'tis not the skin that makes a man mean. Some of them will betray another to curry favor with the master, or to get a new coat, or two or three dollars, and I have noticed the same mean spirit among white men. But there are others who would die sooner than betray a friend.

I bade my wife get ready for a start on the next night, and then I took to the bush again. Meanwhile, the traitor slipped to our master, and asked him if he knew that three of the negroes were going to run away. He told him "No—which three?" He named us. "Where are they going to?" "Ohio State." This aroused my master: he went to the quarters, tied the man, and tied my wife, and took them to a swamp. There they uncovered my wife, and compelled a girl to whip her with the paddle to make her tell where I was. It so stirred me with indignation to think they should so foully abuse my wife, that I could have run a dagger through their hearts and not thought it wrong: nor have I yet got so far enlightened as to feel very differently about it now. She could not tell him, for she did not know. The man also was punished, and put in irons. They had no irons to fit her, and sent to the blacksmith's shop to get some made: and had it not been for some craft on her part that night, I should never have got away. Old Billy, with whom we were usually left, was the blacksmith; and while he was going to make the irons, she was left with a younger man who was a stupid sort of a fellow. It was then nearly noon, and she had had no food for the day. She was then at the quarters. She said to one of the girls, "Maria, you go to the turnip-patch, and get some salad, and I'll go to the spring, get some water, and put on the meat." She expected the fellow would stop her, but he did not. She carried the pail to the spring, about a quarter of a mile, then dropped it, and made for the bush. It was a down-hill way at first, but by and by, there was a rise and then they saw her. Out came master, overseer, and many slaves, in full run to catch her: but she was now nearly half a mile ahead, and ran very fast. She got into the woods which were very thick. Master then ordered a halt,—he had found from the other slaves that I had a pistol, powder, and ball. I had, indeed, and would have used it, rather than they should take me or her. But I was in another place at the time.

I had appointed a place where she was to come to meet me: when I went she was not there. I then drew near the house to ascertain what had happened, and heard a loud laughing and talking in my cabin. I tried to hear what it was about. I heard one of them say, "Lord, how she did run across that field! ha!ha!ha!" She had baked cakes for our journey, and they were making merry over the flour cakes. Presently, I saw a colored man, and whistled to him. He came up, and I learned what had happened, and that all were then out on a hunt for me, being stimulated by a promised reward of ten dollars. All this set me into a tremble; I turned back, and went to the place I had appointed. She was near by, saw me and ran to me, and so we were together once more. We then walked nine miles northwardly to a little village where I had put up my clothes. The man who betrayed us had told our route. I got the things and went to the barn close by: then my wife was exhausted, and fell on the barn-floor. I had a strong constitution, and could travel all the time; but she was so fatigued from the flogging, and the race, and the long walk, that she fell on the barn-floor. I returned to the house, and then walked to a tavern stable, to hook three or four blankets to keep us warm on our way north. If this was wrong, it was taught me by the rascality of my master.

While at the tavern stable, I heard the dog bark at the house I had left; I gathered three blankets and bolted for the barn, expecting the scoundrels would be pursuing my wife. I saw a candle burning bright in the house, and moving from room to room. That frightened me: I seized and shook her,—"wife! wife! master is coming!"—but I could not awaken her. I gathered her up, put her across my shoulder manfully, jumped the fence, and ran with my burden about a quarter of a mile. My heart beat like a drum, from the thought that they were pursuing us. But my strength at last gave out, and I laid her down under a fence, but she did not awaken. I then crept back to the house to see who was there and to get my things. The light I had seen now came down stairs, and moved towards the barn. I was so near that I saw the overseer and six slaves, armed, searching for me.

Oh my soul! it makes my hair stand up to think how near we were to getting caught, and carried back, to be abused and maltreated unreasonably, and without cause.

I was within five rods of them when they went into the barn. They searched it thoroughly, as I saw between the rails of a fence. "Oh you rascals!" I thought, "You're defeated now!"—but 'twas a close run and a narrow chance. When they left the barn, I kept watch of them. They returned the candle to the house, then walked the way they had come, to the place where they had left their mules. They stayed there about a half an hour. I still kept watch of them. I wanted to get my things, but I was wise enough to know that every time a slaveholder is out of sight, he isn't gone; every time his eye is shut, he is not asleep. They then returned toward the house; as they moved, I moved, keeping the same distance from them. When they were within about ten rods of the house, they crouched down in readiness to shoot me when I might approach the house. They had rendered me desperate by their devilment, and knew I would fight: they would not dare take me without shooting me first. I watched them, and they watched for me, until the cocks crowed for morning. It would not do for me to remain any longer to get my clothes and provisions. I went back to the place where I had left my wife; she was then easily awakened, and we hied to the woods to conceal ourselves for the day. We had no provisions but a raw ham. We dared not make a fire to broil it, so we ate of it raw; like a dog. At night, between sunset and dark, I went back to the house in the village—at the door I saw a person with our things. They gave them to me, and bade me God-speed, and that, if ever I was taken, not to betray them. I then put forth, and, with my wife, reached Canada. God save the Queen!

From Jackson to the Ohio River was called one hundred and forty miles,—crossed the river to Cairo; then we footed through Illinois to Chicago; all the way we lay by days, and travelled nights. I forgot the name of that city, and wandered out of the way, and got to a river. It was the Mississippi, but I did not know it. We crossed into Black Hawk territory. There I was so lost and bewildered, that I had at last to go up to a house to inquire the way. I found there a man with true abolition principles, who told us the route. He said a man and his wife had been carried back to slavery from that neighborhood. He did not take us across the river, but we found a way over. Then we walked on,—my wife was completely worn out: it was three months from the time we left home before we slept in a house. We were in the woods, ignorant of the roads, and losing our way. At one time we came to a guideboard, which said "5 miles to Parks's Landing." I had learned to spell out print a little. This was Sunday night. I took the direction I wanted to travel as near as I could, and we went on. On Wednesday afternoon we came back to the same guide-board—"5 miles to Parks's Landing." Many such roundabout cruises we made, wearing ourselves out without advancing: this was what kept us so long in the wilderness and in suffering. I had suffered so much from white men, that I had no confidence in them, and determined to push myself through without their help. Yet I had to ask at last, and met with a friend instead of an enemy. At Chicago money was made up to help me on, and I took passage for Detroit, and then crossed to Windsor, in Canada. That was the first time I set my foot on free soil.

Work was dull among the French at Windsor. We stayed there about six months. We heard of the Queen's Bush, where any people might go and settle, colored or poor, and might have a reasonable chance to pay for the land. We set out to find the Queen's Bush—went to Buffalo—thence to Black Rock—thence to St. Catharines, and there I got straight instructions. We had not a second suit of clothes apiece; we had one bedquilt and one blanket, and eighteen dollars in money. I bought two axes in Hamilton, one for myself, and one for my wife; half a dozen plates, knives and forks, an iron pot, and a Dutch oven: that's all for tools and furniture. For provisions I bought fifty weight of flour and twenty pounds of pork. Then we marched right into the wilderness, where there were thousands of acres of woods which the chain had never run round since Adam. At night we made a fire, and cut down a tree, and put up some slats like a wigwam. This was in February, when the snow was two feet deep. It was about fourteen years ago. We made our bed of cedar boughs from a swamp. Thus we travelled three or four days, seeing plenty of deer: wolves, as plenty as sheep are now, were howling about us, and bears were numerous.

At last I came to a place where I judge, from the timber, the land was good—and so it proved. My nearest neighbor was two miles off. I felt thankful that I had got into a place where I could not see the face of a white man. For something like five or six years, I felt suspicious when I saw a white man, thinking he was prying round to take some advantage. This was because I had been so bedevilled and harassed by them. At length that feeling wore off through kindness that I received from some here, and from abolitionists, who came over from the States to instruct us, and I felt that it was not the white man I should dislike, but the mean spirit which is in some men, whether white or black. I am sensible of that now.

The settlers were to take as much land as they pleased, when it should be surveyed, at various prices, according to quality. Mine was the highest price, as I had taken of the best land. It was three dollars seventy-cents an acre. I took a hundred acres at first, and then bought in fifty.

Myself and wife built us here a little log hut amid the snow. We made it ourselves, shouldering the logs to bring up to the place. We went to the cedar swamp, and split out boards for the roof. We had plenty of firewood, which served instead of blankets. Wolves, any quantity, were howling about us constantly, night and day—big, savage wolves, which alarmed the people. Some men carrying meat, were chased by them. Isaac Johnson was obliged to take up a tree. We got used to them on our way here, and did not fear them at all. In the spring, plenty of bears came about us after sheep and hogs. One day my wife and I were walking out, and we saw four bears in the cherry-trees eating the fruit. My wife went for my gun, called some neighbors, and we killed all four. Now the wolves are all gone, and the deer and the bears are scarce. There are idle men enough about here, colored and white, to drive them away, when they had better be chopping and clearing land.

We went to chopping, day and night; there was no delay; we logged the trunks with our own hands, without cattle, or horses, or help,—all with our own hands, and burned them. I raised that year one hundred and ten bushels of spring wheat, and three hundred bushels of potatoes on land which we had cleared ourselves, and cultivated without plough or drag. All was done with the hoe and hand-rake. This I can prove by my nearest neighbors. I got the seed on credit of some Dutchmen in the towns, by promising to work for them in harvest. They put their own price on the seed, and on my labor.

In the next winter, we went to clearing again. My wife worked right along with me: I did not realize it then, for we were raised slaves, the women accustomed to work, and undoubtedly the same spirit comes with us here: I did not realize it then; but now I see that she was a brave woman. I thank God that freedom has never overweighted us: some it has, but I have worked to support it, and not to discourage it. I thought I ought to take hold and work and go ahead, to show to others that there is a chance for the colored man in Canada; to show the spirit of a man, and a desire to improve his condition. As it is so often said by slaveholders, that if the "niggers" were free, and put in a place where they could be together they would starve to death, I wanted to show to the contrary. I have one hundred and fifty acres of land: one hundred and ten of it cleared, and under good cultivation: two span of horses, a yoke of oxen, ten milch cows and young cattle, twenty head of hogs, forty head of sheep; I have two wagons, two ploughs, and two drags. I would like to show this to that everlasting scoundrel, E— —, my former master, and tell him, "All this I would have done for you cheerfully, and thought myself at home, and felt happy in doing it, if you would have let me: but I am glad that you scarred and abused me, as it has given to myself and my family the fruits of my own labor." I would like to show it to those stout, able men, who, while they might be independent here, remain in the towns as waiters, blacking boots, cleaning houses, and driving coaches for men, who scarcely allow them enough for a living. To them I say, go into the backwoods of Queen Victoria's dominions, and you can secure an independent support. I am the man who has proved it; never man came into an unsettled country with lesser means to begin with. Some say, you cannot live in the woods without a year's provisions,—but this is not so: I have come here and proved to the contrary. I have hired myself out two days to get things to work on at home one. If there is a man in the free States who says the colored people cannot take care of themselves, I want him to come here and see John Little. There is no white blood in me; not a drop. My mother's father was imported from Africa, and both my grandparents on the father's side were also imported. I can prove to him that every thing which was due on the land is paid; that I raised seven hundred bushels of wheat last year, two hundred bushels of potatoes, one hundred bushels of peas, two hundred and fifty bushels of oats, ten tons of hay; fattened fifteen hundred weight of pork, one ox, besides other produce of less consequence. I have now growing fifty acres of wheat, eighteen acres of oats, ten of peas, one acre of potatoes, and twenty acres of meadow grass: I have horses, oxen, cows, hogs, sheep, and poultry in abundance. The man who was "a bad nigger" in the South, is here a respected, independent farmer. I thank God that I am respected in this neighborhood by the best men the country can afford—can lend or borrow two thousand dollars any time I am asked, or choose to ask for it. I don't say this for the sake of boasting—I say it to show that colored men can take care of themselves,—and to answer any who deny that Canada is a good country.

The *"nigger"* who was so "BAD" among Southerners, as to be scarred with whips, put in the stocks, chained at his work, with ankles sore from the irons, months together, legally shot and maimed for life by a boy who was too young to be trusted with a gun, sold into Tennessee, his character *"bad,"* sent after him to debase him there, put in jail after jail, hunted by hounds—stands up here at the North, a man respectable and respected. I don't ask any one to take my word for it, merely. Ask the people of Peel, Wellesley, Woolwich, and Waterloo—those are the places where I am known, and where they can get acquainted with my character; and I am willing it should be compared with that of any slaveholder whatever.

The abuse a man receives at the South is enough to drive every thing good from the mind. I sometimes felt such a spirit of vengeance, that I seriously meditated setting the house on fire at night, and killing all as they came out. I overcame the evil, and never got at it—but a little more punishment would have done it. I had been so bruised and wounded and beset, that I was out of patience. I had been separated from all my relatives, from every friend I had in

the world, whipped and ironed till I was tired of it. On that night
when I was threatened with the paddle again, I was fully determined
to kill, even if I were to be hanged and, if it pleased God, sent to
hell: I could bear no more. If any man thinks slavery a proper thing,
let him go and be abused as I was for years in North Carolina, much
of the time in agony from irons and whips and paddles—then let him
be sold off a thousand miles into Tennessee, and begin to live it over
again, and I think he would be tired of it too.

I want every man that has the heart of a man, to put down upon
slavery with all his heart and soul,—because it is a curse—because it
makes the feeling of dislike to color, leading the white to abuse a
"nigger" because he is a "nigger," and the black to hate the white
because he abuses him.

In making my escape, my main difficulty was in crossing the Ohio
Bottoms, before reaching the river. The water was black and deep. I
bound our packages on my wife's back, placed her on a log as a man
rides on horseback, and I swam, pushing the log, holding it steady, to
keep her up. Had the log turned right or left, she would have slipped
off, and the packs would have sunk her. It would have been death,
sure—but worse than death was behind us, and to avoid that we
risked our lives. When we had crossed one, we would presently come
on another, and have to go through the same again. By and by, I
would think, this must be the last,—but when we had crossed this,
and gone over some little island, there would be another. Oh dear! it
seems as if I could see it now,—I almost repented I had started, but
on I went. There was another and another—good swimming creeks:
but when I had crossed the last one, my spirits rose again—my heart
cheered up, and I thought I could go through all.

After we had got to a place where we intended to pass the night, I
would leave my wife, and go look all around, to see if there was any
white man. I was like an old hunting dog, who, when he has treed a
coon, will not believe his eyes, but goes scenting about to see if the
track has left the tree: if not, he will come back, look at the coon,
bark, and then scent again.

I was hunted like a wolf in the mountains, all the way to Canada.
In three months I had to go to many places to steal our food. I
would have asked for it, but if I **did**, it was, "Where is your pass?" To
avoid this meanness, and the risk of capture, I was obliged to look
out for myself, and I made good use of my time. One night, on

entering a dairy near a farm-house, the door creaked, and an old man called out, "Sa-a-l!" But I took some cakes, and Sal made no answer.

When I was travelling in the North, I found that men worked days, and slept nights without fear, because they were honest. At the South they do not have this comfort. The overseer watches through the day, and the master is on the look-out in the night. I know this, for many times, after my hard day's work, being but half fed, I went out to steal a chicken, or a goose, or a pig, as all slaves have to do,—at night, if the dog barked sharp, I would see master at the window with a gun. Sometimes the window would fly up—"who's that?"—then the man must give an account of himself. They are doing wrong in robbing the slaves, and so they are uneasy nights. When I first got into the North, and heard a dog at night, I would dodge away from the house, expecting to see the man of the house start out with a musket, as I had down south: but I was much astonished to find that they let a dog's bark go for what it was worth. I saw then the difference between free labor and slave labor: the northern man labors in the day, and sleeps soundly all night. He does not spend his day in laying deep schemes to whip a "nigger's" back, and then start up at night, in unexpected places, like a ghost.

One night, in Tennessee, my master heard a dog bark; he started up and ran out in his shirt, like a madman, to the quarters. When he got there, he called to us by name, saying some one had gone up to the house to see his girls—two slave girls he kept at the house. Every man was in his own cabin, but one old man of sixty, who was getting a little wood. He accused him of going up to the great house to trouble his people: the old man begged off, and finally was excused.

How can men, who know they are abusing others all the day, lie down and sleep quietly at night, with big barns of corn, and gin-houses full of cotton, when they know that men feel revengeful, and might burn their property, or even kill them? Even now the thought of my cruel abuses begins sometimes to creep up and kindle my feelings, until I feel unhappy in my own house, and it seems as if the devil was getting the better of me; I feel, then, that I could destroy that tyrant, who, knowing that I was a man, cut me with a whip in a manner worse than I will name. Then I think, "What is the use? here I am, a free man in Canada, and out of his power." Yet I feel the stirrings of revenge. I know that thousands at the South feel the same, for we have counselled upon it; the slaveholders know this—how will they sleep nights? The slaveholder is afraid of his slaves: it cannot be otherwise. Some have been round the borders of slavery, and seen a little of the edges of it, and they think they know a great deal about it, but they are mistaken. I have been in slavery, and know its worst is hid from them. They have all the laws and customs of the country in their favor, and yet they find something to grumble about: how then can they expect the slaves, whose feelings are wretched, even when they are best used, can be happy and contented? They say the slaves are happy, because they laugh, and are merry. I myself, and three or four others, have received two hundred lashes in the day, and had our feet in fetters: yet, at night, we would sing and dance, and make others laugh at the rattling of our chains. Happy men we must have been! We did it to keep down trouble, and to keep our hearts from being completely broken: that is as true as gospel! Just look at it,—consider upon it,—must not we have been very happy? Yet I have done it myself—I have cut capers in chains!

MRS. JOHN LITTLE

I was born in Petersburg, Va. When very young, I was taken to Montgomery county. My old master died there, and I remember that all the people were sold. My father and mother were sold together about one mile from me. After a year, they were sold a great distance, and I saw them no more. My mother came to me before she went away, and said, "Good by, be a good girl; I never expect to see you any more."

Then I belonged to Mr. T– – N– –, the son of my old master. He was pretty good, but his wife, my mistress, beat me like sixty. Here are three scars on my right hand and arm, and one on my forehead, all from wounds inflicted with a broken china plate. My cousin, a man, broke the plate in two pieces, and she said, "Let me see that plate." I handed up the pieces to her, and she threw them down on me: they cut four gashes, and I bled like a butcher. One piece cut into the sinew of the thumb, and made a great knot permanently. The wound had to be sewed up. This long scar over my right eye, was from a blow with a stick of wood. One day she knocked me lifeless with a pair of tongs;—when I came to, she was holding me up, through fright. Some of the neighbors said to her, "Why don't you learn Eliza to sew?" She answered, "I only want to learn her to do my housework, that's all." I can tell figures when I see them, but cannot read or write.

I belonged to them until I got married at the age of sixteen, to Mr. John Little, of Jackson. My master sold me for debt,—he was a man that would drink, and he had to sell me. I was sold to F— — T— —, a planter and slave-trader, who soon after, at my persuasion, bought Mr. Little.

I was employed in hoeing cotton, a new employment: my hands were badly blistered. "Oh, you must be a great lady," said the overseer, "can't handle the hoe without blistering your hands!" I told him I could not help it. My hands got hard, but I could not stand the sun. The hot sun made me so sick I could not work, and, John says if I had not come away, they would surely have sold me again. There was one weakly woman named Susan, who could not stand the work, and she was sold to Mississippi, away from her husband and son. That's one way of taking care of the sick and weak. That's the way the planters do with a weakly, sickly "nigger,"—they say "he's a dead expense to 'em," and put him off as soon as they can. After Susan was carried off, her husband went to see her: when he came back he received two hundred blows with the paddle.

I staid with T— — more than a year. A little before I came away, I heard that master was going to give my husband three hundred blows with the paddle. He came home one night with an axe on his shoulder, tired with chopping timber. I had his clothes all packed up, for I knew he would have to go. He came hungry, calculating on his supper,—I told him what was going. I never heard him curse before—he cursed then. Said he, "If any man, white or black, lays his hand on me to-night, I'll put this axe clear through him—clear through him:" and he would have done it, and I would not have tried to hinder him. But there was a visitor at the house, and no one came: he ran away. Next morning, the overseer came for him. The master asked where he was; I could have told him, but would not. My husband came back no more.

When we had made arrangements for leaving, a slave told of us. Not long after, master called to me, "Come here, my girl, come here." I went to him: he tied me by the wrist with a rope. He said, "Oh, my girl, I don't blame you,—you are young, and don't know; it's that d—d infernal son of a —; if I had him here, I'd blow a ball through him this minute." But he was deceived about it: I had put John up to hurrying off.

Then master stood at the great house door, at a loss what to do. There he had Willis, who was to have run away with us, and the man who betrayed us. At last he took us all off about half a mile to a swamp, where old A— — need not hear us as he was going to meeting, it being Sunday. He whipped Willis to make him tell where we were going. Willis said, "Ohio State." "What do you want to be free for? G— d— you, what do you know about freedom? Who was going with you? "Only Jack." G— d— Jack to h—, and you too." While they were whipping Willis, he said, "Oh, master, I'll never run away." "I didn't ask you about that, you d—d son of a —, you." Then they tried to make him tell about a slave girl who had put her child aside: but he knew nothing about that. As soon as they had done whipping him, they put a plough clavis about his ankle to which they attached a chain which was secured about his neck with a horse-lock.

They took a rheumatic boy, who had stopped with us, whom I had charged not to tell. They whipped him with the paddle, but he said he was ignorant of it: he bore the whipping, and never betrayed us. Then they questioned him about the girl and the child, as if that boy could know any thing about it! Then came my turn; they whipped me in the same way they did the men. Oh, those slaveholders are a brutish set of people,—the master made a remark to the overseer about my shape. Before striking me, master questioned me about the girl. I denied all knowledge of the affair. I only knew that she had been with child, and that now she was not, but I did not tell them even that. I was ashamed of my situation, they remarking upon me. I had been brought up in the house, and was not used to such coarseness. Then he (master) asked, "Where is Jack?" "I don't know." Said he, "Give her h—, R— —." That was his common word. Then they struck me several blows with the paddle. I kept on telling them it was of no use to whip me, as I knew nothing to tell them. No irons were ready for me, and I was put under a guard,—but I was too cunning for him, and joined my husband.

My shoes gave out before many days,—then I wore my husband's old shoes till they were used up. Then we came on barefooted all the way to Chicago. My feet were blistered and sore and my ankles swollen; but I had to keep on. There was something behind me driving me on. At the first water we came to I was frightened, as I was not used to the water. It was a swift but shallow stream: my husband crossed over, and I was obliged to follow. At the Ohio Bottoms was a great difficulty,—the water was in some places very deep,—it was black, dirty water. I was scared all but to death: but I had become somewhat used to hardship. If I had seen a white face, I would have run into the river.

By and by, we succeeded in crossing the last one. Then we struck a light at a shingle-getter's shanty, made a fire with the clapboards and dried ourselves. We were merry over our success in getting so far along, and had a good laugh as we burned the boards and part of the shanty itself. I felt afraid at getting into a boat to cross the Ohio River: I had never been in any boat whatever. Now to get on this in the night, frightened me. "John," said I, "don't you think we'll drown?" "I don't care if we do," said he. We reached Cairo well enough.

We never slept at the same time; while one slept, the other kept watch, day or night. Both of us never slept at one time,—if we had, we would not have reached Canada. One morning, as I was watching by a fire we had made, John sleeping, I saw a dog, and told John. Said he, "'tis some old white man hunting a hog,—however, we had better go from this fire." We went down into a valley and there remained. In the afternoon, an hour before sunset, a white man came suddenly upon us, while we were getting ready for a night's march. I started to run: John stood. The man said, "Stop, there!" But I kept on; his face was so white, that I wanted nothing to do with him. John said, "What did you say?" "Stop, there." John said, "I'll do no such thing." Then hard language passed between them. The man said, "I'll have a pack of hounds after you before night." John answered him with an oath to frighten him, "You had better do it, and be off youself, or I'll blow a ball through you." The man never had heard a negro swear at him before. They are generally so cowed down, that John's swearing at him, alarmed him more than a bullet from a white man. It showed that he was desperate,—and that was the only reason why he used such language. The man struck spurs to his horse, and went off in a hurry. We followed him, as he went the same way we were going, and kept as close to him as we could: for, if the man got hounds he would start them at the place where he had seen us; and coming back over the same route with hounds, horses, and men, would kill our track, and they could not take us. But we saw no more of the man.

Soon after dark, we came to a lake. We found an old white man there in a shanty, who was caring for a slave that had been shot by his master a few days before. We went in and saw him,—he was an old, gray-headed man. His master had threatened him with a flogging, and he took to the river: just as he reached the water, his master shot him behind. But he got across. He was wounded, and without hat or shoes. In this place we were informed about our route. It was in Kentucky.

While we were stopping at the shanty, a day or two, John went out one evening with the old man, to hunt for provisions. I went to bed. By and by the dogs barked; the door opened, and by the fire I saw five white men. One said, "Who you got here?" "Only my own family." I was afraid, and crept out slyly on my hands and knees, and hid behind an ash-barrel until they were gone.

In a few days we crossed the ferry. Then we went on, and were without provisions, except some corn, which we parched. We met here a runaway slave, who knew the route of the country above us. He was returning to his master, where he had a wife and children.

At Cairo, the gallinippers were so bad, we made a smoke to keep them off. Soon after I heard a bell ring. Said I, "John, somebody's dead." It was a steamboat bell tolling. Presently there she was, a great boat full of white men. We were right on the river's bank, and our fire sent the smoke straight up into the calm. We lay flat on the ground. John read the name—Maria. No one noticed us: after the boat was gone, we had a hearty laugh at our good luck. Thinking there was no more trouble, we did not put out our fire. Presently came a yawl boat: they saw our fire, and hailed, "Boat ashore! boat ashore! runaway niggers! runaway niggers!" We lay close, and the boat kept on. We put out our fire, and went further back from the river, but the musquitoes were so bad, we made another fire. But a man with a gun then came along, looking up into the trees. I scattered the fire to put it out, but it smoked so much the worse. We at last hid in a thicket of briers, where we were almost devoured by musquitoes, for want of a little smoke.

Next day I lay down to sleep, while John kept watch. When I awoke, I told him I had dreamed about a white cow, which still seemed a white woman, and that I feared we would be caught. We were in the woods, in a low, damp place, where there was no bit of a road, and we knew not where the road was. We started to find a road, and then met with a white woman. I reminded John of my dream. "Good evening, good evening," said she. My husband asked if she would sell him some bread: this was to make conversation, so he could inquire the road. "Oh yes, just come to my house, I'll give you some bread." We went to the house, and presently her husband came in. He asked, "Have you got free papers?" John answered, "No." "Where are you travelling to?" "To the upper lakes." "We are not allowed to let a colored man go through here without free papers: if we do, we are liable to a fine of forty dollars." He allowed us to remain all night,—but in the morning we were to go before a squire at Dorrety, and, if we were free, we would go on. This was the woman's arrangement: the man did not seem inclined to stop us. She said, "If we stop you, we shall get fifty dollars apiece for you: that's a—good—deal—of—*money*,—you know." The man asked John if he had a pistol. John produced one. The man said 'twas no harm, he would take care of it for him,—and locked it up. They lived in a little, dirty log hut: they took the bed off the bedstead, and lay down on it close to the door, so that it could not be opened without disturbing him. The man took a nice silver-mounted pistol from a cupboard, loaded it, and placed it where he could reach it in the night. We lay on the bedstead—they on the floor. She was the evil one: she had made the plans. Their name was Smith.

At about three o'clock in the morning, husband aroused me,—"I'm going away from here; I don't value them, now other folks are asleep." We both got up. John spoke roughly, "Mr. Smith! Mr. Smith!" He aroused: "we are unwell, and must pass out,—we'll be back very soon." Mr. Smith get up very readily, and pulled the bed away a little, so we could slip out. As John passed by the pistol, he put his hand on it, and took it in exchange for his old one. It is a beautiful rifle pistol, percussion lock,—John has been offered fifteen dollars for it. If the man will come here with John's old flint lock, my husband will exchange back, and give him *boot*. I am very sorry for my friend, Mrs. Smith, that she did not get the hundred dollars to go a shopping with in Dorrety—am much obliged to her for our night's lodging. We went across a small stream, and waited for daylight. Then we went on to Dorrety, and passed through the edge of it, without calling on the squire, as we had not time.

One Sunday morning, being on a prairie where we could see no house—about fifty miles west of Springfield—we ventured to travel by day. We encountered an animal, which we at first supposed to be a dog; but when he came near, we concluded it to be a wolf. He yelped something like a dog: he did not attack us. We went on and crossed a stream, and then we saw three large wood-wolves, sneaking around as if waiting for darkness. As we kept on, the three wolves kept in sight, now on one hand, and now on the other. I felt afraid, expecting they would attack us: but they left us. Afterward we made a fire with elder-stalks, and I undertook to make some corn bread. I got it mixed, and put it on the fire,—when I saw a party of men and boys on horseback, apparently approaching us. I put out the fire; they turned a little away, and did not appear to perceive us: I rekindled the fire, and baked our bread. John managed to keep us well supplied with pies and bread. We used to laugh to think how people would puzzle over who drank the milk and left the pitchers, and who hooked the dough.

I got to be quite hardy—quite used to water and bush-whacking; so that by the time I got to Canada, I could handle an axe, or hoe, or any thing. I felt proud to be able to do it—to help get cleared up, so that we could have a home, and plenty to live on. I now enjoy my life very well—I have nothing to complain of. We have horses and a pleasure-wagon, and I can ride out when and where I please, without a pass. The best of the merchants and clerks pay me as much attention as though I were a white woman: I am as politely accosted as any woman would wish to be.

I have lost two children by death; one little girl is all that is spared to me. She is but four years old. I intend to have her well educated, if the Lord lets us.

CHATHAM

"At Chatham," said Mr. John Little, "the fugitives are as thick as blackbirds in a corn-field." Here, indeed, more fully than anywhere else, the traveller realizes the extent of the American exodus. At every turn, he meets members of the African race, single or in groups: he sees them building and painting houses, working in mills, engaged in every handicraft employment: here he notices a street occupied by colored shopkeepers and clerks: if he steps into the environs, he finds the blacks in every quarter, busy upon their gardens and farms.

The white population of Chatham is reckoned at four thousand: the number of colored persons in the town may be safely estimated at eight hundred. If to this estimate is added the number residing in the neighborhood, the total amount cannot be less than two thousand. A gentleman, holding an office in the town, and who, having been one of the earliest settlers, has seen the town grow up around him, remarked of the colored population, "They are as good a body of people as you can find anywhere:" and their general appearance, and attention to business confirm his opinion.

Among that portion of the whites who put a high value on their prejudices, and a lofty estimate on their own personal importance, there seems to be a dread that some terrible and unpardonable crime, termed "sauciness" may yet become rife among the blacks. A white farmer in the vicinity of Chatham, manifested in conversation a great dislike of the colored residents. His main objection to them seemed to be, that, on one occasion, as somebody had told him, four or five of them kept the side-walk, whereby a white woman was obliged to step off,—"That's the way 'tis with 'em,—they'll get so *saucy*, by and by, that there'll be a rebellion." On mentioning this circumstance to a colored man, he answered, "I have had to step off fifty times for impudent white fellows,—but I do not blame *all* the whites for it: but if a colored man does any thing out of the way, his fault is tacked to the whole of us." And this is too much the case.

In another part of Canada, a white man expressed lively fears that the negroes would yet become "saucy." He explained this term as applicable to "language which would be well enough from a white man, but out of the way from a negro,—because a man won't take from one of them, what he would from a white man." "And why should he not?" "Why—*he won't.*"

In 1832, there were in Chatham, but two or three shops, and a few houses. The oldest deed on record is dated 1801. In 1837, two steamboats commenced plying to Detroit, one occasionally extending its trips to Buffalo. The facilities thus afforded to trade, proved highly conducive to the prosperity of the town: but Chatham "took its great start" in 1852, while the Great Western Railway was constructing. Colored people began to come in at the first settlement of the town: at present they are increasing in a greater ratio than the whites. They maintain separate churches, and attend a separate public school. This the writer visited, and found fifty pupils of both sexes in attendance under a colored teacher. A private school is taught by Mr. Alfred Whipper, a colored man. This school appeared to be in very good condition: fifty-eight colored pupils of both sexes were present.

It was in Chatham, that the writer first heard of the Associations called True Bands. A True Band had just been formed here, enrolling at first three hundred and seventy-five members, and it was continually receiving accessions of numbers. On inquiry, the following was furnished as an answer to the question, what is meant by a True Band?

A True Band is composed of colored persons of both sexes, associated for their own improvement. Its objects are manifold: mainly these:—the members are to take a general interest in each other's welfare; to pursue such plans and objects as may be for their mutual advantage; to improve all schools, and to induce their race to send their children into the schools; to break down all prejudice; to bring all churches as far as possible into one body, and not let minor differences divide them; to prevent litigation by referring all disputes among themselves to a committee; to stop the begging system entirely; (that is, going to the United States, and there by representing that the fugitives are starving and suffering, raising large sums of money, of which the fugitives never receive the benefit,—misrepresenting the character of the fugitives for industry, and underrating the advance of the country, which supplies abundant work for all at fair wages;) to raise such funds among themselves as may be necessary for the poor, the sick, and the destitute fugitive newly arrived; and to prepare themselves ultimately to bear their due weight of political power.

The first True Band was organized in Malden, in September, 1854. It consists of six hundred members. It is represented as having thus far fulfilled its objects admirably. Since its organization, no action at law has been brought by one member against another: their differences being arranged by a committee of arbitration. A small monthly payment is made by the members. The receipts have enabled them to meet all cases of destitution, and leave a surplus in the treasury. In all other places where the bands have been organized, the same good results, as I was creditably informed, have followed as in Malden: thus showing that the colored population possess the means and the will, when acting in concert, to take care of themselves and of the strangers as they arrive. There are now fourteen True Bands organized in various sections of Canada West.

What in the above sketch of the bands is characterized as "the begging system," meets the almost univeral reprobation of the colored people of Canada. Many of them express themselves with indignation against it: "We have heard that thousands of dollars have been raised for us in the United States, but we never received any of it; a great deal of clothing, but it never reached us. Not that we want the money or the clothing; we can support ourselves: but we don't want others begging over our backs: representing us as starving and freezing through our own laziness and vice, and thus injuring our character while they pretend to befriend us,—meanwhile, subserving nobody's interest but their own. What cases of suffering occur, can be taken care of here." Some expressed a wish that those who were disposed to give money, should give it to the fugitive on his way, or use it to relieve those who suffer from having assisted fugitives. One case was named to me of a man who raised a sum of money in the United States for some imaginary persons, whom he called suffering, starving fugitives, and who, on his return, erected for himself a fine dwelling-house. By and by, wanting a fence about his premises, he again raised a sum of money for some more miserable fugitives, and, soon after, his grounds were duly fenced in. Many similar stories are in circulation. What part of them is true, and how much is scandal, it may be difficult to determine: but every one at all acquainted with the present status of Upper Canada, knows that any man there, able to labor, can readily find work, and get his pay for it when it is done. The cases of suffering and destitution occasioned by sickness and improvidence, can best be relieved by local institutions. The annual report of "The Toronto Ladies' Association for the relief of destitute Colored Fugitives" for 1853-1855, states, "During the past inclement winter, much suffering was alleviated, and many cases of extreme hardship prevented. Throughout the year, the committee continued to observe the practice of appointing weekly visitors to examine into the truth of every statement made by applicants for aid. In this way between two and three hundred cases have been attended to, each receiving more or less, according to their circumstances." How much money was disbursed during the year is not stated: the amount of subscriptions and donations for the year was a little more than one hundred and sixty pounds. Of this society, Mrs. Arnold is president; Mrs. Willis treasurer, and Mrs. Henning corresponding secretary.

The Rev. Hiram Wilson succeeded a few years since, in organizing in St. Catharines, a "Refugee Slaves' Friend Society," which embraces many of the most respectable citizens of the place. If these and similar well-managed associations, which practise a judicious system of expenditure, see fit to appeal to friends of the fugitives in the United States, there can be no doubt of a suitable response.

The opinions of a portion of the fugitives themselves on the subject of charities in their behalf will be found among the narratives which follow.

J. C. BROWN

I was born in Frederick county, Va. My father was a white man; my mother a mixed blood. She was given away by a man named N— — to a man named B— —, so that she could not appear at a court against N. on a suit for her freedom and her three children's. B. took her to Kentucky: therefore, myself and brother and sister remained slaves with N. He in a short time removed to Kentucky. At fifteen, I was hired to Capt. George Smith, who volunteered to go to Tippecanoe. I was fifer in his company. The freedom of myself, Moses, and some others was promised us on our return. But the last time I saw Moses, he was bowed down in hellish slavery in Little Rock, Ark., and I had the misfortune to have to pay N. eighteen hundred dollars for my freedom—my step-father and mother hiring my time for six years. Neal was captain of the Silver Greys, who did not go to war, being over forty-five,—they reported whether any negroes were disaffected, and strong suspicion fell on me—but it was false. At that time there were many colored people joined in a conspiracy to get their freedom, and wore as a mark, a plait in the hair over the left eye. This was discovered,—many were whipped, and had the plait cut off. The conspiracy extended over three hundred miles, from Maysville to Henderson.

A free colored man named Freeribbon, who lived four miles from Louisville, was suspected as the author of this conspiracy. F., his wife and daughter kept an inn, and he had a blacksmith's shop to accommodate with farriery those who stopped with him. They searched the shop,—under it they found old guns, butcher-knives, and other implements for killing. He was put in jail and condemned to be hung,—but having many friends, he was reprieved on condition that he should be sent to some Spanish mine, and there remain the rest of his days. He was sent to the mines. After twenty years, a white man in the neighborhood committed murder. Under the gallows he confessed that he had been employed by three near neighbors of Freeribbon, and that they paid him for putting the implements under F.'s floor. One of the three was a congressman, one a colonel, one a gentleman. In consequence of their crime, F. had been sent off, and his fine farm confiscated. When this was made known, the court sent for Freeribbon. He came back, and I saw him—a heart-broken man. The colonel afterward poisoned himself.

After I became a free man, I carried on the mason business in Bardstown, Shelbyville, and Louisville. My misfortunes now began. I had been used well as a slave, for my mistress was my aunt. I was an object of jealousy to the white mechanics, because I was more successful in getting jobs. They threatened me, unless I left the neighborhood, to break every bone in my body. I was then finishing a large building for Capt. Nelson. He said he would see M— —, leader of my enemies, and stop their proceedings: but M— — still continued his threats. About the same time, I saw a free colored man whipped. This grieved and alarmed me. I burst into tears; I went to my mother and told her I would leave a slave country and go to a free country. I had been married about two years. In 1819, under the advice of Stratford Gowen and Benjamin Lundy, I was sent to Texas to find shelter and suitable situations for free people of color. Meeting there with Mr. Black or Blake, then a member of the council of that colony, he told me that Texas was to be a great cotton and sugar-growing country, and would one day be annexed to the United States. He said a majority of the council were opposed to having a free colored settlement in Texas, and it would be useless for me to look further. I then returned to Louisville, and in a short time removed with my family to Cincinnati.

At this time, a white man of a Quaker family, named Hethers, was teaching colored children in Louisville. The slaveholders being very suspicious of him, hired a colored barber named Tillman, a slave, to get Hethers into his shop and ask him to write a free paper. Capt. T – G– – and S– – B– – concealed themselves under the counter in Tillman's shop. Hethers came in, and the colored man asked him his charge for writing a free paper to come to Canada. He told him, if he was to write one, he would not charge him any thing. Tillman said, "No—you must have twenty dollars,"—as he had been instructed. He asked Hethers if he thought the papers would pass him good to Canada. Hethers told him "Yes, but he had better call on J. C. Brown, in Cincinnati, who was, he understood, a very clever man, and could give him instructions." So I got into a scrape without knowing it.

It was a few days after that, I went to Louisville to settle up some business. Hethers had been seized by the two white men and was now in jail. The night I got down, a man named Shaw came to me, and told me that some gentlemen wanted to see me in Dr. Talbot's shop. I went there; M– –, my old enemy was there. He asked me who raised me? "'Squire Neal of Shelby." "You are a sample of some of his raising. Do you know what we sent for you for?" "I do not." He then raised an oil cloth, and showed pistols, bowie-knives, ropes, and cow-hides. Said he, "this is what we sent for you for; and I'll tell you what you are to do. To-morrow morning at 10 o'clock, you are to go to court, where Hethers is to be tried, and testify that Hethers is writing free passes for our *niggers* to be taken to you, and for you to forward to Canada." I denied that it was so, and told them I didn't know Hethers. "Take me to the jail and let Hethers see me, and if he says he ever saw me or knew me, turn the key upon me and give me a trial." M— — was then a Methodist preacher, and is yet. He said, "Hear him,—he wants to be tried like a white man! but we have a trial for you in Bullock's woods." He then told me if I failed to appear and testify as they said, I should be taken to the woods at night, then tied up and receive nine hundred lashes: one hundred apiece from nine of them. They consulted Dr. T— —, as to whether I could take the nine hundred blows and live. He felt of my body and said I was a man of great muscle,—he told them where to chalk me about the shoulders, and so as to avoid the kidneys. I said to them, "Gentlemen, I have a wife and two children, and of what use can I be to them after you have given me nine hundred lashes?" M— — said, "That's their look-out, not ours." They dismissed me with the injunction that I should attend the court. I did not attend it, believing that I had many friends in Louisville who would not let them use me so.

Just after dark, on the evening after the court, I was at my mother-in-law's with my family, and was invited to stop to supper. Knowing that I drank water, the old lady was going to the pump, when she met a mob of white men coming. One of them told her to run to the house and tell me to flee for my life, or my life would be taken. She fainted and fell. While I sat at the table, fearing that all was not right, I came down to the foot of the stairs, and there saw three or four white-hatted gentlemen looking up the stairs, and many others behind them. I walked out through them bareheaded—they did not recognize me—I heard them say, "Hush! hush!" to each other as I passed through the crowd. I got to a steamboat landing, where were several boats going next day, and went on board a Pittsburg boat bound to Cincinnati. I told my situation to a man, who then locked me up in a state-room. Next morning, the slave-holders went aboard all the boats and ordered them not to take me out of the city. We left next morning at 9 o'clock, Capt. Y— — not knowing that I was on board.

After we got twelve miles from Louisville, they rung the bell for passengers to pay their fare. Not wishing any charge against the man who had concealed me, I had come out on deck. The clerk asked my name,—I told him "J. C. Brown." He wouldn't take my money, but went for the captain. He came and said, "I can get more money by running back to Louisville, than I can by going to Pittsburg." I told him he had better do it. He said, "No insolence!" and then told a young man, a deck hand, to "camp me." That fellow's back soon felt the deck, and I made for the captain; he rang the bell, and called help, who seized me, and chained me to the capstan-bar, where I was kept nearly all the distance to Cincinnati. I got a warrant for false imprisonment against Capt. Y. It was to be served by one Doty, but he always pretended he never could catch him. I got no recompense nor justice for that treatment.

Three years after this affair, the law of 1804, known as the Ohio black law, was revived in that State, and enforced. By this law, every colored man was to give bonds in $500 not to become a town charge, and to find bonds also for his heirs. No one could employ a colored man or colored woman to do any kind of labor, under penalty of $100. There were then about 3,000 colored people there—by this law they were thrown out of employment. I was then clearing $600 a year, and refused to give bonds. The colored people had a meeting, and talked about a court of appeals to test the law. Some talked of going to Texas,—we knew not what to do: we were sore perplexed. I spoke to them of Canada, and we formed a Colonization Society, of which I was President. I wrote for the Board to Sir John Colborne, at Little York, now Toronto, to know if we could find in Canada an asylum for ourselves, our wives, and children. Two members of the Board went with the letter to Toronto, and were well received by Sir John. He wrote us to remove into Canada with our wives and children, if we chose to do so; and that so long as we remained true and loyal subjects, we should have every privilege extended to us that was enjoyed by any of her majesty's subjects, no distinction being made on account of color. I have his letter now in my possession—his memorable words. Mr. Hammonds, our friend, editor of a daily paper in Cincinnati, published the letter at my request. The publication made an excitement in the corporation of Cincinnati. Two or three of us, including myself, were sent for by the city government, next day. The reason was, as Mr. Hotchkiss said, that I, as one of the leading spirits, was doing a great deal of mischief; for every one that I took off to Canada was a sword drawn against the United States. At this time Cincinnati was full of women, without husbands, and their children. These were sent there by planters from Louisiana and

Mississippi, and some from Tennessee, who had now got fortunes, and had found that white women could live in those States. In consequence, they had sent their slave-wives and children to Cincinnati, and set them free. They had begun to come about the close of the last war. Cincinnati was the great point for them. I was agent of a man who had eighteen of these headless families in one house. I asked the Mayor, "Now that they have deprived us of work, who is to go begging for these people, to keep them alive?" He said they were taking steps to have the law repealed, and wished me to stay any action about sending people to Canada.

I paid no attention to what he told me, and sent three wagon loads out to Sandusky next day. In three or four weeks I and my family left—came to Sandusky—thence I took a boat, the "Gov. Cass," and went to Little York, where I entered into a contract with the Canada Company, for a township of land, agreeing to pay $6,000 a year, for ten years. It was the township of Biddulph. The black law had now become inoperative in Cincinnati, and the colored people wrote me, that they could now walk without being pushed off the side-walks, were well used, and were living in clover. Of 2,700 who were to have come, only 460 came out. They settled promiscuously in the province, buying land here and there, and getting work. Only five or six families of them settled in Biddulph. Three weeks after they settled, fifteen families from Boston, Mass., met them there, and settled there, where they remain. We only paid for 1,220 acres, which was divided, from 25 to 50 acres a family. Numbers, who came afterward, had to leave for other places. These families in Biddulph are now independent. Their lands now will sell at forty to fifty dollars an acre: it cost one dollar and fifty cents. I settled in Toronto, where I could have some means of making myself useful for them among the white people, and where my trade was good.

My wife became dissatisfied, and I removed with her and my daughter,—my son having died,—to Cincinnati, where I remained for thirteen months. I went on to Louisville, to see my old mother. This was some six or seven years from the M— — scrape. I saw my old mother, and just as I was taking a seat at the table, an officer popped into the room, shook hands with me, and said he wanted to speak with me. I went into another room with him—he put his hand on my shoulder, and said, "You are my prisoner." I was put in jail, charged with running off large quantities of slaves: my accuser, Mr. G— —

D— —, said I had crossed the river at Utica, Charleston, and Madison, with large droves of slaves. The third day I wrote an advertisement for Mr. Penn's paper, offering $100 reward for any credible evidence of my having done as was alleged. The court released me on $2,500 bail: two persons recognized in $1,000 each, and I was taken for the $500. On the evening of the day I gave the bonds, three men came out at me, and drew pistols, which they fired at the ground about my feet: this, my friends supposed, was to frighten me, and induce me to run off, so that my securities might forfeit their bonds. The Grand-Jury failed to find a bill, and I was discharged.

I returned to Cincinnati. My wife had seen so much of my persecution, that she was more anxious to return to Canada than she had been to leave it. We returned to Toronto, and I was a gunner there in the Patriot war. I removed to Dawn, and was elected one of the trustees of the school in that place. From Dawn I came to Chatham about 1849. Chatham was then a little village of frame buildings and log cabins. There were then no masons, bricklayers, or plasterers among the colored men. I went for some, and got them here, and we are now able to build a house from the stump. We can cut the timber and make the brick. The greater part of the bricklaying and plastering is in the hands of the colored mechanics. There are four churches of colored people which are well filled. We have separate schools which are tolerably well attended,–the Sunday School is very numerously attended. There are three charitable societies of men, and two of women, which do much good, relieving the wants of the sick and destitute. There is a great deal of property owned here by the colored people: their number has doubled in two years, mainly by immigration, which continues still—especially of fugitive slaves,–sometimes twenty in one day. Many agents have come here, nominally to assist the fugitives, but some of them have not been so honest as one could wish. They collected money, but the fugitives did not get it. However, what money the fugitives have received has been an injury, rather than a benefit. I have seen cases where the money would have done good, if rightly distributed.

Our children growing up in this country, and not having the fear of any white man, and being taught to read and write, will grow up entirely different from their fathers,–of more benefit to themselves, of more benefit to the government, and will be more able to set good examples to the rising generation. Intelligent parents will raise up intelligent children.

Slavery disarms a man of virtue,—of every thing: it prevents his being a man. Anticipation is what we live for,—it makes us anxious to improve ourselves and our children; but the slave anticipates nothing, but the setting of the sun, or the passage of some law to curtail what little of privilege he possesses. The effects of slavery are perceptible here in our courts. I have seen fugitives, brought as witnesses, afraid to testify against a white man. This is a part of the horrid effects of slavery. The younger ones are better than this. They grow up without slavish fear: they know nothing about it.

PHILIP YOUNGER

I served in slavery fifty-five years, and am now nearly seventy-two years old. I was born in Virginia, went, at ten, to Tennessee; at twelve, to Alabama: was, all the time, body servant of a military man. My treatment was various,—sometimes rough,—sometimes good. Many awful scenes I have seen while moving about. I have had to put chains on men, myself, to go into a chain gang: I have seen men whipped to death,—have seen them die. I have ridden hundreds of miles in Alabama, and have heard the whip going, all along from farm to farm, while they were weighing out cotton.

In Alabama, the patrols go out in companies at about dark, and ride nearly all night. If they meet a colored man with a pass, it is thirty-nine lashes; but they don't stop for the law, and if they tie a man up, he is very well off if he gets only two hundred. If there is a party assembled at the quarters, they rush in half drunk, and thrash round with their sticks, perhaps before they look at a pass,—all must be whipped unless they rush out: I can't paint it so bad as 'tis. Sometimes a stout man will fight his way through.

As a general thing the treatment on the plantations in Alabama is very hard. Once in a while a man is kind, as kindness is out there, and then he is hated by all the other masters. They say "*his* niggers spoil *our* niggers." These servants are not allowed on the other plantations at all,—if caught there, they will put as much on them as they can bear. I have as good a chance to know as any man there,—I have travelled there on the plantations,—I was there before the country was opened,—at the war,—and have seen it grow up by the colored man's labor. I have seen miles of fences around plantations, where I had been through woods with the surveyors. Escape from Alabama is almost impossible,—if a man escapes it is by the skin of his teeth.

There was a free man in Huntsville—a barber,—whose wife—a free woman—was taken by a patrol, as she was walking out at dark, and put in jail, just to disgrace her,—as she was in a little better standing than the patrol was. Her husband grumbled about it,—a rumpus was made, and people collected. It was in front of a tavern door. The folks then called out, "Shoot the d— —d nigger! shoot him!" The patrol stabbed him with a bowie-knife, and he fell in the street. He was carried in, and a doctor dressed the wound, but he was never a sound man afterwards.

I hired my time, and made some money. I bought my wife's freedom first, and sent her away. I got off by skill. I have children and grand children in slavery.

I had rather starve to death here, being a free man, than to have plenty in slavery. I cannot be a slave any more,—nobody could hold me as a slave now, except in irons. Old as I am, I would rather face the Russian fire, or die at the point of the sword, than go into slavery.

We are placed in different circumstances here—some drag along, without doing much,—some are doing well. I have a house; I have taken up fifty acres of land, and have made the payments as required; I have other property besides. Here is Henry Blue, worth twelve thousand dollars: Syddles, worth a fortune; Lucky, worth a very handsome fortune; Ramsay, a great deal of land and other property, at least twelve thousand dollars; all these were slaves at some time. And there are many others wealthy, through their own skill and industry.

Before I came here, I resided in the free States. I came here in consequence of the passage of the Fugitive Slave Bill. It was a hardship at first; but I feel better here—more like a man—I know I am—than in the States. I suffer from want of education. I manage by skill and experience and industry—but it is as if feeling my way in the dark.

GILBERT DICKEY

I have been in Canada but six weeks: am 55 years old. I was raised a slave until 35. I was born in North Carolina, Guilford Co., where I was the main hand on the farm, where we raised wheat, corn, rye, etc., some cotton. There were about fifteen slaves on the farm, sometimes more, sometimes less. My master has frequently said, that Gil. could carry on the farm better than he could: he had told his neighbors that I and his wife could carry on the farm as well, if he were a hundred miles off. I never had a day's schooling in my life—went to a Sunday School a few times, but that was cut off. I have no learning but what God has put into my head. My master was hasty and high-tempered, but was always kind to me owing to some peculiar circumstances. He was more kind than most who own servants in that country, and more so than his companion. Some thought him a hard man, but I never thought him so hard as some I have seen. When he *did* whip, he whipped severely, I tell you; he was high-strung when he got up. I suppose there's no doubt that he and his father-in-law—a severe old man—whipped one slave man to death. They whipped him over the head with a loaded whip, shamefully. He was one of those that could not be whipped. He was sold after the beating, and died two months after. The ferrule came off the whip they used, and the whalebone bursted out.

At nine years old, I was bought into this family, being transferred to pay a debt of three hundred dollars. At the death of my master, I was hired out sixteen years, until my young master came of age. I had then made up my mind to buy my time and was preparing to do it, by laying up my money as I could earn overplus. I have made fifty dollars in a winter by working after 9 o'clock nights while buying my time. It is hard work ever since I was seven years old, which has broken me down: I now have rheumatism, coughs, etc. I worked at all kinds of work,—every thing a man would call on me to do, exept stealing, my hands were ready to do it. I worked at fencing, laying stone wall, digging wells, carpentering, etc. During the sixteen years, I paid up five hundred and seventy-five dollars; that left four hundred dollars to be paid, which I borrowed by giving names. I was then free, but had to work to raise the four hundred dollars, which took me nearly two years.

I was whipped at one time by my old master, because I could not work. It was brought about by a mean white man who was working in the field, and told master that I was not sick. My master cursed and swore very wicked. He did not tie me up, but he gave me a severe whipping. It did not cure me: I had to go and try to work, but could not do much.

I have seen sixteen men chained abreast for market, and driven from that place. I have seen a woman chained and handcuffed in the gangs, leaving a child only nine days old: the child raised by hand, and when a woman nearly grown, she was sold.

After the old man died, and before I was hired out, two of the colored children were sick—one died, and I watched with the other by the corpse. On the next day evening, when we came back from the burial of the child, the other was dying, and the doctor was there. The child died that evening. My mistress then requested me to mend a pair of shoes for her daughter that night. I told her I would rather not, as I had been up the night before, and a corpse was in the house. She flew into a passion, said she would have it done, or her father should whip me. I mended the shoes that night, but it made no difference. Her father came next morning with some work-hands, and told me with an oath, that if he had a knife he would cut my d— —d throat. I drew a knife from my pocket, opened it, handed it to him, opened my shirt-collar, and told him to cut it. He pretended to do so, and drew blood on my throat—the mark remains. I went away a piece, then changed my mind and came back. They tied my hands, I was so mad, I hardly knew what they did. He gave me thirty blows. I told him afterwards, that I had no place appointed to die or to be buried, and I cared not when it happened; that I would not be whipped any more, and that the first man who struck me I would kill. I was never punished afterward, although I was sometimes threatened. If they find a man determined and resolute not to be whipped, they will sometimes let him alone: but in other places, they will do it at any rate.

No man, who has not been in slavery, knows the real curse of it. A northern man can't tell half how bad it is.

When I began to be hired out, I felt more liberty than on the place—where I had to do whatever a man said—where it was never too wet, nor too cold, too hot, nor too dry—where I could not go to the next house, no matter how near it was, without a permit.

I lived in Indiana for nine years before I came here, and did well. I have been doing business for myself some twenty years: I never considered that I was doing business for myself till I got out of debt. I was making money in Indiana, and had plenty of friends. I liked there, all but one thing—slavery was there, as it is all over the United States. One or two days in the year they acknowledge a colored person to be a man; that is, when he works on the road, and pays his tax: all the rest of his time he is a brute. I came on purpose to a country where I could be a free man, and to encourage men of my color to take hold of work; to set them a good example, and to make their condition here better, if my assistance could do any good.

WILLIAM J. ANDERSON

I was a slave from birth, until thirty-two years old, on Red River, Bayou Rapide. I belonged to a man who kept me at home until twenty-one years of age. He was a constable, and I was the turnkey some two or three years. After twenty-one, I hired out to work on a steamboat, paying my master $25 a month, and supporting a family: and at the age of thirty-two I had $500. I was steward and cook. One day, at New Orleans, I heard the news of my master's death. I felt that I had lost my only friend; for although a mean man, he had some good qualities—he could not bear a man that drank, and yet he was drunk all the time himself. On hearing his death, an acquaintance of mine said, "Now is your time *to put.*"

I packed some clothes, took my $500, started for the North, and reached Cincinnati. I was robbed of my money on the passage. I opened a shop, and did very well by cooking at the hotels. After four years, I had some words with a man named Magee, who was a run-away, who had come barefoot, and I had given him employment to keep my grocery. He went down to the place where I came from, and informed where I was: he was retaken, and held in slavery.

I married in Ripley, Ohio. One day I heard a gentleman in Cincinnati talking to his brother about buying "niggers" and horses: one of them said, "Old Atwood is dead." I asked my wife if her name really was Atwood. She applied to the men, and found that

Atwood had left her mother and the balance of the servants free—say ten—and left $8,000 to each of them. Part of this I invested in Ohio, and a part I brought with us to Canada. Her father was her master, and had brought her to Ohio when she was six years old.

I had a brother named Charles, who carried a basket of eggs on board a boat named Red River, that ran up Red River. When he came off, he did not get the money for the eggs, as was expected by Mr. T— —, a Frenchman, who had hired him. He belonged to my master. When he went back, the Frenchman jumped on him, and beat him severely. Charles, however, struck the Frenchman. My master said, "Charles will certainly be hung for striking a white man: so you fix four stakes, and I'll whip him." I drove the four stakes into the ground for my brother: he was fourteen, and I thirteen years old. Master asked me if the stakes were ready. Said I, "Charles, before I'd be whipped for that Frenchman, I'd cut my throat." He did cut his throat, and ran into the river, where he beat off five men who tried to get him out. Then he came out himself, and was clear—was not whipped. In a few weeks he got well: he meant to kill himself.

I have seen many whipped till they could not stand up. S— — P. S— — whipped a man in Red River jail while I was turnkey, until he burst a bloodvessel, and died. I saw this done: no notice was taken of it.*

HENRY CRAWHION

Was born in Louisville, Ky. As soon as able to work, I was hired out on a steamboat, and have mainly followed steamboating. Master died, and I remained with my mistress: young master being a sporting character, I had to be sold to pay his debts. Was sold to a

---

*Female slaves enciente were formerly tied up for punishment: but to avoid the pecuniary loss which sometimes ensued, the masters adopted the *humane* method said to have been first practised by the French of Louisiana. The woman's limbs are fastened to four stakes driven into the ground; a portion of the earth having been previously removed in the centre of the space staked out. The traveller in Canada West will hear of this mode in almost every town and village; from old settlers and recent immigrants; from persons who came from different slave States, and from parts of the same State remote from each other.

trader in L., who took me to South Carolina, where I was employed three months to take care of race-horses. While there, I undertook to escape. I packed up in a carpet-bag, went to depot, and bought a ticket for Montgomery. A black man suspected me, because I had changed my trunk for the carpet-bag,—they came to the cars and took me out. They put me in chains, and kept me confined in the stable about two months; then I found a man who would buy me and take me to Louisville. I was put in the trader's yard, but nobody wants to buy out of the yard, because they think they are put in for some fault. I was then taken down to Port Gibson, Miss., and traded off for fifteen mules. I stayed there three weeks, and was then taken to Baton Rouge, where I was set up for sale. Here I found a man who bought me to take to Louisville, where I had a wife, on the condition that I would find a man to buy me there. But I could not find a man who would buy me. I went to see my wife, and left for the North. I got here last night. I don't feel reconciled, on account of my wife and family. I am anxious now to get work. [He got employment in the course of the day.] I would prefer Louisville, if I could be free there. It is hard on me that I am obliged to live away from my family.

I cannot express what I think of slavery, I have so horrible ideas of it. I was taken to Savannah on my way to Charleston, and staid in Savannah four weeks. On the farms around Savannah, I saw them using bucking-paddles on the women. There were overseers and drivers behind the workmen on the farms. If a man lagged, he got a cut with a whip,—if any reply was made, he was *bucked down*. The bull whip is used freely all around there,—I have heard them crack like a pistol almost. In the city, a black man must get off the side-walk if he meets a white man, or stop on the curb-stone and raise his hat: if he meets a lady and gentleman he must step clean off the walk and raise his hat.

While in Charleston, S. C., I did not know the law of the country, and lit a cigar at my boarding-house and walked towards the stable smoking. I was taken up and put in the calaboose. Several others were put in for being out after nine at night. In the morning, they gave each of them ten lashes apiece, and let them go. I asked them why they did not whip me and let me go. They said I had committed a crime, and must go before a magistrate. I asked them "what crime?" "Smoking in the street." I told them I was a stranger, and did not know the law. That made no odds, however; I was sentenced to nine and thirty lashes, and received them in the calaboose with a leather strap cut into three or four strips. White people smoke in the street, but 't is against the law for a colored man.

MARY YOUNGER

I was reared a slave, and have seen a great deal of barbarity in the State I came from. Many a time I have looked out in the moonlight, and seen my little children, just able to walk to the fields, carrying buckets of water to the hands. They used to carry the buckets on their heads: they would wear off the hair, and I used to make pads to protect the sore places where they carried the buckets.

If those slaveholders were to come here, I would treat them well, just to shame them by showing that I had humanity.

A woman who lived near us, used to beat her cook, and burn her with hot irons. I have seen the burns with these eyes. The same woman whipped at different times three of her slave women to death. The last one I was sent for by her mother to see: I found her dying. She died while I was standing by. Her mother wanted me to shroud the corpse: but the mistress interfered, and made the dead woman's mother do it. The house where these cruelties occurred, was so near ours that we could talk over the palings.

If a white man passes by a house, and a person is whipping a servant, he goes straight by—he don't see it.

I did not know, when I was a slave, that any white person had any sympathy for me. I thought all white people were alike, and had no sympathy for colored people. I did not know the difference until I reached a free State, when I saw the white people use the colored people like folks. I did not hear such terms applied as "wenches," "heifers," etc. Where I was raised, my children were often whipped till the blood ran, and then they would call me to see if I looked rumpled about it, and unless I looked pleased, I knew they would whip me.

I often wish that people from the North could just go through the southern country at harvest time, and see and hear what is done there.

There was a man whipped there one day, and at night I took pity on him and greased his back,—he died on my floor.

The barbarity of slavery I never want to see again. I have children now who have got the yoke on them. It almost kills me to think that they are there, and that I can do them no good. There they are—I know how it is—it brings distress on my mind—there they are, working till late at night; off before day; and where there is no humanity—where the lash is not spared.

EDWARD HICKS

I was born and raised in old Virginia, Lunenburg county, and was sold when a well-grown boy—was put on the block at the court house and sold. I was frightened at being up there on the block, and was afraid of being carried out of the country. A trader on his way to New Orleans bought me. He took me to his pen at Brunswick court house. I being very obedient, he thought I wouldn't run; but I determined to run if I could, for I thought if I got to New Orleans, I *was* at the shutting-up place. He waited a day or two to attend another sale fifty miles off, us with him—perhaps forty or fifty. We went by stages. I being so obedient, he turned me out to bring water and do errands in general, while he waited for the sale at Brunswick court house. In this time I thought about my mother and brother in the place where I was raised, and thought 'twas about time to run. I ran; but did not know what way to go, and took into the pines. Now, after I had done this, I began to study what I should do for something to eat: then I was in a strange country. I continued there for four days without any food except sassafras leaves, and I found water. After that, I found an old colored man. I told him how the case was with me, and asked for a bit of bread. He told me to come to his house at night, at a certain hour, and he would give me a mouthful to eat. I went to the house, got some food; and behold, the patrollers were out that night, and they came within one of catching me. Just as I had stepped out of the house, they came right in. The old man came out a little before day and whistled. I went to him, and he put me on the way to Lunenburg.

I travelled on about twelve miles, when it was so dark I dared not walk any further. I made for the bush, and laid a stick with the big end the way I was to go. That night, about dark, I got up and started again. I went on, and struck a creek near midnight, called Earn's Creek,—from Earn's Creek, I came to Stony Creek. Day overtaking me, I had to make into the willows on the creek. The bloodhounds that day, of their own accord, having such knowledge, gave me a little race: I went down into the creek, nothing out but my head, among big water moccasin snakes, which I kept off with a stick. The dogs I saw,—they heard me, but there was no one to hearken them on. At night I left the creek, and went up into the neighborhood of the house where I was born and raised: I saw some of my friends and brothers there, and I got something to eat. I was then advised (as the advertisement was just out from the *nigger*-trader) to go on to an old house where cotton was kept, and there stay until the advertisement was over. For they drive for runaways there with bloodhounds, and a great many men moving abreast, so that they will have a man unless he is a long distance under the ground. I went to the cotton house, and got under the cotton, and stayed till the drive was over—some two or three days.

I came out then, and made for the bush. I stayed till that trader went down with that company of colored people, and sold them and came back. I was out all the winter in caves and barns. In the spring the trader came back. There was a white man in Lunenburg, that wanted to buy me. The trader heard of it, and said, "I'll sell him, if you think you can get him: a *nigger* that will stay in the woods all winter, I won't have him. What will you give me for him?" It was settled at eight hundred dollars: then he sent out some of his boys to tell me, and in a few days I went to him.

He had four farms. I commenced to work right at the great house. I stayed there three years, I guess: then he died. Then every man had to come up to be appraised: about sixty of us were appraised. The same old trader (S— — N— —) came up to buy me again, chains and handcuffs all in his hand. He swore that the "nigger" that ran away from him, was the one he'd have, and the chains should not leave him, till he'd got him to Orleans. At twelve o'clock, I went to the kitchen to get my breakfast, and stepped right on, out into the bush. The sale was coming on in about a week, and the trader had come on to brag what he would do,—I stepped out right in the bush.

I was appraised and given to a young lady who thought it necessary to hire me out, right in the bush, where I was. A man hired me at about half price. He was a good man,—no bad man will hire one in the bush, because he won't come to him to save his life, and only the big traders can afford to have driving done. After I got to him, he put me to work at the great house, and he liked me so well, he bought me.

He got a man to oversee at the great house, who was determined to make more than any farmer in that country. He began to fight, kick, and knock over. We were going along, suckering tobacco one day; a couple of worms were found—these big, horned worms—lying on the ground in the rows: we had not seen them as we were breaking the suckers. He called the two men who went by them, and made each take one of the worms and bite its head off. I passed a small worm,—"G- —d d— —you," says he, "you bite that worm's head, and suck the stuff out of him: you may run away,—you've got to a place now, where if you run nine miles into h— —, we'll go in for you up to our armpits. You've made three runs, now you've made a bad stand." I told him I shouldn't bite the worm's head off: it was a thing I never had done, and I wasn't used to it, and wouldn't do it. He made to me with his bull whip, very long, and struck me three or four times; the third or fourth time, I got hold of it. He then turned to strike me with the butt,—but being too anxious, he let too much of it go over my shoulder, and I caught the other part, that he was going to knock me down with. S— — H— —, if he gets hold of that paper, he'll know all about it. He hollowed for help,—he wanted the other colored people to help him. They all passed on with their rows, but would not. I then having hold of both ends of the whip, jerked it out of his hands and ran. I did not intend to carry the whip far, but there was no stop for *me* then. I went on to the bush; he mounted his horse, and started off for men and bloodhounds. He then came back with the company and the hounds, stripped the head man and whipped him, because he did not help take me. I was then preparing to keep the bloodhounds from following me. I had gathered up some wild onions, and knew what to do.

The master now came home. He tells the overseer, that he shall pay a dollar a day for every day that I was gone, for he had no business to make that disturbance among the people. They chased me that day, but could not follow me beyond the place where I had put on the onions. It takes a mighty old hound to follow that track. I stayed three weeks, and then went in home. When I got home, the old man got hold of it then, and I was not flogged. At the end of the year, my lost time was brought against the overseer. The overseer left, and went to oversee for another man, named S— — S— —, at the edge of Brunswick Co. My master being sickly, in some way, his boys being sportsmen, and gambled, got involved, and had to sell part of his hands, at sheriff's sale I suppose. I was again put on the block and sold, and that overseer, S— — H— —, persuaded his employer, S— —, to buy me so he could get his spite of me. S— — bought me and sent me on to the quarter: put on leg goggles, a band of thin iron round each ancle, with a piece of wood, banded with iron, sticking from each with a rivet. A man cannot run with them on: the iron plays round and the long piece whips his legs as he runs. Each goggle weighs about three pounds. The overseer put them right on, as soon as I got there.

The master had plenty of dogs, four of which were regular "nigger bloodhounds," worth one hundred dollars or more apiece. That was the first time I began studying head-work. I had been running about in the bush without much object, but now I began studying head-work: while in this condition, it put my mind off to study what to do now. Every day I was sure of my whipping though—that was sure—with the loaded bull whip—loaded at both ends: every blow would cut through the skin. I couldn't run—couldn't get away. I lay down studying, and got up studying, how to get out of the condition I was placed in.

One night it came to my mind that I would go to the blacksmith's shop. After every person was asleep, and every thing appeared still, I got into the window and got a rasp. I put it away where I could get hold of it, knowing that if I cut it part through, they would see it, and band me stronger. That night I studied that I would go down deep, right there in the yard, where they machine cotton and pack cotton, right down among the seeds—way down—five feet I guess I went down,—and that the bloodhounds would not find me, as they would look round for me outside. I studied that as hard as a Philadelphia lawyer ever studied a case: if he studies as hard as I studied that, he'll give a right judgment.

I went down the night after I got the rasp, taking the rasp with me. The cotton seed and motes tumbled in after me as I went down, and buried me up entirely. They walked over me: I could feel the rattling

over me. I could not rifle in there. The next night I came out, and
commenced rifling to get off the goggles. They had been out all the
day with some drivers and the bloodhounds, expecting, as I had the
goggles on, to catch me directly. I sat up on the upper floor, where I
could see by the light of the moon or stars, and there I rifled away; I
rifled faithfully, and got one off that night,—but I had to break it
away some, and got the skin off my leg. Before day I went down into
the hole again.

The next night I came out and rifled off the other: it came off
easier than the other. Now I've got to go down again. Into the same
hole I went—'twouldn't do to come out yet. They had driven the
second day, and I was afraid they would the third. I had eaten
nothing all this time, nor drank a drop. The next night about dark, I
jumped out and went into the bush. I knew all about that
neighborhood, and which way to go. I got me an old scythe-blade,
and broke off a piece and made me a knife. This I found at the
machine as I was on the way to the bush. Then I killed me a pig,
took him on my back and walked five miles. I dressed him, singed off
the hair, and before he was fairly dressed, I had his ears on the coals
broiling.

Another consideration struck me now. It would be death to go
back to that place: I must get to a free land now. I had got the irons
off—that I knew. I came out of that county, went into a neighboring
county, into the bush, and staid out six months. I heard of some free
people coming on to the Ohio, and I thought I would get in the
crowd. We came on with a white man who had formed an
attachment to a colored girl, and as she was coming, he determined
to leave too, although he was a regular patroller. I came on with him
as a waiter and servant, and very faithfully I worked too. We
travelled with horses and wagons, but some had to walk. I had to pull
at the baggage,—I would have pulled a wagon all through myself but
what I'd have come. I was concealed the first part of the way; all the
food and clothes piled on me in the wagon, which was very
uncomfortable. You don't know how much I endured. At night I
would get out and walk. We succeeded until we got to Point Pleasant;
within three or four miles of the ferry, we met men at different
times, telling this tale—"If you take your slaves this way they'll all
get free,—for you'll get 'em on the Ohio side: I wouldn't take that
man; if you want to sell him, you can get your money right in this
place," etc.

He began to fear that they'd think he was running away slaves. "Look here," says he, "to-night you'd better take a skiff and cross the river—these folks have got passes to show, and you have not." This made me uneasy- I knew nothing about paddling a skiff: I might get off into the middle of the river, and then paddle back to the same shore. I then said to him, "It is a matter of course that we go on, and I go on as you said, and you've a right to take your slave wherever you please." Now he told me, "Do you go off, and come up to us when we get to the ferry-place." I said, "That won't do." We reasoned considerably about it: he was a man that would hear to a little reason, and so we reasoned. Now he told me, "Suppose I sell you, and I come back and steal you, and we divide the money?" He was turning now; he'd been into the town that day: enough wanted to buy me, but they didn't want the women. I told him, that wouldn't do—that wasn't our bargain—I had worked for him all the way, and his agreement was to take me over the ferry, and go on to the farm he was to take, and work for him one year at clearing, etc. We came on, all hands, down to the ferry at Point Pleasant,- some were for putting me in the wagon, and covering me, but they would search the wagon. So I walked with the rest.

At the ferry, the guard who watches all who cross the ferry—a great, big white man, who looked rather severe, quizzed my master, whether I was his slave, and questioned so close, that the white man began to grow weak in the knees, and I saw it: he trembled. I was scared for him, and I was scared about being taken myself—it was a scaring time. The guard told him the consequences—of going to the penitentiary, if he were going off with another man's slave. He trembled, and got weak, so that he did not get over it, till he got way out into the Ohio. We were commanded to get aboard the ferry-boat, and over we went. I walked on behind him, as he went up the hill: he yet trembled, and so did I, not knowing what might take place yet. I felt joyful that I had got over, but it was no time to rejoice there. We put the man in the wagon, and dragged him: he was more scared than he ought to have been.

I went to work with him in Ohio, according to promise. After we had begun, it got clear back to where I started from, that I was in Ohio. I made out that I was a man from Cincinnati, and was hired for money: but it got back home, that I was in Ohio. He then told me to leave. I understood that there was a reward of five hundred dollars offered to any one who would take me over the river to the

Kentucky side. I had been there as near as I can tell about six months when I got this news. I left him and was concealed at Gallipolis, at old man Isaac Browner's house—he is dead now, and 't wont do any hurt to mention his name. He put me in a bedtick on which he placed his children, who were sick of measles. I was in the straw-tick, the feather-bed was above me, and then the children. This was so, that if they came to search for the sake of the reward, they might not move the sick. I stayed there one day: I cared nothing for the heat, discomfort, nor sickness. All I thought of was to get off clear. At night-fall, I all alone came to the wharf to hail a boat—he told me how—to hollow "passenger." The boat was for the salt-works at Kanawha. If I had gone on board they would have taken me sure, because the boat was going to the place I did not want to go. The boat did not, however, put in for me, and I had to go back and get concealed again. The next day, they disguised me,—I went down to the wharf—a boat was coming which was bound for Pittsburg: it touched the wharf-boat,—there was no freight and only three passengers; a gentleman and a lady, and myself; they stepped aboard, and so did I,—a little bell rung, and away went the boat: when, looking back, I saw two men whom I knew, standing on a place, where they could see every man who came down to the boat. But they did not know me and the boat came on.

The river was high, and we came on slowly. I did not sleep for four nights at all- dozed a little in daytime. There was another boat coming behind,—"Clipper, No. 2,"—and I was afraid she was in pursuit of me. I fired up harder on that account: although I expected to get nothing for my work, I worked sharp. After we had started out, the clerk came round with his book and pen. I tried to dodge, but when he touched me, I thought I was gone. But he only wanted the money: I gave him all I had, and he returned me ten cents. I had my victuals for my work. At Pittsburg, I left a handkerchief of victuals, which I had put up, I was in such a hurry. I went up into the town, and inquired for the country, where I could get work. I worked not many miles from Pittsburg, and got a little money, and then concluded to come to Canada, where I would be safe.

I have been here about six years. I like Canada well,—I am satisfied with it. I have got a little property together, worth some two thousand dollars.

Liquor is right along the road here, and some make fools of themselves: but I mind my business, and am doing well.

My opinion of slavery is, that it ought to be broken down. If the white people were to set the slaves free, and offer to hire them, they would jump at the chance: they wouldn't cut throats.

We have got some good white friends in the United States. If it had not been for them, I would not have got here.

HENRY BLUE

I learned the trade of a blacksmith in Kentucky. I should have been perfectly miserable to have had to work all my life for another man for nothing. As soon as I had arrived to years of discretion, I felt determined that I would not be a slave all my days. My master was a kind and honorable man; purchased no slaves himself: what he had, came by marriage. He used to say it was wrong to hold slaves, and a good many who hold them say the same. It's a habit—they mean, they say, to set them free at such a time, or such a time,—by and by they die, and the children hold on to the slaves.

I purchased my freedom, and remained in Kentucky awhile; then removed to Cincinnati; thence to Chatham. Every thing goes well with me in Canada: I have no reason to complain.

I think that if a slaveholder offers his servant freedom, on condition that he will earn and pay a certain sum, and the slave accepts freedom on that condition, he is bound in honor to pay the sum promised.

Some poor, ignorant fellows may be satisfied with their condition as slaves, but, as a general thing, they are not satisfied with being slaves.

AARON SIDLES

By the law of Almighty God, I was born free,—by the law of man a slave. I was born in South Carolina: was raised in Murfreesboro', Tenn., until nineteen. I was taken into Kentucky, and sold three times. Then I was sold to one of the worst negro-traders that ever was, to be taken five miles below Baton Rouge. While he was purchasing more, I gave my guard the slip, and went into the bush five months. In this time I slept in no man's house nor barn: I felt that there were only two persons in the world I could trust: one girl, Lavina Robinson, who brought me food from a white man, and that white man himself, Timothy Guard. Mr. Guard knew me well,—I was his foreman—cooper. He offered $1,000 for me: the trader wouldn't take it. Guard lent me the money—I offered it for myself. The trader said, "I know you had that money of Guard, and I won't please him. I want *you*—you'll make a first-rate *nigger*-driver." I felt I would rather be killed than go. I was only afraid they'd chain me: I think they were afraid to undertake it. I was. a stout man, and have lifted seven hundred and fifty pounds—a steamboat shaft. It was on a bet; a Southerner bet a new coat he had against five dollars, that I could not lift it. I lifted it with ease, and took the coat.

I took to the woods as I said. The trader got discouraged, and sold the chance of me to Guard for $1,000. The conditions were, if Guard ever saw me in the United States, he was to pay the money. He saw me the next night, for I went in. I had a previous understanding with Guard, that if he bought me, I was to have a chance to buy myself. He gave me a paper signed before witnesses, that I was to be free, when I paid him $1,600. He also gave me papers stating that I was allowed to trade for myself: if I would not pay, he would, and if any one would not pay me, he would compel them. I went to work as steward of a steamboat. At first, I got $35 a month, which raised till I got $100 a month. I paid off Guard between six and seven years after: still remained on the boats, and, in all, I worked eleven years with one man at $100 a month,—and he would give me that now, if I would go back.

On passing up or down the Mississippi, between slave States, the first thing I heard in the morning was the sound of the great bells, which are rung to call the slaves. The next thing, before it was light enough to see, I heard the crack of the overseer's whip, and the cries of the slaves, "Oh! pray, Mas'r! Oh! pray, Mas'r!" Every morning I heard it from both sides of the river.

Living in Indiana, I was dissatisfied with the laws of the country. I had a good deal of property there; it was not safe, for any loafing white might destroy or steal, and unless a white man were by to see it, I could get no redress.

One time in Indiana, seven white fellows, without provocation, threw brickbats at my house, and broke my windows. I was so mad, that I seized my gun and pursued them, and put some small shot in the backs of two of them. Dr. F. would not take out the shot, unless they would tell him where they got them. They told him they had been to steal watermelons; had not got any; and on passing my house, they threw the brickbats because colored people lived there. The Dr. blamed them, said I was as much esteemed and respected as any man there. They owned they had no cause. I afterward made it known that, as my oath was good for nothing, if any white man interfered with me, or trespassed on my property, I would *make him* a witness.

I removed to Canada, where I would have an equal oath with any man, when any thing occurred; where I would have every right that every man has. I brought ten thousand dollars into Canada with me, and I find profitable employment for my capital here.

Excepting for the oppressive laws, I would rather have remained in Indiana. I left one of the most beautiful places in that country—everybody who sees it says it is a beautiful place. I had a two-story frame house, with piazza—good stable—and every arrangement about the premises was nice and convenient. I had abundance of apples, peaches, quinces, plums, and grapes. I paid my taxes, and felt hurt and angry too, that I was not allowed my oath—there was no justice in it. The road tax, I *would not* work out. They threatened to sue me. I told them I would stand a lawsuit first, and take it to the Supreme Court. "What!" said I, "shall a white man drive against me, on this very road, and break my wagon, and I get no redress? No! when you give me my oath, I'll work on the roads." They never sued me. I suffered oppression in being obliged to leave my place to claim my rights as a man.

I blame for this the tories and turncoats of the free States. They don't put in right men, that are true to their country. They are chosen to represent the free States, but they act with the South. Just exactly what they call dough-faces.

I was never taught to read or write.

JOHN C— —N

I live at the concession line and farm about four miles from Chatham. I was many years a slave, and have been up and down the Mississippi a great deal. In the morning the great bells ring on the plantations. Before you can see persons on the farms, you hear the whips crack and the slaves cry out. I have heard them every morning, when passing up or down the river,—"Oh Lord! master!—Oh Lord! master!" It seems to me always as I heard them in the dark, as if hell was there, and I heard the cries of them who were just going into it.

REUBEN SAUNDERS

I was born in Greene Co., Georgia. At about twelve years old, our family was broken up by the death of my master. I was the oldest child: there were three brothers and two sisters. My master's children had grown, and were married, and settled in various parts of Georgia. We were all separated,—no two went together. My mother's master was about half a mile from where the youngest child was. They did not think it would know enough to learn the way. Some of them carried her once to see her mother, and she learned the way. She used to go over to where her mother lived, and creep under the house, where she would wait till her mother came into the yard and then run to her. There were bad dogs there, but they did not trouble her. My mother's master tried to buy this child but her owner would not sell her under six hundred dollars. He did not mean to sell. I have not seen my mother since the sale. I remained there from twelve to twenty-four years of age, and was well treated.

I was never caught there with a book in my hand, or a pen. I never saw but one slave in Georgia, who could read and write, and he was brought in from another State.

The treatment about there, seemed to depend on the number a man had. If few, they got on well, if many, they fared worse. If a man used his slaves with kindness more than the others, they disliked it.

From Georgia, I was removed to Mississippi,—that being considered a money-making place. I was the only slave my master had. I went on with him. At first he engaged in rafting cypress timber, then kept a wood-yard on the Mississippi. I stayed there sixteen years. Then he brought me and my wife and children to Indiana, and set us free. He had made money fast, and he made a good use of it,—for he bought my wife and three children, and my wife's brother, on purpose to set us free. My family cost him thirteen hundred dollars, and the brother, seven hundred and fifty dollars. He afterward went down the Mississippi with eight hundred dollars, and to sell some land and wind up. He was lost off the boat and drowned: some thought he was robbed and pushed overboard.

I don't think any man can of right, hold property in another. I like the condition of freedom,—what I make is mine. I arrived here last April.

THOMAS HEDGEBETH

I was born free, in Halifax Co. North Carolina, where I lived thirty-five years. About ten years ago, I removed to Indiana. My father was a farmer, half white, who ran through his farm. If a white man there brings a great account, the white man would carry it against the colored,—the law there does not favor colored people. I cannot read or write. A free-born man in North Carolina is as much oppressed, in one sense, as the slave: I was not allowed to go to school. I recollect when I was a boy, a colored man came from Ohio, and opened a school, but it was broken up. I was in the field ploughing with my father,—he said he wished we could go and learn. I think it an outrageous sin and shame, that a free colored man could not be taught. My ignorance has a very injurious effect on my prospects and success. I blame the State of North Carolina—the white people of that State—for it. I am now engaged in a troublesome lawsuit, about the title to my estate, which I would not have got into, had I known how to read and write.

There were lots of slaves in the neighborhood where I was raised. After I grew up to take notice of things, I found I was oppressed as well as they. I thought it a sin then, for one man to hold another. I never was allowed to visit among the slaves,—had I been caught visiting them, I should have been fined: if a slave had visited me, he would have been whipped. This prevented my having much intercourse with them, except when I was hired to work by the masters. The conversation among the slaves was, that they worked hard, and got no benefit,—that the masters got it all. They knew but little about the good of themselves,—they often grumbled about food and clothing,—that they had not enough. I never heard a colored man grumbling about that here. They were generally religious,—they believed in a just God, and thought the owners wrong in punishing them in the way they were punished. A good many were so ignorant that they did not know any better, than to suppose that they were made for slavery, and the white men for freedom. Some, however, would talk about freedom, and think they ought to be free.

I have often been insulted, abused, and imposed upon, and had advantage taken of me by the whites in North Carolina, and could not help myself.

When I was twenty-one, I went to vote, supposing it would be allowed. The 'Squire, who held the box objected, and said no colored man was allowed to vote. I felt very badly about it,—I felt cheap, and I felt vexed: but I knew better than to make an answer,—I would have been knocked down certain. Unless I took off my hat, and made a bow to a white man, when I met him, he would rip out an oath,—"d— —n you, you mulatto, ain't you got no politeness? don't you know enough to take off your hat to a white man?" On going into a store, I was required to take off my hat.

I have seen slaves with whom I worked, nearly starved out, and yet stripped and whipped; blood cut out of them. It makes my flesh creep now to think of it—such gashes as I've seen cut in them. After a whipping, they would often leave and take to the woods for a month or two, and live by taking what they could find. I've often heard it said that's the cause of colored people in the South being dishonest, because they are brought so as to be obliged to steal. But I do not consider it dishonest—I always thought it right for a slave to take and eat as much as he wanted where he labored.

At some places where I have worked, I have known that the slaves had not a bite of meat given them. They had a pint of corn meal unsifted, for a meal,—three pints a day. I have seen the white men measure it, and the cook bake it, and seen them eat it: that was all they had but water—they might have as much of that as they wanted. This is no hearsay—I've seen it through the spring, and on until crop time: three pints of meal a day and the bran and nothing else. I heard them talk among themselves about having got a chicken or something, and being whipped for it. They were a bad looking set—some twenty of them—starved and without clothing enough for decency. It ought to have been a disgrace for their master, to see them about his house. If a man were to go through Canada so, they'd stop him to know what he meant by it—whether it was poverty or if he was crazy,—and they'd put a suit of clothes on him. I have seen them working out in the hot sun in July or August without hats—bareheaded. It was not from choice,—they couldn't get hats.

I have seen families put on the block and sold, some one way, some another way. I remember a family about two miles from me,—a father and mother and three children. Their master died, and they were sold. The father went one way, the mother another, with one child, and the other two children another way. I saw the sale—I was there—I went to buy hogs. The purchaser examined the persons of the slaves to see if they were sound,—if they were "good niggers." I was used to such things, but it made me feel bad to see it. The oldest was about ten or eleven years. It was hard upon them to be separated—they made lamentations about it. I never heard a white man at a sale express a wish that a family might be sold together.

On removing to Indiana, the white people did not seem so hostile altogether, nor want the colored people to knuckle quite so low. There were more white people who were friendly than in North Carolina. I was not allowed my vote nor my oath. There were more who wished colored people to have their rights than in North Carolina,—I mean there were abolitionists in Indiana.

I came here a year last spring, to escape the oppression of the laws upon the colored men. After the fugitive slave bill was passed, a man came into Indianapolis, and claimed John Freeman, a free colored man, an industrious, respectable man, as his slave. He brought *proofs* enough. Freeman was kept in jail several weeks,—but at last it turned out that the slave sought, was not Freeman, but a colored man in Canada, and F. was released. The danger of being taken as Freeman was, and suffering from a different decision, worked on my mind. I came away into Canada in consequence, as did many others. There were colored people who could have testified to Freeman's being free from his birth, but their oath would not be taken in Indiana.

In regard to Canada, I like the country, the soil, as well as any country I ever saw. I like the laws, which leave a man as much freedom as a man can have,—still there is prejudice here. The colored people are trying to remove this by improving and educating themselves, and by industry, to show that they are a people who have minds, and that all they want is cultivating.

I do not know how many colored people are here—but last summer five hundred and twenty-five were counted leaving the four churches.

WILLIAM BROWN

[An old man, apparently eighty years of age, nearly bald: what little hair he had was grey. His countenance wore a pleasant but subdued expression.]

I am not eighty—only sixty-three—but I am worked down, and worn out with hard work. Work all the time in the South—in Fauquier county, Va. When I began work in the morning, I could usually see a little red in the east, and I worked till ten before eating: at two I would eat again, and then work, at some seasons, until ten at night. Then I would have a pint of meal and a roasted herring. Tired and hungry—tired and hungry,—the slaves are obliged to steal; they are so hungry, that they will steal whatever they can find to eat.

I could generally find the tobacco worms by a hole through the leaf. But in the heat of the day, they get under a leaf and do not eat: and the hands passing along, breaking off suckers, don't always see them; then the overseer follows along behind looking, and if he finds the worm, the man is called back to kill it, and he gets five or six blows from the hickory or cow-hide.

In hoeing corn, the overseer will perhaps stand in the shade of a tree, where he can see the slaves; if they slacken work, he calls out to hurry them up, but he don't like to leave the shade of the tree, it is so hot. But sometimes, if a man drops behind, the overseer comes up, gives him some lashes, and then goes back to his tree.

The slaves work and the planter gets the benefit of it. It is wrong for him to have the money for their labor, and if a man goes to him for ten cents, to be refused. But they can't prosper: Providence won't let 'em. My master got all broke up at last, and started with his slaves for Missouri. I have a wife and three children that belonged to another master. When my master was about moving, the man that owned my family came to him and said: "William is old, and his family are here; his work won't amount to much now. I will give you two hundred and twenty dollars for him, and let him stay with his family." But my master cared nothing for that. "I can get that out of him in Missouri in three years," says he. I had to leave my family behind.

When we got to Cincinnati, he put all the slaves but me in a boat and kept them on the Kentucky side. I took care of his five horses on board. He came on board just at night, and said, "Have you fed the horses?" "Yes, Mas'r." "I want you to stay on board and look out for the horses, for I can put more dependence on you than on the others. Don't leave the boat, nor go up into the city to-night, for there are men here that catch all the *niggers* they can, and take them to New Orleans: so be sure, don't go ashore." I said, "No, mas'r,"—but that no meant yes. In the evening, while he was on the other side, I looked for my bag of clothes which I had left on the top of every thing,—but I couldn't find it: that fellow had hid it. I searched among the things, but I couldn't find it anywhere. I went up into the city and passed a great many folks, but they took no notice of me. I wanted to find some abolitionists or quakers. At last, I saw two white men standing together, and spoke to them. They were friendly, and it was not long after that, I got into Canada.

It is three years ago that I left my family, and I don't know whether they are dead or alive. I want to hear from them.

MR. — — — —

[The name and former residence of the person who furnished the following testimony of his experience as a slave, and his present doings as a free man, are suppressed, on account of the circumstances connected with his escape. The writer has suppressed several interesting narratives and parts of narratives for similar reasons.]

At sixteen years of age, I went in a chain-gang to Mississippi, where I was sold and taken to another State. There they calculated to work me down. Taking my shirt off and whipping me, was a new thing to me—it was what was never done by them that raised me. Then 't was cut on some two or three hundred. Once I received a very severe whipping—the colored people told me it was two hundred—with the paddle. I had no friends there. The colored people were as eager to catch me as the whites. I wanted to find some friend. I made my way back to the place where I was raised, and saw my old mistress who had raised me from an infant. Her second husband, while I was stopping around there, secreted me, but was watching the advertisments, to let the reward run up high, so as to get a great sum. The mistress told me he was calculating to pocket the reward, and return me into the hands of my owners. She said there was a free country, called Canada: she gave me a few dollars, and told me to follow the north star. If it was too dark to see the north star, to feel of the trees, and on that side where the moss was longest, was my way. I followed her directions, and travelled through the woods, exposed to wet and cold and starvation.

On my way I was caught and put in jail, where I was kept six weeks. They could find no master. I was hired out one month. They calculated to keep me twelve months, advertising me, in hopes my owner would appear. I was again hired out, on the second month, to a drunken dog,—but I had learned better sense than to follow the plans he was determined on. While his guard was at supper, I made my escape. I was pursued the next day, and saw my pursuers, but they did not see me: I made my escape by hiding in the brush. The first friend I met was a white man at last—an abolitionist. He kept me two weeks till I got recruited.

I leased a piece of ground, and went to clearing up. It was heavily wooded. I have cleared four acres, and cut it into cord-wood; have got it under good fence,—have raised one crop, and have a prospect of another. I was to have it three years more if I wished—if I leave it, I am to be paid for my improvements. I can understand about written agreements, but do not know how to write, and have suffered losses from this cause.

Slavery is one of the greatest curses that ever was. There could not be one so despised in the sight of God. I believe that the place of punishment was made for those who separate husbands and wives, and traffic in their fellow men: killing babes—I have seen one with its brains dashed out against a red oak tree. Tired of carrying it, its mother being in the gang, and troubled with it, as any man would be, they put it out of the way.

ISAAC GRIFFIN

I am from Trimble county, Ky. I was a slave in Kentucky forty-six years. Then I had $500 for self, wife, and child. I left eight children in bondage, who undertook to escape. The oldest got here; the others were retaken, and sold in Texas.

Two years ago, I saw one hundred men chained, besides women and children, going down south.

I have often been down the Mississippi on flat-boats,—following the river every year for five or six years. Mornings I would hear something like a bell—it is a clock though,—then the hands have to rise; if they don't, the overseer is among them.

Just before day, the first time I went down, as I was floating down the Grand Gulf, I heard the whip cracking, and a man crying, "Oh Lord! Oh Lord! Oh Lord!" I was afraid somebody was murdering: I called my master,—he said, "Somebody is whipping his slave." We had to put in there. I saw the man: he was put over a log, his feet tied, and his hands tied, and a rail put between. They would whip him, and then rest upon it. They flogged him off and on until daylight. His back . . . . .

At one time I went down on a boat. There were many slaves on board, and one yellow girl with a child. At Natchez, a man came on board who wanted to buy a yellow girl without children. Her master told her to say she had none. The man bought her, and the trader gave her child, six weeks old, to a white woman.

Slavery is the greatest curse on earth. Nothing exceeds it for wickedness. A slave in the South suffers death many times before he does die.

I felt, when free, as light as a feather—a burden was off of me. I could get up and go to my work without being bruised and beaten. The worst thought was for my children,—what they might have to go through. I cannot hear from them.

I have lived in Canada one year. I find the people laboring well generally: as industrious as any men. The law is the same for one as another. We have our meetings and gatherings here, and have no trouble at all.

I am doing as well, for a poor man, as I can expect—I get a good living.

WILLIAM STREET

I am from Middle Tennessee, where I worked as a blacksmith, another man taking my wages. All I got was my victuals and clothes, and not much at that. Twenty-five years I was a slave,—was bred and born a slave, and cannot read or write.

My mother has several times told me that her father was sick, and his mistress drove him out of the house, and he leaned his breast over the fence and died. She often showed me the place where he died. I was hired out when very young—did not get the lash. It was never "Can you do it?" or "Will you do it?"—but "you must go and do it." Sometimes I would do a good day's work, and then have another job put on me. I can't paint it as bad as it is. I have seen a man at the iron-works—Perkins's—who said he did not believe that there was a bit of skin on him that he was born with,—they had whipped it all off.

If a northern man were to go right into a slave State, he would not see the worst of slavery. By the time he was up in the morning, the slaves would be a mile off—he would see but little of the evil—he wouldn't get to see it.

My master died when I was seven; my mistress when I was twenty-five. Then we were divided out: I fell to a son who lived in Mississippi. I had been living with a doctor two years, and I asked him to buy me. But my master wouldn't sell—the doctor offered $1,100 for me. I was put in jail five days—I and my brother, who had fallen to the same man, were there. Our owner came in with irons and handcuffs, and put them on, and took us to the blacksmith to have them riveted. I left two men in the jail who had run away from Mississippi, and had lain there eleven months,—in one month to be sold. One of them was a great fellow to pray: I'd hear him praying every morning for the Lord to help him. He said he wished the doctor would buy me. The rivets were fixed: we went to Nashville, and were put on board a steamboat, I and my brother chained together. They were loading the boat, which takes two or three days. I heard some one tell a colored man to pump the boilers full, and they'd put out in the morning. I said to my brother, "When you hear me say to-night, *the dog's dead,* then we'll put out."

At 11 o'clock we laid down. I made believe that something ailed me, and kept going out. By and by, I said *"the dog's dead."* We crept into the wheelhouse, and down on the wheel, to the outside of the guard, and got on board a stone-coal boat. We walked eighteen miles that night,—but we were not away yet—yet had no thought about Canada. I had heard of it, but had no thought about getting to it. We laid down, meaning to stay till next night.

Two men went out to hunt partridges, and at about one o'clock they came across us. "What are you doing here, boys:" We had broken off the chains, but the handcuffs were on each of us. "I am going to Columbia—didn't you see that wagon with the boiler on it?" They said, "Come, go this way," and one threatened with his gun. We up and ran. The slaveholders both followed us. We ran across a field about half a mile: when we got across there was a mill and a creek. We ran through the creek: there was a big hill. I went one side, and my brother the other: they followed after me. I stopped and hailed, "What do you want?" They thought I was coming in to give up,—but I passed them and went into the creek, where I fell down, and got wet all over. I crossed at the mill; they after me: there was a horse tied there, and there were several men about the mill; one a colored man, who had the horse. "Can I take your horse?" "No." I took him anyhow. I cut the bridle, jumped on, and started. Then a white man put his gun over a tree and shot me—some eight or ten small shot went in—they are most of them in me now. The horse then put out with me—then I was shut of them. They had no horse—he put out like lightning—I did not know where I was going,—I rode two miles, got off, hitched the horse, and went away and left him. Thinks I, they've gone from the mill now—I'll go back and get my clothes now,—I had left them in my hurry. As I went back to the mill, I saw them and took them, and then I saw the men coming back from pursuing my brother. I heard them say, "Yonder he is! yonder he is!" I ran to an open field where there was a little grass, and laid down. They did not see—they hunted about and gave it up: then I went to an old house that had hay in it, and put my clothes in there. I then walked right before the door of a house where were slaves at work—nobody spoke a word to me. After I got through them, I saw an old colored man with a wagon. He told me, "You go this way, and when they come I'll tell 'em you've gone that way." I did as he advised me, and got into a tree that had been burned out, and stayed in it till night: then I went and got my clothes, and started for the old place where I was raised.

I went on to where my oldest brother lived in Tennessee, and told him the circumstances. I was then told to go into the barn-loft, and stay there,—I did—stayed three days hid in the wheat: then I went in the woods, and stayed eight months without ever going into a house,—from Christmas until the last of August. Then my owner came from Mississippi, with a man named T— —, who brought three bloodhounds along with him. A white man who saw me the day before, told them where they had seen me. They went to that place, and put the bloodhounds on my track. I had never seen a bloodhound, but I heard them, and I spoke to myself; says I, "I'm gone." I had a pistol, a big stick, and a big knife. Then I ran out of the corn field into a little skirt of woods, and the bloodhounds got over the fence when I did. I wheeled and shot one of them through and through. He never got away from the place at all. I got back to the corn field, the others both with me in the field; one hold of my wrist, the other of my leg. I have the marks—here they are on my wrist. I struck at the dog with my knife a number of times—but he dodged every time. Then my master came up with a pistol, and said if I didn't stand, he'd put a ball through me. T— — came up and struck me with a hickory stick five or six blows, on the back of my neck. I cried, "Oh Lord! Oh Lord!" then T— — made the dogs let go. He then took out his handcuffs and chains, and put them on, and took me to a blacksmith's, to have them riveted, putting in another chain between the cuffs, to make 'em strong, so I couldn't get away anyhow.

They concluded I must know where my youngest brother was, but I did not and could not tell them any thing about it. They didn't believe that. I was standing up; a great many gathered round to see me: I was chewing tobacco. T— — said, "G— — d— — you, quit chewing tobacco, and tell us where your brother is, for I know you know." Some fellow asked my master what he was going to do with me,—he said he was going to give me up to T— —, because I had killed the bloodhound,—T— — wouldn't have taken five hundred dollars for him; said "he was worth more than him, d— —n him." He was the fastest one they had; before they brought them from Mississippi, they had caught a man and torn out his entrails,—T— — told me so himself. They kept me going round from that day, Tuesday, to Friday, trying to find my brother,—chaining me to the bedstead at night. Thursday morning they thought they had heard of him; went eighteen miles to Shelbyville. A great many went with them for the fun of the thing. This was in the beginning of September, 1851.

I was now at the old place where I was bred, and was left with master's brother-in-law, in his care. At three o'clock, the brother had some sheep to shear: he took me into the stable, put on shackles, and took off my handcuffs, so I could shear. After dinner, said I, "Mr. E— —, won't you give me some grease, if you please, to grease my boots?" "Oh, yes." I went into the kitchen where my mother had lived, close by, and thought over all things that had passed before. Pretty soon he told me to fill a kettle with water. The kettle was some fifty yards from the house; there were some six men on the piazza, who could watch me. I filled the kettle. "Did you see my boys?" says he. I told him, "Yes—behind the barn." The barn was further off than the kettle. "Shall I go and tell them to make a fire about the kettle?" Says he, "Yes." They wanted to kill a shoat against the folks got home with my brother. I stepped to the barn to tell them; I looked round,—no one was looking. I told them. They all started for wood, etc. I looked up to the sun, and said to myself, "it's three o'clock." I threw my boots over a stump, and drew them so I could run, I kept my boots, and ran off to Canada . . . . .

It is above my language to tell how overjoyed I was on getting into Canada. Nothing harasses a man so much as slavery. There is nothing under the sun so mean: after a man is dead, they won't let him rest. It is a horrible thing to think of, the ignorance slaves are brought up in. There is not a man born, who can represent slavery so bad as it is.

I work here at blacksmithing: I own this shop. I have plenty of work, and good pay.

BUXTON

The Elgin Settlement, or, as it is more commonly called, King's Settlement, is in Buxton, in the township of Raleigh, county of Kent. The colored population of Buxton numbers eight hundred. Nearly all the adults have, at some time, been slaves, but many resided in the free States before entering Canada.

King's Settlement comprises nine thousand acres of land,—a tract some six miles in length, by three in breadth,— and is situated between the Great Western Railway and Lake Erie: its boundary being about a mile and one fourth from the lake shore. A company has been chartered by the Provincial Legislature, for the purpose of constructing a railroad to connect Niagara with Amherstburg. This road is to pass through the southern portion of the settlement, and will afford a ready market for all the firewood, of which there is abundance on the lands.

The settlement at Buxton, was first projected by the Rev. Wm. King in 1849. Mr. King was formerly a slaveholder in Louisiana; but not being "to the manner born," he manumitted his own slaves, about fourteen in number, (for whom he had been offered nine thousand dollars,) and brought them with him to Canada, where he settled them on farms or on lands recently purchased of the government. From long acquaintance with the colored people in the South, and from their previous history, Mr. King was satisfied, that, when placed in favorable circumstances, they could support themselves as well as the emigrants from Europe, and would be capable of making the same progress in education. The colored people and their friends owe a debt of gratitude to Mr. King, for having successfully conducted the experiment at Buxton.

In furtherance of Mr. King's views, an association was "formed in Upper Canada by divers persons resident therein, under the name of the Elgin Association, for the settlement and moral improvement of the colored population of Canada, for the purpose of purchasing Crown or Clergy Reserve Lands, in the township of Raleigh, and settling the same with colored families resident in Canada, of approved moral character." The association under the above style and description was incorporated on the 10th of August, 1850.

The land is divided into farms of fifty acres each, and so situated that a road runs past each man's farm. The houses are set thirty-three feet from this road, facing streets, so that the whole settlement, when cleared up and opened, will present a uniform appearance. The land is sold to the settlers at $2.50 per acre, the government price, and is paid in ten equal annual instalments, with interest at the rate of 6 per cent. But although ten years were allowed to the settlers to pay for their farms, a number have taken out their deeds already; and there is no doubt that before the ten years shall have expired, each settler will have his deed in possession: for which he will be indebted to his own exertions—since the settlers receive no money, no grants of land, no farming implements,—nothing but protection and advice. Whatever they have is purchased by themselves, and as far as the supply of their physical wants is concerned, they are self-supporting.

The houses in the settlement are built of logs, after a model prescribed by the Improvement Committee. The model was 18 feet by 24, and 12 feet in height, with a gallery running the whole length of the front. While no house was allowed to go up inferior to the model, the settlers were allowed to build as much better as they pleased. The first actual settler entered in December, 1849.

The third annual report of the directors, September, 1852, says, "The number of families of colored persons settled on the lands of the association up to August 1, 1852, is 75—and the number of inhabitants 400. By these settlers not fewer than 50 houses have been erected. Besides the regular occupants, about 25 families of colored people, attracted by the advantages of the settlement, have purchased lands in its immediate proximity. Including these 100 colored families, about 500 individuals are now comfortably settled on their own property in that district. The number of acres cleared on the Elgin grounds to August 1, is 350; and 204 of those have been under crop this season. The land is best adapted for the culture of wheat; but it also produces corn, tobacco, and hemp, equal to any that is grown in the Western States. With regard to the moral state of the people, sobriety is so general that no case of drunkenness has occurred; and as a guaranty for peace among the settlers, a *court of arbitration* has been set up, before which *five* cases only have been brought, which were decided easily and amicably, and without expense to either party. The day school has 73 on the roll; the attendance is good, and the number increasing. About 20 of the present number are the children of white parents. The Sabbath school has 53 attending it. The church, which is supplied by Rev. Mr. King, the indefatigable and able missionary to the Elgin settlement, is attended by from 100 to 140 persons; and the desire for the administration of the word and ordinances seems to be on the increase. A Latin class was opened last November, which is attended by 6 colored youths; and it is hoped that some of them may be found qualified for teaching their brethren, or for filling the office of the Christian ministry."

Mr. King is chiefly paid by the Home Mission Committee of the Presbyterian (Free) Church of Canada, which has always borne testimony against the evils of slavery.

The fourth annual report of the directors, made in September, 1853, states: "Up to this time, 130 families have settled on the lands of the association, and improved farms in the neighborhood: these families contain 520 persons in all. 500 acres are cleared and under fence; 135 cut down and partially cleared. Of the cleared land, 236 acres are in corn; 60 acres in wheat; 29 in oats, and 90 in other crops: making in all 415 acres under cultivation. The number of cattle in the settlement is 128. There are 15 horses, 30 sheep, and 250 hogs. The temperance principle is strictly acted on through the whole settlement,—no intoxicating drinks being either manufactured or sold. The Sabbath is generally observed; and most of the settlers attend some place of worship. The number of children at the day school is 112; at the Sabbath school, 80. They were all improving, both in secular and scriptural knowledge: a number of the more advanced pupils were studying Latin, with a view to future usefulness."

The fifth annual report, September, 1854, shows that the settlement was making good progress. It informs us, that "several houses have been built during the past year far above the model, and one person has contracted for a brick cottage, the first on the lands of the Association; [this has since been completed;] others, both of brick and frame, will be erected in a few years. The clay on the land is found to make excellent brick: 250,000 have been made during the last year, and the same number will be furnished during the next year. About 150 families are on the association lands and farms in the neighborhood; 77 houses have been built after the model, most of them inclosed with a picket fence and whitewashed: 8 are above the model. The rest are making arrangements to have their houses put up during the ensuing year. The number of acres cleared and under fence is 726; the number chopped down and ready for clearing is 174. Of the cleared land, 334 are in corn, 95 in wheat, 48 in oats, and 100 in other crops, making in all 577 acres under crop. This shows an increase over last year of cleared land, 226 acres; and of crops, 162. The number of cows and oxen is 150; of horses, 38; of sheep, 25; and of hogs, 700. The health of the settlement continues good; peace and harmony reign among the people. The Sabbath is strictly kept as a day of rest. Temperance prevails; nothing that intoxicates is made or sold in the settlement. The schools and church are well attended; 147 are on the roll in the day school; 120 in the Sabbath school. Progress has been made in secular and scriptural knowledge. The population has increased so fast during the last year, that, one school failing to accommodate all, the residents in the northern part of the settlement, anxious that their children should receive education, have erected a neat school-house at their own expense, with a view of getting a teacher for it, at least six months in the year."

The value of the oak timber on the lands of the Association has been estimated by good judges at $57,000; of the maple, hickory, etc., at $70,000. Lumber, however, has hitherto been of little avail to the settlers, for want of a saw-mill and a market. A steam saw-mill was, however, completed, and ready for operation on the 4th of July,1855: and a plank road is contemplated, which, extending eight miles from the Great Western Railway to the Lake, will give the settlers two markets—one on the Lake, and another on the Railroad.

The annual report for 1855, states that "the colored population have manifested a more fixed determination to raise from the soil what will support themselves and their families, without going abroad to work, a part of the year, for money to purchase the necessaries and comforts of life . . . . . Nearly all the settlers have made a steady advance in clearing and cropping: the quantity of land clear and under fence is 827 acres, besides 216 acres that have been chopped down, and will be ready to put in fall and spring crops. Of the land cleared, 180 acres have been sown with wheat; 340 with corn; 50 with potatoes; 40 with oats; and 200 with hay, buckwheat, and turnips. Besides these crops, there is considerable quantity of tobacco,—the leaf of which is said by competent judges to be equal in quality to any raised in Virginia and Kentucky . . . . . During the past year, but little has been done in raising stock. It has been found that sheep and horses cannot be raised with much profit, till there is more open land, and more hay to support them during the winter. The number of cows in the settlement is 140; of oxen, 50; of horses, 40; of sheep, 38; and of hogs, 600 . . . . . The improvement in the buildings has not made the same progress this year as last. Several buildings after the model, have gone up, and some above the model, but none of them have been finished for want of lumber. That difficulty will now be obviated. A good saw and grist-mill has been erected. The saw now supplies abundance of lumber for the settlement: so that, during the next year, there is a prospect of having more houses finished than during any one year since the settlement commenced . . . . . One hundred and fifty children have been going to school during the last year; and some of them have made considerable progress in the higher branches of education . . . . . The health and morality of the settlement continue good."

The settlers at Buxton are characterized by a manly, independent air and manner. Most of them came into the province stripped of every thing but life. They have purchased homes for themselves, paid the price demanded by government, erected their own buildings, and supported their own families by their own industry; receiving no aid whatever from any benevolent society, but carefully excluding donations of any kind from coming into the settlement.

Mr. King having full faith in the natural powers, capacity, and capabilities of the African race, is practically working out his belief, by placing the refugees in circumstances where they may learn self-reliance, and maintain a perfect independence of aid: trusting, under God, on their own right arm.

A few testimonials from residents of Buxton are appended. Those of Mr. and Mrs. Isaac Riley are the most favorable to the "peculiar" institution, of any that the writer listened to in Canada—and yet they tell against slavery with tremendous force. Comparatively well treated as was Mrs. R., she was yet urged by a young white man to make her escape from "darkness," and from evils which impended over her.

ISAAC RILEY

In Perry county, Missouri, where I was raised, I never saw an overseer, nor a negro-trader, nor driver, nor any abuse, such as is practised in other places. I've never seen any separations of families. I always from a small boy meant to be free at some day. After I had a son, it grieved me to see some small boys in the neighborhood, who were hired out to work twenty miles from home. I looked at my boy, and thought if he remained, he would have to leave us in the same way, and grow up in ignorance. It appeared to me cruel to keep him ignorant.

I escaped with my wife and child to Canada. Among the French near Windsor, I got small wages—2s. or 1s. 6d. a day, York: and morning and night up to my knees in water,—still I preferred this to abundance in slavery. I crossed over and got work and better pay in Michigan. They would have liked to have me remain, and offered to build a house for me. But I did not feel free in Michigan, and did not remain. I went to St. Catharines, and got fifty cents a day. By and by, I heard of Mr. King's settlement,—I came here, and have got along well. My children can get good learning here.

MRS. ISAAC RILEY

I was born in Maryland, and raised in Perry County, Mo. Where I was raised, the treatment was kind. I used to hear of separations of families, but never saw any. I never saw the lash used, nor the paddle, nor ever heard of the abuse of slaves until I came into Canada. I see many here, who have suffered from hard treatment, and who have seen it practised on others,—but I never saw an overseer, nor a negro-trader in my life; if I did, I didn't know it. I never knew any thing about places they call "the quarters," in my life. I could not go when I pleased, but was sometimes allowed to go out without a pass ten or twelve miles from home. I was never stopped on my way by patrols—never heard about such things where I was raised. I was never sent to school,—but my master, who had owned my mother, and raised me from the cradle, was very kind, and taught me to read and spell some,—but not to write.

I used often to think that I would like to be as free as the white people were. I often told them, when they made me angry, that they had no more business with me, than I had with them.

My master was very particular about my having clothing and food enough. When I first came to Canada, the colored people seemed cold and indifferent to each other; and so it was with the white people and the colored. It seemed as if the white people did not want to speak to us. I took this very much to heart, for where I grew up, the white people talk freely to their neighbors' colored people. I felt so about it, that if they had come for me, I would have gone back willingly.

In Missouri, when my first child was young, up to seventeen months old, when I left, I had no care of it, except to nurse it,—the white people took all the care of it.

For two years before I left, my husband talked of coming to Canada. I felt no desire for leaving. But [a young man, a relative of my master] often persuaded me to leave for Canada,—and he talked with a great deal of reason. He said he would not, if he were I, bring my boy up to be a slave: "you don't know," he would say, "how long [the old gentleman] may live,—and when he dies, you may come under altogether different treatment." At last, when there was a camp-meeting, I told my husband we had better leave, as it might be so by and by, that we could not leave at all. We left, and made a long camp-meeting of it.

We crossed over at Windsor, and had rather hard times about Potico, among the French,—there's where the people seemed so distant. I thought if Canada was all like that place, it was a hard place. We stayed there a few months, and went to St. Catherines, where we did better. After a while, we heard that Mr. King was buying a place to settle the colored people. We came up here before it was surveyed, and Mr. Riley helped the surveyors. He took one hundred acres of land, and we are well contented. If I do not live to see it, perhaps my children will, that this will one day be a great place.

My two oldest children go to school. The oldest is well along, and studies Latin and Greek. The other three are not old enough to go to school. We have good schools here,—music and needlework are taught.

I think my present condition here far preferable to what it would have been in slavery. There we were in darkness,—here we are in light. My children also would have grown up, had I remained there, in ignorance and darkness.

HARRY THOMAS

I was born in Brunswick, partly raised in Southampton, ten miles below Bethlehem, Virginia. Was then bought by a "nigger-trader," J— — B— —, and was sold to J— — S— —, in South Carolina. The treatment there was barbarous. At sixteen years old, they gave me a task, splitting rails, which I did in the time, then went to take my rest. His wife was harder than he was,—she told me to make lights in the road, setting fire to rubbish, it being a new place. I got through at ten o'clock: boss came home, I went in again. She ordered me to put on water to scour the floors, etc. I wouldn't,—I went over to her father's "nigger-house" all night. Next morning, the master came for me, took me home, stripped me stark naked, made a paddle of thick oak board, lashed me across a pine log, secured my hands and feet, and whipped me with the paddle. His little boy saw it and cried,—he cursed him away,—his wife came,—he cursed her away. He whipped till he broke the paddle. After that, he took me to the house, and hit me with a hickory stick over the head and shoulders, a dozen times or more: then he got salt and water, and a corn cob, and scrubbed me. Then he sent me to water the hogs, naked as I was, in January. I ran into the woods, and went back to the same house, and the colored people gave me some old rags to keep me from freezing.

I recovered from that beating, and at length ran away again, because he refused to let me go to see my friends. I was caught by a colored man, who took me to my master's step-father's,—he whipped me till he was satisfied, then master came, and whipped me with a leather strap. I ran right off again; was caught and put in a potato-house. After that I was put in the field to knock along the best way I could, but I was not able to work.

My master removed to Mississippi, taking me with him, the year before Gen. Jackson commenced fighting the Creek Indians.

This big scar on my left cheek, I got in a runaway scrape. A man who got up with me, jobbed me with the muzzle of a gun, which knocked me back into the mud: then he tied me. That time, I received three hundred lashes; one of the slaves who helped tie me, fainted at seeing me so abused. I have a cut with a knife made by J— — S— — after I had worked for him all day, because he could not flog me, as he liked.

I staid awhile, then ran away again,—then a man caught me, and another came with him home, who wished to buy me. I was a smart-looking boy—he offered one thousand dollars for me: master wouldn't sell. For running away, I received a hundred lashes on the bare back. I was then sold to his cousin, J— — Y— —, in Mississippi. I lived with him ten years; I suppose I must have been about thirty-two. At first, Y.'s treatment was fair. I was foreman. He got rich, and grew mean, and I left him. I was caught and taken back again. He took me to the blacksmith's shop and had a ring made of axe-bar iron, which I wore on my right leg from the middle of May to the middle of September. I worked with it on, and slept with it on, all that time.

After he got it off, I worked awhile,—again I went off, went into Alabama, was out from October to March,—then was put in jail, where I lay three months, as they could not hear from my owner, who had moved off to the Choctaw purchase. My boss came and took me out of jail, chained me to his horse with plough traces, and was taking me on his way, when Gen. S— —, of Georgia bought me. He put me in his kitchen to cook for him. But I was not satisfied with him, although he used me well. The fact is, I wanted to be free. I ran away and left him,—he had me caught, and sold me to S— — N— —, who took me to New Orleans. Nobody there liked my countenance at all—no one would give a cent for me. N— — took me to Natchez and sold me, after a week, to a young man named G— — S— —, who had a cotton plantation a few miles above Natchez. He treated me well at first. He would not allow any to leave the place to see their friends without a pass from him or the overseer. I went out to see my friends, and was flogged with a bull whip on the bare back—a whip heavier and larger than a horse-whip, with a buck-skin cracker on the lash. I ran away again—they caught me and put plough traces around my body, and put me to work hoeing cotton and corn. Not long after, they put on an iron collar. I made an errand—went to the woods—and the overseer sent all hands to hunt for me. They found me, and brought me back to the driver. The old driver gave me two blows with the bull whip; the young driver stopped him. The overseer came up and knocked me down with his fist by a blow on the head. I fainted, was taken to a tree, and when I came to, the overseer was bleeding me. Word came to the overseer, from my master's grandmother, the same day, that my master was gone away, and unless he took off my chains, I would die before his return. The overseer took them all off.

At night, I dressed up and started off, steering by the north star. I walked seven hundred and fifty miles nights,—then, in Kentucky, I was betrayed by a colored man, and lay in jail fifteen months. I wouldn't tell them where I belonged. Then, under terror of the whip, I told them all about it. A Dr. J— — N— — had bought the chance of me,—he took me to Nashville, where I waited on him, his partner, and took care of his horses about four years. I started to run away from him on his partner's horse—I had one hundred and fifty dollars with me. He overtook me and took away my money. Then he put me in jail and sold me to an old broken down trader. I left him, proceeded north, was caught in Indiana, and taken to Evansville jail. They would not receive me there, and I was taken to Henderson, on the Kentucky side, and put in jail there. My owner put on handcuffs and locked me into the wagon besides with plough chains. I travelled three days thus in succession—he chaining me at night to his bedstead. On the third night, I was eating in the tavern kitchen where we stopped; I concluded to try for the North once more. I went out and hammered off my chains—found some assistance to get off my cuffs, and came on my way, travelling altogether nights by the north star, and lying in by day. In Ohio, I found the best kind of friends, and soon reached Canada. When I first came, I joined the soldiers just after the rebellion: then practised up and down the province as a physician, from the knowledge I had obtained from a colored man in Mississippi, who knew roots and herbs,—but there were many kinds I wanted which I could not find here.

I am now hiring a piece of land in Buxton. My calculation is, if I live, to own a farm if I can. My health is good, and the climate agrees with me—and it does with colored men generally.

Slavery is barbarous. In my view, slaveholders, judged by the way they treat colored people, are the worst persons on earth.

R. VAN BRANKEN

I was born and brought up in New York State. I have suffered in the States somewhat on account of my color: in travelling, not being allowed the same privileges as others, when they took my money: not having cabin fare like others, when I paid cabin passage. If my work was that of an hostler or cook, or any thing of that sort, I did not think that my place was the parlor; but when clean and well dressed, in occupations not offensive, then I think I am as good as anybody, and deserve as good treatment.

I have four acres and a half of land here, and a fifty-acre wood-lot on the fourteenth concession, and can make a good living here.

Among some people here, there is as much prejudice as in the States, but they cannot carry it out as they do in the States: the law makes the difference.

I am acquainted with many of the colored families here, and they are doing well. We have good schools here.

The separate schools and churches work badly for the colored people in the States and Canada. In Rochester, N.Y., it injured them very much, although the separate school was petitioned for by a portion of the colored people themselves. In Cleveland, Ohio, they have separate churches, but no separate school. In Chatham, the separate school was by request of themselves. I never was in favor of such a thing.

HENRY JOHNSON

I have lived in Canada four years—in Buxton one year. I came originally from Pennsylvania.

The situation and circumstances of the colored people in Canada are better than in the United States. I have a large family—ten persons—and know. I have bought, paid for, and have a deed on one hundred acres of land. The people here are very prosperous—they came into the woods without means, depending on their own hands; they never begged a meal here,—nor have any goods nor old clothing been distributed. If any were sent, I should want it sent back. In other places, where money and clothes have been given, the tendency is to make men lazy,—that I know, for I saw the bad effects in Amherstburg. I would n't receive any of their help: I did n't want it: I felt 't would do more injury than good.

We look upon the steam saw and grist-mill, just finished, as of great benefit to us here.

I left the States for Canada, for rights, freedom, liberty. I came to Buxton to educate my children. I lived twenty-three years in Massillon, Ohio, and was doing well at draying and carting—wanted for nothing—had money when I wanted it, and provisions plenty. But my children were thrust out of the schools, as were all the colored children—one *must* know how I would feel about it. My daughter was doing well—advancing rapidly. She began to climb up into the higher classes, among the ladies, and the noblemen of the town thought it wouldn't do. The teacher liked her, but she was thrust out. The teacher called about it, but I could not send her there again: had they altered the law, I would have been too spunky to send her again. We were careful to keep her cleanly, and to dress her nicely and well. Her mother took a great deal of pains with her, because she was going to a ladies' school. I went to see the trustees: they told me the vote was passed—nothing was the matter only she was black. The white children of her class wished her to remain, and voted in the school against the law,—the teacher told me so—but I said I could not send her on account of the law.

DRESDEN; DAWN

Dresden is situated at the head of navigation on the Big Bear Creek, just above the bend in the river which indents the lands of the Dawn Institute. It is in the gore of Camden, being part of the township of Camden. The village contains about 100 whites and 70 blacks. There is not land enough cleared and under cultivation to supply the wants of the inhabitants: their principal business is in lumber, especially staves. One individual had, in the spring of the present year, 125,000 ready for shipment, worth, as I was informed, from $55 to $60 per M.; and as many more had been manufactured by others. About one fifth of the labor on these was performed by colored men. Many of the colored settlers were attracted to Dresden and Dawn by the proffered advantages of education, on the industrial plan, in the Dawn Institute. Their children at present attend a school situated on the Institute Farm, but not under the supervision of its managing agent; it is in the hands of trustees, connected with the common school system. Twenty-four children were assembled about the house, a little before the hour for opening school. The white and colored do not attend the same school

The colored people in the neighborhood of Dresden and Dawn are generally very prosperous farmers—of good morals, and mostly Methodists or Baptists. But here, as among all people, are a few persons of doubtful character, who have not been trained "to look out for a rainy day,"—and when these get a little beforehand, they are too apt to rest on their oars.

Some of the settlers are mechanics,—shoemakers, blacksmiths, etc. About one third of the adult settlers are in possession of land, which is, either in whole or in part, paid for.

BRITISH AMERICAN INSTITUTE

In the early history of its settlement, this was known as the Dawn Institute. In 1840, £350 was raised in England, mostly among Quakers, for the purpose of establishing an Industrial or Manual Labor School for the benefit of refugees and their children. Three hundred acres of land were purchased and deeded to trustees, solely to subserve educational purposes.

The Dawn Institute Farm, lies partly in the gore of Camden, and partly in the township of Dawn. It is beautifully situated on a bend of the river Sydenham, (the Big Bear Creek of the maps). At one extremity of the curve, where the river "comes cranking in," with "deep indent," is a windowless, uninhabited, two story frame building, against which props are placed to keep it from falling. This house was injured by fire soon after its erection, and has never been repaired. At the opposite extremity of the bend, and nearly half a mile distant, is situated a dilapidated steam saw-mill, which has not fired up for about two years: huge logs, brought to the mill long ago, lie rotting on the ground. The ruined dwelling-house on the one hand, and the old, unused saw-mill on the other, and the unbroken stillness of a spot so well fitted for the home of busy men, give an unfavorable and melancholy impression to the mind, which the sight of the growing grain on the farm, and of the deep and beautiful river, winding from view among lofty woods, can scarcely dispel. An unfreighted canoe, paddled down the stream by a colored man, and a larger boat which a youngster was pushing to the shore, assisted by two lads tugging at a line, was the only navigation observable.

I was hospitably and kindly received by John Scoble, Esq., resident superintendent, who expatiated with pleasing enthusiasm on the natural advantages of the place, and accompanied me in a walk along the bank of the river, to point out the site where the church is to be erected, on either side of which is to be a school-house, one for boys, the other for girls. The cultivated clearing, across the stream, he pointed out as the spot where the college is to be erected. In a beautiful piece of woods, a little above the ruined dwelling-house, and extending from the Dresden road to the river, trees have been felled, to open an avenue to the shore: and when the obstructions shall have been removed, and the road gravelled, this avenue will add much to the beauty of the place. The ground opposite the avenue on the right of the Dresden road, rises gently in a wooded knoll,—the trees are to be "thinned out," leaving a magnificent grove, and, on the summit of the elevation, a cottage is to be erected, from which the superintendent will be able to survey all parts of the farm.

The Rev. Hiram Wilson originally conceived the plan of establishing here an Industrial School; and he directed and managed the school for nearly seven years from its commencement in the wilderness. At that time there were no more than fifty colored persons in all, in the vicinity of the tract purchased. Mr. Wilson began the school with fourteen boarding scholars, received the refugees as they arrived, and did what he could for their encouragement. About seven years ago, Mr. W. left the Institute: it was then a little embarrassed, but was considered to be in good condition for accomplishing the main design. The saw-mill was in process of erection, about the time Mr. Wilson resigned.

The original purchase was two hundred acres, to which one hundred were subsequently added. Nearly half the tract has been cleared, and is well cultivated. Three or four colored families support themselves on the Institute Farm. Mr. Josiah Henson resides here, but as he was absent at the time of my visit to Dawn, I had not the pleasure of an interview.

The First Annual Report to the Anti-Slavery Society of Canada, presented March 24, 1852, says of the Educational Institute, "About sixty pupils are attending the school. The Institution is soon to be placed under the management of the British and Foreign Anti-Slavery Society, a change likely to prove favorable to its future success." The property of the Institute has since been conveyed through John Scoble, Esq., by "lease and release."

The whole number of colored persons in Dawn and Dresden, who are within reach of the place where the church and school-houses are to be built, does not exceed five hundred.

There is not a single colored person coming into Dawn or Dresden, who if he have health and industrious habits cannot support himself within one week of his arrival. Refugees need no pecuniary or other aid, except on first arriving, or in sickness, or with young children.

Mr. Scoble is ready to assist in any enterprise which would be of advantage to the Institute. Sydenham River is deep and bold; from its banks commerce may be carried on with St. Clair and the adjacent lakes,—nay, with the Atlantic itself. What is wanted is, the hearty cooperation of wealthy, energetic, and enterprising men.

WILLIAM HENRY BRADLEY

This is my name since I left slavery: in slavery I was known as Abram Young.

I left Maryland with my wife and two children in 1851. While body-servant, I was well used—while a farm-hand, had more hardship.

In Baltimore, I was acquainted with Mr. M— – L. N— –.

I look at slavery as the most horrid thing on earth. It is awful to think of the poor slaves panting for a place of refuge, and so few able to find it. There is not a day or night that I don't think about them, and wish that slavery might be abolished, and every man have his God-given rights.

I have prospered well in freedom. I thank the Lord for my success here. I own fifty acres of land, bought and paid for by my own energy and exertions, and I have the deed in my house.

If there were a law to abolish the use of liquor as a beverage, it would be a good thing for Canada.

I own two span of horses, twelve head of hogs, six sheep, two milch cows, and am putting up a farm barn.

There is a great deal of prejudice here. Statements have been made that colored people wished for separate schools; some did ask for them, and so these have been established, although many colored people have prayed against them as an infringement of their rights. Still, we have more freedom here than in the United States, as far as the government law guarantees. In consequence of the ignorance of the colored men, who come here unlearned out of slavery, the white people have an overpowering chance. There are many respectable colored people moving in, but I have not much hope of a better state of things. Public sentiment will move mountains of laws.

Steam-engines don't work harder than a man's heart and veins, when he starts from his master, and fears being overtaken. I don't understand how an honest man can partake of any principle to carry him back.

If a man could make slaves of mud or block, and have them work for him, it would be wrong,—all men came of the hand of the Almighty; every man ought to have life, and his own method of pursuing happiness.

Mr. Scoble is doing all he can for the benefit of the colored people. His plans are all for their good, but they don't seem to see it, and so don't help along as they might.

WILLIAM A. HALL

I was born seven miles from Nashville, Tenn., Davidson county. I lived one year in Mississippi. I saw there a great deal of cotton-growing and persecution of slaves by men who had used them well in Tennessee. No man would have thought there could have been such a difference in treatment, when the masters got where they could make money. They drove the hands severely. My mother and brothers and sisters, when they changed their country, changed their position from good to bad. They were in Mississippi the last I heard of them, and I suppose they are there yet. It makes me miserable to consider that they are there: for their condition has been kept fresh in my memory, by seeing so much suffering and enduring so much. I went from Mississippi to Bedford county, Tenn. My master died here, and I was in hopes to go to see my mother. The doctor who attended my master had me sold at auction, and bought me himself, and promised he would never sell me to anybody; but in six months he tried to sell me. Not making out, he sent me to his father's farm in Tennessee, where I was treated tolerably well.

I remained there one year, then he took me horse-driving to Louisiana and back.

I saw some of the dreadfulest treatment on the sugar farms in the sugar-making season. The mill did not stop only to gear horses. People would come to my master and beg money to buy a loaf of bread. I saw them chained. I saw twelve men chained together, working on the levees. I saw three hundred that speculators had, dressing them up for sale. The overseers were about the mills, carrying their long whips all the time and using them occasionally.

When they wanted to whip severely, they put the head and hands in stocks in a stooping posture.

The last two years I was in Tennessee, I saw nine persons at different times, made fast to four stakes, and whipped with a leather strap from their neck to their heels and on the bottoms of their feet, raising blisters: then the blisters broken with a platted whip, the overseer standing off and fetching hard blows. I have seen a man faint under this treatment. I saw one about eighteen years old, as smart as you would see on the foot, used in this way: seven weeks after he fainted in consequence; his nerves were so shattered that he seemed like a man of fifty.

The overseer ·tied me to a tree, and flogged me with the whip. Afterwards he said he would stake me down, and give me a farewell whipping, that I would always remember. While he was eating supper, I got off my shoe, and slipped off a chain and ran: I ran, I suppose, some six hundred yards: then hearing a dog, which alarmed me, l climbed a hill, where I sat down to rest. Then I heard a shouting, hallooing, for dogs to hunt me up. I tried to understand, and made out they were after me. I went through the woods to a road on a ridge. I came to a guide-board—in order to read it, I pulled it up, and read it in the moonlight, and found I was going wrong—turned about and went back, travelling all night: lay by all day, travelled at night till I came where Duck River and Tennessee come together. Here I found I was wrong,—went back to a road that led down Tennessee River, the way I wanted to go. This was Monday night,—the day before they had been there for me. A colored man had told them, "For God's sake to tell me not to get caught, for they would kill me:" but that I knew before. I got something to eat, and went on down the river, and travelled until Saturday night at ten, living on green corn and watermelons. Then I came to a house where an old colored man gave me a supper: another kept me with him three days. My clothes were now very dirty: I got some soap of a woman, and went to a wash-place, and washed my clothes and dried them. A heavy rain came on at daybreak, and I went down to the river for a canoe—found none—and went back for the day,—got some bread, and at night went on down the river; but there were so many roads, I could not make out how to go. I laid all day in a corn field. At night I found a canoe, 12 feet long, and travelled down the river several days, to its mouth. There I got on an island, the river being low. I took my canoe across a tongue of land,—a sand-bar—into the Ohio, which I crossed into Illinois. I travelled three nights, not daring to travel days, until I came to Golconda, which I recognized by a description I had given on a previous attempt,—for this last time when I got away was my fourth effort. I went on to three forks in the road, took the left, travelled through the night, and lay by. At two, I ventured to go on, the road not being travelled much. But it seemed to go too far west: I struck through the woods, and went on till so tired I could walk no further. I got into a tobacco-pen, and stayed till morning. Then I went through the woods, and came to where a fire had been burning—I kindled it up, roasted a lot of corn, then travelled on about three miles completely lost. I now came to a house, and revolved in my mind some hours whether to go or not, to ask. At last I ventured, and asked the road—got the information— reached Marion: got bewildered, and went wrong again, and travelled back for Golconda,—but I was set right by some children. At dark I went on, and at daybreak got to Frankfort—13 miles all night long, being weak for want of food. A few miles further on I found an old friend, who was backward about letting me in, having been troubled at night by white children. At last he let me in, and gave me some food, which I much needed. The next night he gave me as much as I could carry with me.

I went on to within five miles of Mount Vernon. At 4 a.m., I lay down, and slept till about noon. I got up and tried to walk, but every time I tried to stoop under the bushes, I would fall down. I was close to a house, but did not dare to go to it; so I laid there and was sick—vomited, and wanted water very bad. At night I was so badly off that I was obliged to go to the house for water. The man gave me some, and said, "Are you a runaway?" I said, "No—I am walking away." "Where do you live?" "I live here now." "Are you a free man?" "Why should I be here, if I am not a free man?—this is a free country." "Where do you live, anyhow?" "I live here, don't you understand me?" "You are a free man, are you?" "Don't you see he is a free man, who walks in a free country?" "Show me your pass—I s'pose you've got one." "Do you suppose men need a pass in a free country: this is a free country." "I suppose you run away—a good many fugitives go through here, and do mischief." Said I, "I am doing no mischief—I am a man peaceable, going about my own business; when I am doing mischief, persecute me,—while I'm peaceable, let no man trouble me." Said he, "I'll go with you to Mount Vernon." "You may go, if you have a mind to: I am going, if it is the Lord's will that I shall get there. Good evening;" and I started out of the gate. He said, "Stop!" Said I, "Man, don't bother me,—I'm sick, and don't feel like being bothered." I kept on: he followed me,—"Stop, or I'll make you stop!" "Man, didn't I tell you I was sick, and don't want to be bothered." I kept on,—he picked up a little maul at a wood-pile, and came with me, his little son following, to see what was going on.

He walked a mile and a quarter with me, to a neighbor of his—called—there came out three men. He stated to them, "Here's a runaway going to Mount Vernon: I think it would be right to go with him." I made no reply. He said, "We'll go in with him, and if he be correct, we'll not injure him,—we'll not do him no harm, nohow." I stood consulting with myself, whether to fight or run; I concluded to run first, and fight afterward. I ran a hundred yards: one ran after me to the edge of the woods, and turned back. I sat down to rest,—say an hour. They had gone on ahead of me on horses. I took a back track, and found another road which led to Mount Vernon, which I did not reach until daybreak, although he said 'twas only five miles. I hastened on very quick through town, and so got off the track again: but I found a colored friend who harbored me three days, and fulfilled the Scriptures in one sense to perfection. I was hungry, and he fed me; thirsty, and he gave me drink; weary, and he ministered to my necessities; sick, and he cared for me till I got relieved: he took me on his own beast, and carried me ten miles, and his wife gave me food for four days' travel. His name was Y——. I travelled on three nights, and every morning found myself close to a town. One was a large one. I got into it early,—I was scared, for people was stirring,—but I got through it by turning to my right, which led me thirty miles out of my way. I was trying to get to Springfield. Then I went on to Taylorville. I lay out all day, two miles out, and while there, a man came riding on horseback within two feet of me. I thought he *would* see me, but he wheeled his horse, and away he went. At dark I got up and started on. It rained heavily. I went on to the town. I could discover nothing—the ground was black, the sky was cloudy. I travelled a while by the lights in the windows; at last ventured to ask the way, and got a direction for Springfield. After the rain the wind blew cold; I was chilled: I went into a calf-lot, and scared up the calves, and lay where they had been lying, to warm myself. It was dark yet. I stayed there half an hour, trying to get warm, then got up, and travelled on till daybreak. It being in a prairie, I had to travel very fast to get a place to hide myself. I came to a drain between two plantations, and got into it to hide. At sundown I went on, and reached Springfield, as near as I could guess, at 3 o'clock. I got into a stable, and lay on some boards in the loft.

When I awoke, the sun was up, and people were feeding horses in the stable. I found there was no chance to get out, without being discovered, and I went down and told them that I was a stranger, knowing no one there; that I was out until late, and so went into the stable. I asked them if there was any harm. They said "No." I thanked them and pursued my way. I walked out a little and found a friend who gave me breakfast. Then I was taken sick, and could not get a step from there for ten days: then I could walk a little, and had to start.

I took directions for Bloomington,—but the directions were wrong, and I got thirty miles out of my way again: so that when I reached Bloomington, I was too tired to go another step. I begged for a carriage, and if they had not got one, the Lord only knows what would have happened. I was conveyed to Ottawa, where I found an abolitionist who helped me to Chicago. From about the middle of August to the middle of November, I dwelt in no house except in Springfield, sick,—had no bed till I got to Bloomington. In February, I cut wood in Indiana,—I went to Wisconsin, and staid till harvest was over; then came to a particular friend, who offered me books. I had no money for books: he gave me a Testament, and gave me good instruction. I had worn out two Testaments in slavery, carrying them with me trying to get some instruction to carry me through life. "Now," said he, "square up your business, and go to the lake, for there are men here now, even here where you are living, who would betray you for half a dollar if they knew where your master is. Cross the lake: get into Canada." I thanked him for the book, which I have now; settled up and came to Canada.

I like Canada. If the United States were as free as Canada, I would still prefer to live here. I can do as much toward a living here in three days, as there in six.

WINDSOR

Windsor, at the terminus of the Great Western Railway, is in the township of Sandwich. It was incorporated January 1, 1854, with a population of 1000 souls. It is now estimated to contain one thousand four hundred inhabitants. There are settled in various parts of the village fifty families of colored people, some of whom entertain as boarders a number of fugitives from bondage. Assuming an average of five in a family, the colored population may be set down at two hundred and fifty. The general appearance of these is very much in their favor. There are many good mechanics among them: nearly all have comfortable homes, and some occupy very neat and handsome houses of their own.

Appearances indicate that the inhabitants of Windsor will unite in supporting good schools for the rising generation, without distinction of color. Where separate schools exist, the advantage in respect to buildings and teachers is for the most part on the side of the whites; and unless the separate schools are abolished, there is reason to fear that the progress of the colored people in education will be very much retarded in the greater part of the province. Mrs. Mary E. Bibb, widow of the late lamented Henry Bibb, Esq., has devoted herself to teaching a private school in Windsor, and with good success. During the last spring term, she had an attendance of forty-six pupils, seven of whom were white children.

A gentleman of Windsor who has long taken a deep interest in the welfare of the African race, is of opinion that immigrants who have been engaged in agricultural pursuits in Pennsylvania and other free States are more industrious and "more to be depended upon than those who come into Canada directly from a state of slavery." The same gentleman assured me that the best and most dexterous blacksmith he had ever known was a refugee: he had not such tools as he wanted, nor would take good ones on credit, for fear he might not be able to pay: yet he would make or mend various utensils, while other smiths could not. He is now at Buxton.

While in Windsor, I was repeatedly informed by those who have the best means of knowing, that "there is no need of raising money to aid the colored people here, unless for a day or two when a fugitive family first comes in. Women get half a dollar for washing, and it is difficult to hire them at that."

A circumstance which fell under my notice in this township of Sandwich,* reminds me of what I might with propriety have said in referring to other parts of the province, that it is fortunate for some conscience-stricken slaveholders, that Canada affords a refuge for a certain class of their household victims—their slave-wives, or slave-children, or both. If it be a crime to assist slaves in reaching a land of freedom, it is not a crime of which those terrible fellows, the northern abolitionists, alone are guilty. Slaveholders may pour contempt on the names and the deeds of northern philanthropists: but these have no slanderous epithets to hurl back upon the southerner, who snatches his children and the mother of his children from the threatening hammer of the auctioneer, and hurriedly and tearfully starts them for the North with the parting injunction, "Stop not short of Canada!" We rejoice with him that England offers a place of refuge where his wife and his offspring may be free. Yet, of any head of such a family, a northern fanatic might be prompted to ask, Is this course honorable and manly? Do not these children need *both* parents to look after their interests? and does not this slave-wife, ignorant and among strangers in a strange land, need your presence, your counsel, your direction? He that provideth not for his own household is worse than an infidel, and almost as bad as an abolitionist: but your family are in arrears for board, and are quartered upon the charity of persons who are themselves poor refugees.

Mr. David Cooper, who lives on the lands of the Industrial Institution, has furnished a statement which will be found below, showing the position of affairs where he resides.

---

*See the narrative of J. C. Brown, Chatham.

REFUGEES' HOME

At about nine miles from Windsor, in the townships of Sandwich and Madison, the Refugees' Home Society have made a purchase of nearly two thousand acres of land, on which reside some twenty families, each on a farm of twenty-five acres. Forty 25 acre lots have been taken up. A school is maintained there three fourths of the year.

Mr. Henry Bibb, who was himself a fugitive from the house of bondage, originated the idea of establishing a society which should "aim to purchase thirty thousand acres of government land somewhere in the most suitable sections of Canada where it can be obtained for the homeless refugees from American slavery to settle upon." This was soon after the passage of the fugitive slave bill.

The society was organized and a constitution adopted in August, 1852. The object of the society is declared to be "to assist the refugees from American slavery to obtain permanent homes, and to promote their social, moral, physical, and intellectual elevation." The society propose to purchase of the Canadian government, fifty thousand acres of land, at a cost of one hundred thousand dollars. Money for the purchase is obtained in part by contributions; and one half the moneys received for the sale of lands is devoted to the purchase of other lands. The other moiety of moneys received is to be devoted to the support of schools.

By the constitution adopted in 1852, it appears that each family of actual settlers receives twenty-five acres of land, five of which they receive free of cost, provided they shall, within three years from the time of occupancy, clear and cultivate the same. "For the remaining twenty acres, they shall pay the primary cost in nine equal annual payments, free of use, for which they shall receive deeds." This article may be varied to favor the aged, etc. "This Society shall give deeds to none but landless refugees from American slavery." "No person receiving land by gift or purchase from the Society shall have power to transfer the same under fifteen years from the time of the purchase or gift." "All lands becoming vacated by the removal or extinction of families, shall revert to the Executive Committee."

Here, too, as in Buxton, the claims of temperance are kept fully in view. A by-law provides that "No house shall be used for manufacturing or vending intoxicating liquors on any lot received from this Society."

The Refugees' Home Society, its officers and agents, possess the entire confidence of the American public: at least of that portion which sympathizes with the wandering outcasts from the United States. It will be seen by some of the testimonials which follow, that some dissatisfaction exists among the settlers: having its origin doubtless, in some misapprehension or mistake. Still, I have not felt at liberty to depart from my original plan—that so far as the limits of a single volume may extend, the colored people of Canada might express their own opinions, and tell their own story of their slavery in the past, their present condition, and their future prospects.

The second report of the Canada Anti-Slavery Society (for 1853), remarks: "There is doubtless a better state of things amongst the fugitives, than existed at the time when such a plan was proposed. The panic produced by the fugitive law, having subsided, the poor refugees have had more time allowed them to prepare for the change, and, in consequence, their wants have been diminished. The true principle is now to assume that every man, unless disabled by sickness, can support himself and his family after he has obtained steady employment. All that able-bodied men and women require, is a fair chance, friendly advice, and a little encouragement, perhaps a little assistance at first. Those who are really willing to work, can procure employment in a short time after their arrival, so that what is specially needed, is such associations of friends at the different places where fugitives land, as will interest themselves in the colored man, put him in the way of finding employment, and extend to him such encouragement in the way of grants of land or otherwise, as his altered circumstances may require. In some places, fully to accomplish this, aid from abroad may be necessary, though in most places local charity will, we think, prove sufficient."

A True Band has been organized by the residents of the Home, and other persons in the vicinity.

THOMAS JONES

I was a slave in Kentucky, and made my escape five years ago, at the age of thirty. The usage in Kentucky on the front part of the State is pretty good,—back, it is rather tight.

I came here without any thing. I had no money or aid of any kind. I went right into the bush chopping wood. I brought my lady with me, and we were married on the way at Bloomingsburg in Fayette Co. I have one child. With what I earned by hard licks, I bought land and have built me a frame-house. I now follow plastering and any thing I can find to do. I am worth three or four thousand dollars, and pay about thirty dollars a year tax.

If a man have aid furnished him, he does not have so much satisfaction in what he has,—he feels dependent and beholden, and does not make out so well. I have seen this, ever since I have been here,—the bad effects of this giving. I have seen men waiting, doing nothing, expecting something to come over to them. Besides, it makes a division among the colored people. The industrious are against it, the other class favor it; and so they fall out. My opinion is, that the fugitive on the road, should be assisted, but not after he gets here. If people have money to give, they had better give it to those who suffer in trying to help them here. For those who come sick, or actually stand in need, there is a society here among ourselves to take care of them.

In regard to aid from societies on the other side, there are many who know that money is raised for the poor travelling fugitive, and they take advantage of it: free people of color from the States come over pretending to be fugitives, who never were fugitives. They come in a miserable condition, often drinking men, worthless, to get the money that is raised. I have known six or seven such cases.

The colored people are doing very well. They are poor, some of them, but are all able to have enough to eat and wear, and they have comfortable homes, with few exceptions,—and some of these are in a way to have them. Some few don't seem to care whether they have good houses or not, as is the case among all people.

In the Refugees' Home they are not doing very well. Land was to be sold to the refugees at cost, giving them five acres, and they to buy twenty. Some dissatisfaction exists because there has been an advance made of four shillings an acre for surveying, although the land had been surveyed once. The refugees all refused to pay it. They were to clear up the five acres in three years. They have altered the constitution bringing it down to two years. Some had not been on three years, but went with that understanding. Alterations were made, too, enlarging the size of the houses. One of them has left the lands in consequence, and more talk of doing so. They doubt about getting deeds, and they begin to think 'tis a humbug. The restrictions in regard to liquor, and not selling under so many years, nor the power to will his property to his friends, only to his children, if he have any, make them dissatisfied. They want to do as they please. If they want to exchange and get a bigger place, they want to do it without being cramped.

In addition, the men who have settled there, have been a bother to the society. As they were dependent, smart men would not go, and it has been occupied by men who expected aid from the other side.

The colored men must rely on their own two hands, or they'll never be any thing.

The colored people are temperate and moral.

WILLIAM S. EDWARDS

I was born in Springfield, Ohio. My mother was, to the best of my belief, a free-woman. While I was a little child, a man claimed my mother as a slave woman whom he had lost seven years before, and took both her and me into Kentucky,—as I have been told to Burlington. He took us to Louisville to sell us, and there 'twas proved that she was not his, but another man's slave; that other man took us back to Burlington. Here was another dispute, and another man examined, and found more marks than the other, and proved that she belonged to him. After passing through several hands she was sold, and I have not seen her since, nor do I know where she is. I have heard that when she was sold, it was left her, to take me with her into slavery, or remain there and be free. She chose to let me remain. I stayed with the family until, at thirteen, I was put to the trade of a tobacconist: remained until twenty-one. Then I did not dare to talk about freedom. I dared not name it,—I still stayed working at the business. After a while, hearing some talking about my rights, I questioned as closely as I could, but not to awaken distrust.

When I was about twenty-five, we had a dispute about a holiday, and then I first claimed my rights to his teeth, telling him that I was free. He said I must stay two years more. A man offered to lend me two hundred dollars, to buy my time: he refused. I then hired to another man, paying my claimant twenty dollars a month, for a year and five months.

I kept on inquiring, until I found the man who first carried me into Kentucky. He told me a very straight story,—that he had found the woman whom he had lost in New Orleans—she having been absent from him fifteen years and six months, having been in New Orleans all that time. I searched the records at the Recorder's office, but there was nothing on the books,—the whole being a rascally scheme, therefore they took no account of it on the books. The clerk said there surely was no trial or transaction in the court; if there had been, it would have been on record. But the man who brought me said there was a trial; he acknowledged that neither me nor my mother ever belonged to him; that it was a mistake.

Another man went with me to search, but found no scratch of a pen from ten years back to forty. I then got a white man to go to the persons who pretended to own me, and he told me, in their presence, that if a man were half white and born free, he ought to be free; and you are all of that. My boss said that I would be free after a time—that he never meant to keep me over time. He probably meant my time as long as I lived,—as a master told his slave once, "When you die, I'll give you your papers." He said I couldn't pass without papers: he went with me, saying to get papers, and then he would not, but said I must stay a while longer before I could get them; that he could not give them to me just yet. Things went on in this way two or three months, until I was nearly twenty-seven years old. At length my mistress's son, by her consent, gave me free papers. I went to Ohio: then came into Canada, and settled down in Chatham.

I have five children. One goes to school; we are not able to send all on account of the price partly, as we have to pay fifty cents a quarter for each child, at the public school. I went into Chatham with nothing, and I want the children some in the family.

I have seen many things practised in slavery which are too horrible to name.

MRS. COLMAN FREEMAN

I am a native of North Carolina. I was born free, and lived with my father and mother. My father was a quadroon—my mother a mulatto. My father fought the British in the Revolution. His brother was drafted, but being sick, my father volunteered to take his place, and was in the army seven years. When he returned his brother was dead. He did not get a pension until three years before he died, not knowing that he was entitled to one, until, on some abuse from white men, he went into court, and the lawyer said, "Will you suffer injustice to be done to this white-headed old man, who has faced the cannon's mouth, fighting for our liberties; who has maintained himself and family without drawing a penny from the government?"

When colored persons had their meetings in the groves, white men would stand with their whips where they were coming out, to examine for passes, and those who had passes would go free,—the others would break and run, like cattle with hornets after them. I have seen them run into the river. I remember one time, I was going with my brother, and saw them at the meeting, trying to get away from the patrollers. I could not help shedding tears to see the distress they were in. They ran into the river, and tried to get away. Said I to my brother, "What are they running so into the river for?" He hunched me, and said, "Don't you see the patrollers?" This was because they wanted to hear preaching, and learn a little about Almighty God that made them. They were not allowed to meet without patrollers.

I knew a slave named Adam who experienced religion, and wanted to be baptized. Saturday night the overseer told him he should not be baptized. He went to his mistress, and she gave him a pass for the purpose. Next day, I went down to the shore of the mill-pond to see the baptizing. Just as Adam was ready to go into the water, the overseer rode up, and cried out, "Adam! Adam! if you get baptized, I will give you a hundred lashes to-morrow morning!" Adam said, "I have but two masters to serve, my earthly and my heavenly master, and I can mind nobody else." I know that overseer very well; —— —— his name was: I was standing right by him. Then he forbade Mr. L—— from baptizing him. Mr. L.: "If there is a God I will baptize Adam; if not, I will not baptize him." The overseer stood up in his stirrups, and cursed so that he frightened all the people on the beach: his eyes glowed like two lighted candles. As soon as Adam came out of the water, he ran for home to get protection from his mistress. She prevented the overseer from punishing him.

I came away from North Carolina in consequence of persecution. There was a rebellion among the slaves in Virginia, under Nat Turner, near where I was. A doctor near me had his mother and brothers and sisters, except two, killed in that rebellion. The white people that had no slaves would have killed the colored, but their masters put them in jail to protect them from the white people, and from fears they had themselves of being killed. They came to my mother's, and threatened us—they searched for guns and ammunition: that was the first time I was ever silenced by a white man. One of them put his pistol to my breast, and said, "If you open your head, I'll kill you in a minute!" I had told my mother to hush, as she was inquiring what their conduct meant. We were as ignorant of the rebellion as they had been. Then I made up my mind not to remain in that country. We had to stay a while to sell our crop: but I would not go to church there any more.

I lived in Ohio ten years, as I was married there,—but I would about as lief live in the slave States as in Ohio. In the slave States I had protection sometimes, from people that knew me—none in Ohio. I understand the laws are better in Ohio now than they were then. In the slave States I had no part in the laws: the laws were all against the colored men: they allowed us no schools nor learning. If we got learning, we stole it.

We live here honestly and comfortably. We entertain many poor strangers.

BEN BLACKBURN

I was born in Maysville, Ky. I got here last Tuesday evening, and spent the Fourth of July in Canada. I felt as big and free as any man could feel, and I worked part of the day for my own benefit: I guess my master's time is out. Seventeen came away in the same gang that I did.

WILLIAM L. HUMBERT

I am from the city of Charleston, S.C., and have been in various parts of South Carolina and Georgia. I used to run in a steamboat from Savannah to Charleston.

I left Charleston in September, 1853. I lived in the free States some months, but finally left on account of the Fugitive Slave Bill. This was a law of tyranny, and I had to come to Canada to avoid the ten dollar commissioner. I would rather die than go back,—that's a settled point with me—not on account of ill-treatment of the person; but I could not stand the idea of being held by another man as a chattel. Slavery itself is cruel enough, without regard to the hardships which slaves in general have to undergo.

I do not believe that any slaveholder under the canopy of heaven can see God's face; that is, if I read the Bible right. Slaveholding is against all reason. All men are from the same mother dust, and one can have no right to hold another as a chattel. I know three or four preachers of the gospel who hold slaves. As the minister goes, the congregation goes. The ministers preach to please the people, and not in the fear of God. I never knew but one exception there. I have seen a minister hand the sacrament to the deacons to give the slaves, and, before the slaves had time to get home, living a great distance from church, have seen one of the same deacons, acting as patrol, flog one of the brother members within two hours of his administering the sacrament to him, because he met the slave in the road without a passport, beyond the time allowed him to go home. My opinion of slavery is not a bit different now from what it was then: I always hated it from childhood. I looked on the conduct of the deacon with a feeling of revenge. I thought that a man who would administer the sacrament to a brother church-member, and flog him before he got home, ought not to live.

DAVID COOPER

There was an institution started here in Sandwich about six years ago, called the Industrial Institution. The land was bought by Rev. Mr. Willis, colored Methodist preacher, with money raised in the United States. It comprised two hundred acres, and was divided into ten-acre lots, and sold to any colored men who were disposed to buy, at three dollars on taking possession, and then six dollars the two subsequent years—then they were to have a deed. The land has never been wholly occupied. Some bought the land, but never went on it. There are now eight families on this land, who have forty acres cleared. A part of them can principally support themselves on what they have cleared, but they have to work out to keep their families supplied.* The roads there are very bad,—being wet and muddy. We have had a school there, but it is not kept up. We attend here at church—[at the Refugees' Home.]

I was from Virginia originally, but was brought up in Pennsylvania. My wife was a slave.

JOHN MARTIN

I was born in Virginia, raised up in Tennessee, ran into Ohio, and emigrated to Canada, in order to avoid the oppressive laws of the States.

The Refugees' Home in Sandwich was commenced in 1851. It comprises between sixteen and seventeen hundred acres of land,—I

---

*The same evil hinders to some extent the advance of the Elgin Settlement at Buxton: the Directors of which, in 1854, report as follows:—

"Could it be so arranged that all the settlers could work on their own farms during the whole year, the improvement in clearing and cropping would be very easily doubled. We do hope, before another year, that some arrangement will be made by which the settlers will be enabled to spend more time on their own farms, and with their families."

do not know how many families reside on it. I commenced here in the bush three years ago, and have gone over about eight acres—I think the biggest clearing there is. Those near round me are well satisfied with their homes, excepting the oppression they have tried to raise on us as to the price. They were to have it at the original price, but they bought more land at a higher rate, and wanted to average it on all alike. The old settlers are dissatisfied and will probably leave, if this is enforced.

We have a school here. I cannot tell whether it is good or not, as it has just commenced under a new teacher: the former one did well.

The prospect is, that if the new arrangements about the price are given up, the settlers will go on clearing, and progress in the best way we can: I believe the lands will be taken up, and that the colored people will have good farms here.

Slavery is a dreadful thing. Slaveholders—I know not what will become of them. Some of them I love,—but I know they deserve punishment, and leave them in the hands of God.

The people have been told absolute falsehoods about our freezing and suffering, and money has been raised which does no good. It has been reported to us, that thousands of dollars have been raised for our benefit, of which we have never received the first red cent. I say so—I am fifty-five years old, and have ever tried to keep the truth on my side.

I was not sent to school in slave States, but have since learned to write, as witness my hand,

(Signed)   John Martin

DANIEL HALL

I escaped from the neighborhood of New Orleans, seventeen years ago; had some difficulty about getting through Illinois—there were many slaveholders in heart in Illinois—but I got through. I settled in Malden at Amherstburg. It was then a dense woods—with but little cleared land. There were very few colored people when I got there. If a man had half or three quarters of an acre of corn, he thought he had a large patch: now they have twenty-five or thirty acre lots. The clearing has been done by colored and white, mostly by colored men, as I know, for I cleared up a great deal myself. On the Lake Erie shore, the colored people have raised in past years, a great deal of tobacco, but now they raise corn, wheat, potatoes, and buckwheat.

I look at slavery as being heinous in the sight of God. And as for slaveholders, what is to become of people who take the husband from his wife, and the infant from its mother, and sell them where they can never see each other again?

What the colored people want is land and education. With these, they will do well here.

By the blessing of God, I have been enabled to become possessor of fifty acres in Colchester, of which six or seven acres are cleared.

LYDIA ADAMS

[Mrs. A. lives in a very comfortable log-house on the road from Windsor to the Refugees' Home.]

I am seventy or eighty years old. I was from Fairfax county, old Virginia. I was married and had three children when I left there for Wood county, where I lived twenty years: thence to Missouri, removing with my master's family. One by one they sent four of my children away from me, and sent them to the South: and four of my grandchildren all to the South but one. My oldest son, Daniel—then Sarah—all gone. "It's no use to cry about it," said one of the young women, "she's got to go." That's what she said when Esther went away. Esther's husband is here now, almost crazy about her: they took her and sold her away from him. They were all Methodist people—great Methodists—all belonged to the church. My master died—he left no testimony whether he was willing to go or not . . . . I have been in Canada about one year, and like it as far as I have seen.

I've been wanting to be free ever since I was a little child. I said to them I didn't believe God ever meant me to be a slave, if my skin was black—at any rate not all my lifetime: why not have it as in old times, seven years' servants? Master would say, "No, you were made to wait on white people: what was niggers made for?—why, just to wait on us all."

I am afraid the slaveholders will go to a bad place—I am really afraid they will. I don't think any slaveholder can get to the kingdom.

J. F. WHITE

I have served twenty-five years as a slave; born in Virginia, and brought up, or rather whipped up, in Kentucky. I have lived in Canada two years—I have bought one hundred acres of land in Sandwich, suitable to raise any kind of grain.

I want you to tell the people of the United States, that as far as begging for fugitives is concerned, that we are amply able to take care of ourselves: we have done it, and can do it. We want none to beg for us; let them give to the fugitive on his way, and to those who are assisting him on his way. Money has been raised—an immense quantity of it too, but we don't get it—indeed, we don't want it. We have a society here to take care of our brothers when they get here, and we can do it without assistance. If people send things through pure motives to the suffering, we thank them for their intentions,—still, there is no need of their doing even that.

LEONARD HARROD

I was born and bred in Georgetown, D.C., where I had a wife and two children. About six o'clock one morning, I was taken suddenly from my wife; she knew no more where I had gone than the hen knows where the hawk carries her chicken. Fifteen hundred miles I wore iron on my wrist, chained in a gang from Georgetown to Port Gibson. There I was sold and put to receive and pack cotton, etc., for six years. Then I was sold to Nashville, Tenn., one year; then to New Orleans fifteen years; then I took up my bed and walked for Canada. I have been in Canada nearly two years. I was poor—as low down as a man could be who is not underground. It was in winter,—my wife was in a delicate situation,—and we had nothing for bedclothes at night but what we had worn through the day. We suffered all the winter for things we left on the way, which were never sent us. My wife is now under the doctor's care in consequence.

I have hired a place to work on, and have bought two acres of land.

A man can get more information in Canada about slavery, than he can in the South. There I would have told you to ask master, because I would have been afraid to trust a white man: I would have been afraid that you would tell my master. Many a time my master has told me things to try me. Among others, he said he thought of moving up to Cincinnati, and asked me if I did not want to go. I would tell him, "No! I don't want to go to none of your *free* countries!" Then he'd laugh,—but I did want to come—surely I did. A colored man tells the truth here,—there he is afraid to.

SANDWICH

This beautiful and quiet town, two miles from Windsor, has a population of about fifteen hundred, including twenty-one colored families, which number, perhaps, one hundred persons.

The colored population have the right to send their children when qualified, into the grammar school. None have hitherto availed themselves of this right. Here, as in many other parts of the province, the colored people by accepting of that provision of law, which *allows* them separate schools, fail of securing the best education for their children. The colored teachers who present themselves are examined with a great deal of "lenity,"—and some who cannot even spell, are placed in charge of the young.

The prejudice against the African race is here very strongly marked. It had not been customary to levy school taxes on the colored people. Some three or four years since, a trustee assessed a school tax on some of the wealthier citizens of that class. They sent their children at once into the public school. As these sat down, the white children near them deserted the benches: and in a day or two, the white children were wholly withdrawn, leaving the school-house to the teacher and his colored pupils. The matter was at last—"compromised:" a notice—"Select School"— was put up on the school-house: the white children were selected *in,* and the black were selected *out.*

Still, the prejudice here is not deeply seated: it is only skin-deep. Some slight affairs on the border prove that if a slaveholder were to set his foot in the township with any sinister intention, the true sentiments and feelings of the people would manifest themselves in the most decided and unmistakable manner. The people of Sandwich, as one of them jocosely remarked to me, are "awful independent:" and such is their strong old-fashioned English hatred of oppression, that the population would rally, almost to a man, to defend the rights of the humblest negro in their midst,—even of "crazy Jack," the butt of the village boys.

It is to be observed, moreover, that the law allows separate schools not only to colored people, but to Catholic and Protestant sects, when these are in a minority.

The colored people have also their separate churches here. The Methodists contemplate erecting a building for public worship, and a member of that society remarked to me that he for one, would like to have aid for that purpose, as he did not see how it could be done without; but that the sentiment of his brethren generally was against begging. I asked him why they did not attend the churches of the whites of the same denomination. His reply indicated that they thought they would not be welcomed there with a single exception: "One church," said he, "has thrown open its doors to us; and that is the English Church—Mr. Dewey's—they have invited us all in, and they say if it is not big enough, they will make it bigger." Whether I advised him to comply with an invitation so truly Christian in character, the reader, if he is a Yankee, and cares to take the trouble, can readily guess.

There is a school now open here registering thirty colored children, and having an average attendance of twenty-four. It is under the charge of an able and accomplished lady teacher—Miss Gifford—who informed me that the school was established by the Refugees' Home Society.

GEORGE WILLIAMS

I was from Maysville, Ky., but belonged in Fairfax county at first. Left Virginia at fourteen years old,—am now fifty-three; have lived in Sandwich about fourteen years. When we removed from Virginia, my mother left her husband and two sisters behind. She was much grieved at leaving her husband: the children were taken from her before. This separation of families is an awful thing. At ten or twelve years old, the thought grew in me, that slavery was wrong. I felt mad every day when I thought of being kept a slave. I calculated on buying myself, and offered my master two hundred and fifty dollars. He wanted me to work a year first, going with me to another town. I did not want to go, and came off peaceably.

I remained about six years in the free States. In some respects, I suffered in them on account of my color. Many looked on me with contempt because I was a colored man. My oath was not taken as a white man's. I had a farm in Ohio, and was doing well, but a law was then passed requiring security for good behavior. A white man represented it worse than it was, so as to take advantage, as myself and two others had a heavy crop standing. I lost by coming off before harvest: all I got was a few bushels of wheat. It was a great damage breaking us up at that time.

I work at whitewashing, etc. I rent a house, and own a small piece of land. The colored men here get a living. The greater part of them have no learning,—almost all of them have been slaves. Some of them have homes of their own; but most of them hire. Most of them send their children to school. But we have to rent a house, and although the rent is low, yet we get behind on the rent, till some of us make a sacrifice and pay up. The school is not kept up through the year. We have not had regular schooling,—we do not send to the same school as the whites. There were too few of us to raise money for a separate school. We received £18 from government, but could not carry it on, and gave it up. There is one school now supported by abolitionists in the United States.

I do not go so strong as some against receiving assistance. I have seen many cases of destitute suffering people, who needed aid, and our people could scarcely help them. But the best way would be to manage by means of societies corresponding with those of the States. In some places, the colored people can manage without aid,—but here not.

HENRY BRANT

I was from Millwood, Frederic Co., Virginia. I was brought up by Col. N— —'s widow. I remained in bondage until twenty-three, hired out at different places. I had very little chance to get money,—perhaps two or three dollars a year. Usage was, compared with farming usage, good, as when I was hired out, there were restrictions, that I should be well used.

It always appeared to me that I wanted to be free, and could be free. No person ever taught me so,—it came naturally in my mind. Finally I saw that my case was pretty bad, if I was to live all my lifetime subject to be driven about at the will of another. When I thought of it, I felt wrathy at the white men. At length, I said—this will not do—if I stay here I shall kill somebody—I'd better go.

In 1834, my mistress being old, I feared that in event of her death, I might be placed on some farm, and be cruelly used. I sought a chance to get off. I found friends among those who were in the interests of the slaveholders, and by their instructions reached Canada without trouble, and had the satisfaction of having a friend come too by my persuasion. He is in Canada, but I have not seen him since. I settled in Sandwich.

I received on coming into the country neither victuals, clothes, nor money,—I received only a welcome,—that was all I wanted, and I was thankful to get it. I did just what work I could find to be done. I managed to save up what little I got pretty well. I invested in a home. I got me a house and lot. I own ten acres in the bush.

Comparing the condition of the colored population here with an equal number of families of white laborers, I think they are about equal in means.

Slavery is abominable,—I think slaveholders know it is wrong: they are an intelligent people and they know it. They ought to have done their duty,—given me my freedom, and something to live on for what myself and forefathers had earned. I don't see how a man can obtain heaven, and continue to do as the slaveholders do. A man may do wrong a long time and repent,—but if he continues it, as they do, I think it a hard case for him.

MRS. HENRY BRANT

I am from Maryland. I suffered the worst kind of usage: that of being held as a slave.

I was fortunately among those who did not beat and bruise me. I was gambled off to a trader by my owner. I made such a fuss, (and the people told him 'twas a shame to let me go to a trader,—that I was too good a girl for that, having taken care of him in sickness,—that I ought to have had a chance to find some one to buy me,) that he felt ashamed of what he had done, and bought me back. Then he gave me a chance to buy myself,—gave me one year to pay

$270: before the year was out, I offered him $150 in part payment,—he wouldn't take that unless I'd pay all. I then asked him, would he take that, and security for $120, payable six months after, and give me my papers down. He refused. Then I said to myself, "If you won't take that, you shan't take any." I started for Canada, and travelled in style,—he couldn't take me.

My sister was a free-woman. She was to buy me, and pay $270, and I was to be the security. But he overreached himself: for he drew the paper in such a way, that he could not get the money of my sister. Had I overstayed the year, I would never have seen Canada; for then I would have been carried back to the eastern shore.

One thing which makes it bad about getting our children into school here is, we are so near Detroit. The people here would feel ashamed to have the Detroit people know that they sent the white into the same school with the colored. I have heard this from a white woman.

AMHERSTBURG

Contains a population of more than two thousand. The colored portion is variously estimated at from four hundred to five hundred,—the latter number probably being nearer exactness. Some of these, who had resided in the free States, before emigrating to Canada, assured me that here the colored people are "doing rather better than the same class in the United States."

A separate school has been established here, at their own request: their request was given them, but leanness went with it. I visited the school. There was an attendance of twenty-four,—number on the list, thirty. The school-house is a small, low building, and contains neither blackboard nor chair. Long benches extend on the sides of the room, close to the walls, with desks of corresponding length in front of them. The whole interior is comfortless and repulsive. The teacher, a colored lady, is much troubled by the frequent absences of the pupils, and the miserably tattered and worn-out condition of the books. Two inkstands were in use, which, on being nearly inverted, yielded a very little bad ink. The teacher appeared to be one of the working sort, disposed to bear up as well as she could under her many discouragements: but the whole school adds one more dreary chapter to "the pursuit of knowledge under difficulties." But there is a better time coming. Malden (Amherstburg) is one of the stations at which the Colonial Church and School Society propose to establish schools, "expressly for the benefit of the colored race, but open to all."

The colored people are engaged in the various mechanic arts, and as shopkeepers, etc. One of the best hotels is kept by a very intelligent colored man. In an evening walk about town, his was the only house from which I heard the cheerful sound of vocal and instrumental music: and this was occasionally interrupted by some "saucy" white boy shouting, as he passed, a stave of our national, Union-saving air;

the same which was played in State street, Boston, by a full band, when Massachusetts swallowed so bitter a dose, that the whole world made up faces: when, with all the pride, pomp, and circumstance of glorious war, it sent one poor "fugitive black man" "to old Virginia's shore." It was all right, no doubt,—for on examining the Scriptures, a "passage" from the Constitution, "No person held to service or labor," etc., was found so snugly pasted over Deut. 23:15, that if it were possible, it might deceive the very elect. Therefore, said the people, Burns must be sent back: and the poor fellow was marched off, surrounded by beings who differed mainly from Southern "negro dogs," in not being worth, morally speaking, the remotest approximation to "$100 apiece." It is said that pepper was thrown at them: this was in bad taste,—it had been better to offer them salt—*Turks* Island—as a very useful antiseptic for men who could scarcely boast soul enough to prevent the action of decomposing chemical forces. The reader is requested to pardon this digression, the only one we have made hitherto. It is difficult to speak with calmness when reminded of so disgraceful an action as the surrender of Anthony Burns. The time has come for Americans to adopt the motto of De Witt Clinton—"Patria cara, carior libertas." [Dear is my country, liberty is dearer.]

CHARLES BROWN

I was born in Virginia, and was raised a slave. My grandmother was a free-woman in Maryland. One day, as she was washing by a river, a kidnapper came up, gagged and bound her, carried her into Virginia, and there sold her into bondage. She there had four children, my mother, my mother's sister, and my mother's two brothers. After about twenty or twenty-five years, when I was a very small boy, a man from Maryland, named Hanks, came through Virginia. He saw my grandmother, and knew her. "What!" said he, "are you here?" She told him how she had been kidnapped. He said, "You are free, and I'll get you your freedom." Her oath was good for nothing, but by Hanks's oath, she would get free. At night she was jerked up and carried to Orleans, and sold on a cotton plantation. She wrote on, a good while after, that she would get free, and come back and free her children. She got free herself, as I have heard, but 'twas when she got too old to do any more work. My mother and all the folks there in Virginia knew about her being stolen, and about Hanks's coming there.

I was used kindly, as I always did my work faithfully. But I knew I ought to be free. I told my master one day—said I, "You white folks set the bad example of stealing—you stole us from Africa, and not content with that, if any got free here, you stole them afterward, and so we are made slaves." I told him, I would not stay. He shed tears, and said he thought I would be the last one to leave him.

A year after, I left for the North. I have been cook for large hotels. My health is now very poor,—I have had a bad cough for two or three years, from overwork–cooking sometimes for three hundred persons in a hotel. I have always supported myself, and have some money by me yet. I reside in Chatham, and came here to see a physician.

JAMES SMITH

I was raised on the head waters of the south branch of the Potomac, in Pendleton Co., Va. The treatment there is mild, if there can be any mildness in it. I remained there until my escape in 1847. My father was a white man, and was my master too. My mother's father was also a white man. My master was an Englishman, born in the city of London. When I was five years old, he gave me to his son, who was my half-brother, and he raised me. This son had then children about my age. These children were sent to school, but I was not. These children talked about learning me, but they said, "we musn't—father says he'll write a pass and run off." I have learned to read since I came away. I was ordered about like the other slaves. I ate in the kitchen while they, (my brother's family,) ate at a table by themselves. I was stuck off one side. Other people mentioned my relation to my master, but I never mentioned it to him, nor he to me. His sons had it thrown at them that we favored one another: it was looked on as a stigma. My mother often told me how it was, but told me not to mention it as it would make it worse for her. She died before her master.

My old master was a very wicked man and died a miserable death. My brother was present. My master always had a custom of cursing and swearing, and he died in the same state. Nothing was said about giving me my freedom.

I used to drive to Richmond, and stop at a tavern with white wagoners. I would notice the landlord's countenance, viewing me very much to see if I had colored blood: the wagoners would look at me and wink. They got me in on purpose to joke and bother him. I ate with the other wagoners, excepting a single time. He followed me out into the kitchen where I was eating, and asked me if I was a slave or not. I told him I was. He said I was too white to be a slave. It is often the case that these rascals feel for their own blood—they will say to a man of my color, "It's a pity you're a slave—you're too white to be a slave."

My half-brother got involved and sold me for four hundred dollars to a person in the same neighborhood. I lived with him about two years and six months, clearing up farm six months, balance of the time at grist-mill. His treatment I count well for being a slave. His name was N—— E——.

After my father's death, my brothers and sisters, (also my father's children,) four in number, were hired out at auction to the highest bidder. E—— came home and told me all about it. I then thought, "I'm doing well enough now, but I don't know how long it will last,—I'll try next fall to get my liberty."

The next fall, I made arrangements and walked away. This was in the fall of '47. After travelling fifty miles, I came right along in the road, and nobody asked me any questions, except one man who knew me, and who proved to be my friend. I stayed upwards of three years in the free States, married there a few days before I left in 1850, and came to Canada. I left the United States, in consequence of the Fugitive Slave Bill—it's only a *Bill*. It vexed me as I was leaving in the boat, to hear the Germans, whom I could understand, laughing about the "niggers" having to leave, and come to Canada. One man was taken away from his wife and three children and carried back before I left.

I am doing tolerably well in Canada, and am getting a very comfortable living. I own a lot of land worth about two hundred dollars, and have other property. I keep a grocery, and sell to all who will buy, without distinction of color.

REV. WILLIAM TROY

From Essex county, Va. My father was a slave of ―― ――, Senator of the United States. My mother was a free-woman.

I lived there until twenty-one. I left there 11th March, 1848. I saw scenes there that made my heart bleed. I can particularize the breaking up of R―― P. W――'s farm, some five hundred slaves, many of whom were my associates, with whom I had often been to meeting, belonging to the same church. We had many meetings together, sometimes broken up by patrols. When we had meetings, it was at late hours, to avoid the patrols―yet sometimes they would run us away, and sometimes we would get our meetings through. They were sold to different persons―Judge ―― and others. About the time a part of them were leaving, I went to bid them farewell. Many had their hearts so full of grief that they could not speak―they could only give me their hands.

Another lot who belonged to the same man, aroused me by singing about nine at night, passing my father's residence, singing, bidding farewell to all their friends; many left father, mother, and children behind them. I may mention here that one of these slaves, a woman named Martha Fields, who was hired out at the time, was taken early one morning, without time to get her clothes, hurried off to Richmond, and sold to the highest bidder. From Richmond she went on to New Orleans, put into a slave-pen, and bought by Mr. A――, a celebrated negro trader, and put on his farm, where she married A.'s slave. A. gave them free papers, and they now reside in Cincinnati. She says she has suffered enough herself, and seen so much suffering, that she believes that all those who hold slaves, and those who uphold slavery will, if there is any such place as one of torment, will be sure to go there.

I was aroused at Loretto, Va., by the sale of a slave named William, who was sold by his master. I heard the boy hollowing in the swamp; from hearing his shrieks, I made towards the boy,―when I went there, I found him in the act of catching the boy to have him sold. His mother, who grieved much at the sight, was told if she did not hush, her back would be cow-hided. This same man, soon after that, took her into the stable to whip her, and finding some difficulty about getting off her clothes, took his knife and cut them from her, and whipped her until she bled. Before I came away, he had sold the last one of her children. This man was N―― S――.

These are facts which cannot be denied by the persons whom I have named, and I intend to be a terror to the system while I live.

Personally, I have suffered on account of my color in regard to education. I was not allowed to go to school publicly,—had to learn privately. The reason of my coming away was, I knew that I was open to the assaults of any ruffian, if he were a white man, and if I made any reply, I was liable to nine and thirty before what they call a justice of the peace. Further, I could not educate my children there, and make them feel as women and men ought—for, under those oppressive laws, they would feel a degradation not intended by Him who made of one blood all the people of the earth.

I have been here a few weeks only—am settled as pastor over the First Baptist Church; about one hundred usually attend divine service here, most of whom have been slaves. They seem to enjoy religion and freedom very much indeed. None are desirous to return to the corn-cobs of Egypt.

At Enorn Church, Essex county, Va., colored and white meet together. On the first Sabbath in the month the colored assemble with the white pastor to attend to their church business after sermon. Sometimes a few whites are present on this Sabbath. I used to go to church regularly, but never heard them preach from, "Masters, render unto your servants that which is just and equal:" but I will write down as near as I can, (and I recollect all his points,) a sermon preached by Rev. Mr. ——, on the first Sabbath in the month, and the church proceedings.

SERMON PREACHED AT THE BAPTIST CHURCH CALLED ENORN, BY THE REV. MR. ——

Eph. 6:5. Servants, be obedient to them that are your masters according to the flesh, with fear and trembling, in singleness of your heart as unto Christ.

First,—Let me state relative to the different positions we occupy in life: I am not a lawyer, neither am I a senator, nor a judge of any court,—still I am contented, because Providence has placed me so, and I am willing to submit to his Divine will; and the Apostle tells us, that godliness with contentment is great gain.

Secondly,—Now, you brethren that suffer affliction, should endure it as good soldiers, enduring all hardness. Paul says to his son Timothy, "Let as many servants as are under the yoke count their own masters worthy of all honor, that the name of God and his doctrine be not blasphemed." And they that have believing masters, let them not despise them. These are holy injunctions, and must be adhered to. Be contented under all circumstances with singleness of heart to God, not giving railing for railing, but with fear do the will of your master. Count not your slight affliction dear, for God your Father hath so decreed from all eternity that you should suffer, and if you despise the imposition of God, you cannot enjoy his spiritual benefits.

Again,—we will have to take into consideration the base action of one of our brethren who ran away from his master. When we go into this work, you must consider the obligation that the servant is under to his master; then examine the text, and you will know that we shall be compelled to excommunicate brother Reuben Smith for running away from his master, Mr. —— ——.

Now the Deacons (colored) who are present will state the case, and we will take action on it. Deacon R——, you will state what you know about Reuben's running away.

Deacon R. Yes, Sir; I know that he ran away from his master, and so far as I know about such conduct, I believe it wrong, and can't be tolerated by us.

Minister. Will Deacon Edmund ——, come forward? State what you know about the case.

Deacon E. It is true, Sir, that Reuben ran away, and we must exclude him for it.

Minister. Now, brethren, you hear the statements of your deacons, what will you do with the case?

Deacon R. I move that we exclude brother Reuben, for running away from master.

Deacon E. I second that.

Minister. All that are in favor of that motion will hold up your right hand. It is unanimous. Well, brethren, we have done God's will, let us sing and conclude our meeting. Billy, will you sing?

> "Jerusalem, my happy home!
>   Oh, how I long for thee!
> When will my sorrows have an end,
>   My joys when shall I see?"

Receive the benediction.—May the God of peace crown our efforts with success, and save us all in the end, for the Redeemer's sake. Amen.

Reuben Smith was a preacher, and an intelligent man: that's the reason he ran away. He was caught in the city of Washington, and sold into Louisiana.

WILLIAM LYONS

I have worked in Amherstburg at joining—have worked here two years. I get 15s. York, a day. My family are in Detroit. I was free-born in Virginia, and have been ill-treated in the free States, on account of my color. I went into Columbus, Ohio, to work at my trade; I was employed in a shop. The journeymen all left the shop—wouldn't work in the shop with a colored man—wouldn't think of it. I persevered, and got employment from one who defied the prejudice of the city,—Mr. Robert Reardon. After that I found no difficulty at all, and was treated like a gentleman. The people there who had employed me wished me to remain. I own property there now.

The colored people here are industrious and doing well. They are doing as well as those in the States. There is less whiskey drinking by colored people here, than in any place I know of. They use less, in my opinion, than the whites in general.

JOSEPH SANFORD

At 10 years old I was moved to Kentucky, from Madison Co., Va. I remained in Kentucky till about 50.

My father always advised me to be tractable, and get along with the white people in the best manner I could, and not be saucy. My mother always taught me to serve the Lord—which has ever been my aim; in which I am not the least tired, and am more anxious to go forward than ever. I could almost lay down my life for an abolitionist, for had it not been for them I should have been in slavery still. I believe the Lord will bless them. They have done every thing for me, and it makes my soul melt towards them.

I recollect that my master in Virginia was a monstrous bad man, but not half so bad as some others. I recollect that my mother wanted some salt to put into bread. My mistress, whenever we came down stairs, would search our pockets, to see if we had taken any thing. I went up to get some salt for my mother, and put half a pint in my pocket. My mistress said, "Let me feel your pocket!" I was afraid and ran. She called her son to catch me, as I had got something. He caught me and punished me very heavily with a cowhide—he beat me till I was out of breath.

In Kentucky, after a few years, the old man died,—I fell to one of his daughters—she hired me out to a brother-in-law. She was very good to me. I was hired out eight years to different persons. My mistress then died. She wanted me to be set free. Some of her kinsfolks said no,—that her brother had had bad luck, and she had better will me to him. She, being bad off, being sick, and not knowing how to carry her mind,—she did so: she willed me to her brother. He kept me seven years working on the farm. He was going to move into Campbell Co. I had a wife and four children. To leave me, he swapped me for another man. I lived with him about thirteen years. He was a very clever man. He was pretty rich—a sportsman, gambler, horse-racer, etc. He came to get broke. Then we were seized and sold. J—— G—— bought me. My master was now a most cruel man. There was a great many who had a high regard for me. I was respected by everybody—could be trusted, no matter with what. I used to do his marketing, going to Cincinnati, sell his butter, flax-seed, potatoes, apples, peaches, yarn—every thing—and took every copper home. I wanted to be free, but was afraid to undertake it; for I thought if I were taken and carried back, it would be a great disgrace to me, as I was always trusted. They thought no more of trusting me with fifty or sixty dollars in their stores than with half a dollar. I made enough raising tobacco nights and Sundays to come to more than seventy or eighty dollars a year. I had always been trusty, and had been foreman on the farm.

My master concluded that he must get an overseer. The overseer made the bargain, that he was not to interfere with the hands at all—what he wanted, he was to go to the overseer, who was to order the hands. The overseer carried on very well. He kept us moving from Monday morning until noon, Saturday—then we left work until Monday. This did not suit master nor mistress—it was a little too much privilege. If the fourth of July or a holday was a Friday we had it, and Saturday afternoon as before. This troubled my master more than ever. He began to get very uneasy. I had not had a whipping for twenty years, and I said if they would put a hand on me, that I wouldn't stop any longer. The overseer observed, that he had made a rule that three boys were to make a turn about, one one Sunday, and another the next, to see things correct on the place. I had a wife at home, and was there more or less every Sunday. I always wanted to go to meeting: sometimes I would stop after meeting, but was always at home early to do the business.

The next Sunday after, the overseer was not satisfied, because none of us had stayed at home. He called me down to the barn,—he had a cow-hide under his coat. He said, why didn't you stay at home yesterday? I told him I wanted to go to church, and came home in the afternoon, after the church was out. "I told you to stay at home," said he, "and whatever I tell you to do, you've got to do it." The whipping he gave me did not hurt me so much as the scandal of it,—to whip so old a man as I was, and who had been so faithful a servant as I had been: I thought it unsufferable. This was about the time the year rolled round. The overseer's time was out, and the master took his place. I don't suppose I could tell in two hours what I went through . . . . . In the spring about the 1st of May, he had the corn ground broken up completely. Planted the corn, three of us, fifty acres. After it came up we ploughed in it before holiday. I worked hard to try to please my master. He came home and asked me, "Where have you been ploughing?" "Such and such a piece." "Is that all you've ploughed?" I told him it was. "Well," says he, "I could plough more land in one day, than you and Dave both have ploughed." It was as big a lie as ever was told, but I did not dare contradict him. The same day, he started away to buy up cattle. "Now," says he, "I'll tell you what you've got to do: you've got all this field to weed out, replant, chop all the big briers out, then go to the high-tower place, weed out that, chop out all the big briers and replant it: then go down to old Archy Rendle, and do the same there." "I can't do that," says I, "to-day and to-morrow." "I don't tell you to do it to-day and to-morrow," said he, "you've to do it against I come back, if you don't I'll thump you." He told Ben and Dave to plough the same fields over with two furrows in a row. Monday was holiday; but he said, "you must go into Monday too:" taking away our holidays, which was never done to me before.

Finding that he was going to take away our holidays,—we all resolved to break and run away, hit or miss, live or die. There were thirteen of us started away in company,—not all from his place. One of the boys went down to Covington and made the arrangements. On a Sunday night we made our break, and when we got to Covington, it was daybreak; the garrison were up, beating their drums. God was on our side, or we should have been gone. We divided at the last toll-gate. Some going through the gate and myself and little Henry going round. We then found a skiff and oars, got in the skiff and crossed the Ohio into Cincinnati. I was so afraid I'd see somebody that knew me, I knew not what to do. When I got up on Main St., I saw a great black smoke coming out of the chimney of a steamboat as if she was coming right across,—I was certain she was coming after me. I met draymen who said, "Are you travelling?" "No, I'm going up on the hill, to see my brother." My wife was nearly about to give out. "Joe," said she, "do pray stop a few minutes and let us rest." Said I, "I cannot stop,—if you want to stop you can, but I must go on." I caught her by the arm, and helped her on to the top of the hill. There I met a friend——

[Mr. Sandford's narrative was here interrupted. The concluding portion of his fortunes is luckily supplied, however, in the narrative which follows.]

JOHN HATFIELD

I am a native of Pennsylvania; and a mulatto. I was employed as a barber on a steamboat plying from New Orleans to Cincinnati. At one time, while in New Orleans, I was afraid they would take me under the law, and put me in jail. I would not conceal myself on board the boat, but went up and stayed with a friend, until I thought it time for the boat to start. But I was too soon, and came back to the boat the day before she sailed. I was arrested, ironed in the street to degrade me, and put in the jail, where I remained twenty-three hours. I found in the jail men from Boston, New York, Baltimore, and other places. There was a chain-gang in there rattling, one crazy fellow shouting—it was awful! It reminded me of the place of torment more than any thing else. In the morning the whip was cracking, starting out the chain-gang, just as one would start up horses. They measured me, and recorded my name. I had committed no crime. I never felt so degraded in my life. If I had murdered a man or stolen a horse, I could not have been treated with more contempt. A friend of mine sent a bed to the jail for me to sleep on—they would not take it in,—said I had a good bed—it was a plank and a blanket. They fed me on baked beans and pork, and charged me eleven dollars. It was a complete system of robbery. They make thousands of dollars so, out of the poor colored people. Still New Orleans used to be the best place in the Union for colored people, after they got the right of citizenship: but I am told it is getting to be harder on them now.

I was in Cincinnati when thirteen slaves reached there, running from Kentucky. They got there at seven or eight in the morning. They were questioned very closely by slave-catchers. One, pretending to be their friend, put them in a cellar, and was guarding them very closely, in order to get the reward. Among the slaves were Joseph Sanford and his wife. A few of us hearing of it, went there as quick as possible, and found the man stopping up the holes in the cellar to keep people from seeing them. I went in and asked Mrs. Sanford if she knew that man. She said, "No—never saw him before." I said, "You must get out of this." I put a comrade to watch the man, and we took them out two at a time, and hid them in various parts of the city. Their pursuers were there in less than an hour. They offered large rewards to any one who would just tell what square they were in. But the rewards would not fetch them: a million of dollars would not take a slave in Cincinnati out of some people's hands.

They stayed concealed a fortnight, and then myself and others guided them on the way to Michigan, which they reached in safety. However, they were afterwards all captured in Michigan: but they got off before a judge, and were then sent over the line into Canada.

I came into this country on account of the oppressive laws of the United States. I have as good friends in the United States, colored and white, as ever a man had,—I never expect to get so good friends again—but the *laws* were against me.

I never felt better pleased with any thing I ever did in my life, than in getting a slave woman clear, when her master was taking her from Virginia. She came on board a steamboat to Cincinnati. She had got to a friend's house in the city. Word came to my ear that too many knew where she was. I went there and told the friend; he thought she was safe. Then I went home about sundown from there, and about dark he came to me—he told me they had been there,—they came to the back door,—he wrapped her in a blanket, took her out of a front window, and took her across the street. A man asked him what he had there. "A sick man." He took her to another friend's house across the street: that house was next surrounded. I took a young man's clothes (he lived at my house) and dressed her in them,—we came out at a gate near by, we crossed over the street;—there were five or six persons then coming towards us—all I could say was, "walk heavy!" for they came right upon us. They walked with us half a square—I was scared only for her. They stopped a little—we got fifty yards ahead of them. I then told her, "they are coming again,—hold your head up, and walk straight and heavy!" By this time they were up with us again: they walked with us a whole square, looking right in her face, trying to recognize her. We came to where there was a light opposite,—I did not want to have her come to the light,—I turned the corner and said, "Come this way, Jim." She understood, and followed me. Upon this, they turned and walked away as fast as they could walk. What I said *had the effect.* I put her in a safe place, and took a turn back again: I wanted to have some fun. There were about a dozen standing at the corner, near the house where they supposed she was, talking about it. I went into a corner house,—there were several of us in there, and we went to laughing and talking about it: we did this on purpose to make fun of them. They went away to a house, and said they had seen the "nigger" dressed in men's clothes, but that they were afraid to take her, there were so many "niggers" round. There was no one with her but me, but they did not want to have it appear they were beaten so badly. We had a good deal of sport out of it,—the woman we called "Jim," as long as she stayed there. She came to the North at last. I have had fifteen runaways harbored in my house at one time—in one year, twenty-seven.

COLCHESTER

This beautiful farming town, on the northern shore of Lake Erie, contains a population not far from 1,500, of whom about 450 are colored persons.

The reeve of the town, Peter Wright, Esq., informed me that much of the land which has been opened to cultivation was cleared by fugitive slaves. They leased portions of wild land for a term of years, and by the time they had made a good clearing, they were obliged to go somewhere else. The amount of crime among them was no more than might have been expected from so ignorant and unenlightened a people. But as a whole, there is a manifest improvement in respect to honesty, and in their general deportment.

They have the same opportunity to instruct their children as is enjoyed by the whites,—that is, they draw their share of the school funds, and the trustees are bound to employ competent teachers. It would be convenient sometimes to employ teachers from the United States, but in that case they cannot draw government money.

The fugitive slave bill drove into Canada a great many who had resided in the free States: these brought some means with them, and their efforts and good example have improved the condition of the older settlers.

The town clerk of Colchester coincided in the main with Mr. Wright, but expressed himself in more positive terms on the general improvement of the colored race. They have, however, I fear, but few friends among the white settlers. "They ought to be by themselves;" "if we try to encourage them, we shall have to mix with them,"—these and similar expressions are very common. There are not many who wish to see the colored people come up to an equal rank with themselves, politically or otherwise. The True Bands even begin to form an object of groundless distrust.

Mr. Benj. Knapp, a native of the town, an intelligent farmer, and who is one of the assessors, gave me some information, which, with a few items from other sources, and the statements of the colored people themselves, will show the state of things in Colchester.

The school system is not so well organized as in some of the States, sectarianism and prejudice interfere too much: the law allows too many separate schools paid for out of the public funds.

The front part of the township along Lake Erie is well cleared up. The farms in this part belong to white settlers, native Canadians. In the interior there is yet a great deal of wild lands: to clear these up must be a work of time. Back of the cleared farms on the Lake shore, are farms owned mostly by whites, as far back as the fourth concession, with here and there a farm owned by a colored man. These farms are not generally so thoroughly nor so neatly cultivated as those of the whites; though there are some white men's farms no better than theirs.

In regard to fugitives, there is not one who cannot find work within a few hours after he gets here. There is no trouble about that: "we can't get men enough to do our work."

Beyond the fourth concession, "farms belonging to white and colored are mixed in." This is a newly settled part; it is within a few years that farmers have begun to settle there. Colored people have penetrated further into the woods than any of the whites: they are scattered all through the township up to the sixth concession. They are settled both north and south of the old Malden road: none would have ventured there but them: they are all anxious to own land: they go in anywhere they can make a claim, and clear up a patch. But their ignorance stands most wofully, and in some cases insurmountably, in their way. Instances of this sort are said to have occurred: a settler for instance takes a farm of 100 acres, appraised value $200, with ten years to pay for it in. He pays $12 a year *interest* for ten years, supposing meanwhile that he is paying up the principal. *He do n't understand it,*—and when the ten years have come round, he has not got the $200, and must leave his clearing.

The colored people send their children to school, when they have schools, and seem anxious to send their children to school. The "Colonial Church and School Society" have noted this town as a school station.

The settlement spoken of above where the colored people have "penetrated into the woods," is known as New Canaan. It is a prosperous settlement, in which the element of progress is strikingly manifest.

ROBERT NELSON

I was born in Orange county, Va. My mother was sold away from me before I can remember. I was taken from Virginia at seven, and remained there in Kentucky, in Boone county, until forty-seven. While I was in slavery, I belonged to a man who used me as he did his children, except that he gave me no education. I cannot write or read.

My master got involved, and I was mortgaged. The mortgage was out and closed,—the sheriff got after me, and I ran to Canada. I was to have been taken to a cotton farm in Louisiana. This was in April, 1845. I left without money. I had heard about the abolitionists, but was afraid of them: I thought no white men would do what they said the abolitionists would do. I had been told that they would sell us. So I was afraid to trust them. The abolitionists wanted to have a meeting to raise money for me, but I slipped out of their hands. After I got here, I found they were all true.

Some persons who wanted to betray me, told me I could not live in Canada. I came in without a shilling. I now own a house and one hundred and one acres of land. I have averaged about fifteen acres of land a year that I cultivated, having myself two thirds of the crop. This enabled me to support myself and family, and buy land. My wife belonged to another man. I sent on and bought her for $400.

It is reported throughout the world, that colored people cannot live here: I have been here ten years, and have seen no one starving yet. Any man that will work can get $10 or $12 a month, cash, and more if he takes it in trade. I can raise corn sixty or seventy bushels to the acre, as good corn as ever was raised in the South. It has been stated that the colored population are lazy, and won't work. The principal part all work. This report has been got out by begging agents, to fill their own pockets by raising money.

The prejudice is higher here in this place than in any part of Canada. It arises from a wish to keep the colored people so that they can get their labor. They used to work for the whites, but they only received half price, and cases have been known where, for ten pounds of pork, the laborer received five. The fugitive, as ignorant of figures as a hog is of holiday, had cunning enough to go to another place and get it weighed. By these means, the colored people became unwilling to work for the whites, and tried to make themselves independent. They began to take up land and work for themselves: of course the whites could not hire them. They have consequently become freeholders, and are of some consequence at the polls.

The colored people have cleared up two thirds of what has been cleared in this township. Those who came first, bought lands of individuals and lost them again: but when they began to buy of the government, they began to have good claims on the land.

Some, when they first came, would take a lease of a few acres of wild land, for six or seven years. By the time they had got it cleared, and removed some of the stumps, the lease was out. Then the white man said, "you can't have that piece any more,—you must go back in the bush." They found they must do different from this. They began to work on the land for themselves, and to get farms of their own. Now because the white men cannot hire them, they say the colored people won't work.

They say, too, that the colored people steal. It may be that a few are a little light-fingered, they take, perhaps, a few small articles, and the greatest mischief is, it scandalizes us. What two or three bad fellows do, prejudice lays to the whole of us. But some white men have stolen on the credit of the colored. It is very easy to say when a thing is missed,—"O, 'tis some colored man stole it,"—although, it has, to my knowledge, been proved, that when theft was charged on a colored man, it turned out that a white man did it.

There is a settlement here called New Canaan, where was a large body of wild land. Colored people went in and took it up at one hundred acres apiece. I guess there may be now forty families. [In 1852, there were twenty families.] They paid the first instalment, and had ten years to pay in. But three quarters of them have already paid the whole price, and got the deeds, and are making good improvements on their lands, making enough to support their families. The preaching of the gospel is regularly kept up.

My wish to the people of the States is, to give no more money to the begging agencies. If they wish to give money to the fugitives and the sick, it should be given to the True Band societies, who can disburse it as it is wanted. The Band will attend to the fugitives.

DAVID GRIER

I was born free in Maryland,—was stolen and sold in Kentucky, when between eight and nine years old. In Kentucky I was set free by will, and as they were trying to break the will up, some of my claimant's friends persuaded me to come off to Ohio. From Ohio, I came here on account of the oppressive laws demanding security for good behavior,—I was a stranger and could not give it. I had to leave my family in Kentucky.

I came in 1831. I have cleared land on lease for five or six years, then have to leave it, and go into the bush again. I worked so about thirteen years. I could do no better, and the white people, I believe, took advantage of it to get the land cleared. This has kept me poor. I guess I have cleared not short of seventy or eighty acres, and got no benefit. I have now six acres cleared.

EPHRAIM WATERFORD

I was born free; was bound until twenty-one, in Virginia. The man I was bound out to, was to teach me to read and write, but did not—never gave me any education at all.

I came into Indiana in the spring that James K. Polk was made President. I stayed there till about two years ago. I left on account of oppression in Indiana. I had a farm there of forty acres paid for, and I had the deed. A law was passed that a colored man could not devise real estate to his wife and children, and there were other equally unjust laws enacted. I told them "if that was a republican government, I would try a monarchical one." Between thirty and forty of us, little and big, came over at the same time. I have a farm here of two hundred acres wild land: I have five acres under fence in corn now. E. Casey and S. Casey came over at the same time. They are doing first-rate. Both have farms on the 1st concession—I think between twenty-five and thirty acres under fence together.

There is prejudice right smart in some places in this town. We try to live as upright as we can, get a little stock, etc. The whites can easily hire any colored man who has no work to do for himself. A great many are doing hired work about the town to-day—hired more by white men than by colored, the white being more able. I intend to give my child as good an education as I can.

ELI ARTIS

I have twenty-five acres of land, bought and paid for,—about eight acres cleared. I am often hired out, and never refuse to work where I can get my pay, and have often worked when I got no pay. The colored people are industrious, and if any say they are not willing to work, it is a lie, and I'll say so, and sign my name to it.

I suffered from mean, oppressive laws in my native State, Ohio, or I would not have been in this country. I have lived here fourteen years.

EPHRAIM CASEY

I am from the State of Georgia, where I was born free. But the laws were not better about learning for a free man than for a slave. I was never sent to school in my life. My opportunities for religious information were poor. I am now a member of the Methodist Church. At about twenty-three, I emigrated to Indiana, carrying no property. In Indiana, I attended to farming. I had a farm there, and when I left, owned one hundred and eighteen acres. I left on principle—on account of the laws. I like the country very well. The laws bore hard on me before I came away—I had a case in law, and could not prove my side good by the evidence of colored men, which caused me a loss of fifty or sixty dollars. I did not feel disposed to stand this, and emigrated into Canada.

I settled in Colchester, where I bought out a white settler, land and stock, for seven hundred and fifty dollars. The farm was sixty acres, one half improved: seventeen head of hogs, and five head of cattle. There was no good water there. He had dug in a few places, but got no supply. I sunk a well twenty-eight feet, and the water now rises and runs over the surface, a stream eighteen inches deep; enough to supply water for a steam saw-mill. I have growing eight or ten acres of corn, five or six in wheat, two or three in oats, some potatoes, and other vegetables. The land is better than where I was in Indiana.

I moved in, two years ago last May. I have hired colored men to work for me whenever I wanted their help, and have seen them hired by others: but they prefer, so far as I know, to work for themselves, and to get an independent living.

REV. WILLIAM RUTH

I am a native of Bourbon county, Ky., left there at twenty-seven, and have resided principally in Colchester since 1825.

I never met with any rough usage in slavery. It was expected that I would be set at liberty at thirty-one, by the will of my former master; but as there was supposed to be a disposition not to give me a fair chance, I was assisted off by a man who was a slaveholder himself. There are a great many such movements there.

I was young when I left there, but often saw separations of families by sales and by hiring. I happened to fall to an Irishman, who was a good sort of a man—an extraordinary man for a slaveholder—in advance of all the county for kindness to his slaves.

I have fifty acres of land under fence, and had it all cleared and improved years ago. It is well supplied with water. I have an orchard with a good assortment of fruits—apples, pears, and peaches. It is one of the best farms in Colchester. I own seventy acres besides in New Canaan.

New Canaan is going to be one of the finest and most beautiful places. It has every advantage necessary to make it a fine settlement. It is covered with heavy timber, and has a first-rate soil. The settlers are doing extraordinarily for the time they have been there.

The colored people have their inferior class as well as other people; I mean a careless, loafing, negligent, vicious class—and they have their turn in prison, like other persons of that sort. We don't claim to be better than other pople, but we claim to be as good.

In regard to education, we are destitute of it, as a general thing. But the prospect is advancing. The government schools are kept up. The rising generation are improving.

My candid opinion in regard to raising money in the United States for fugitives is, that they should have an agent here whom they can place confidence in, and have him expend it under the direction of a committee of white men belonging to the province. I would have the board white, in order to bring the races more to an understanding and better feeling towards each other; another reason is, that the colored population have not generally had the opportunity to learn how to transact business. They might, as they improve, be placed on the board.

The society over which I am placed, is connected with the Wesley or New Connexion in Canada. I preach every Sabbath, generally two or three times a day. They pay good attention to religion, and as a general thing are a moral people. The laws of chastity are well observed: in this they excel the whites.

GOSFIELD

Numbers nearly 2,600 inhabitants. The whole colored population, by actual count, is 78.

Of the heads of families, all but two or three are freeholders, and some of them have very good farms. James King, Esq., Clerk of the Courts for the County of Essex, C. W., thus characterized the colored people of Gosfield: "They are good, loyal subjects, and good, honest people. They are as moral as any people. There is no fault to be found with them at all."

JOHN CHAPMAN

I was originally from Kentucky, but removed into Indiana at fourteen. I did not feel safe in Indiana, and removed with my family into Canada at Gosfield. Then it was pretty much all bush. The farmers raised but little more than they wanted themselves. One raises as much now as twenty did then. It was hard to get a start when I came to this country.

There are now seventy-eight men, women, and children: when I came there were but three colored. We live like rich folks, but when we came I was almost discouraged.

They are generally getting along as well as could be expected. All make a good living. Most of them own houses and land. They generally attend divine service, and send their children to school when it is open. It is not kept up in the summer.

THOMAS JOHNSON

I was raised in Virginia, which I left with my master for Kentucky, at the age of twenty-one. Twenty years after we moved, my master died, and I remained with my mistress taking care of the farm. I used to take a great deal of care of the place, seeing to the farming operations, and have been to Cincinnati to sell produce. The people all considered me trustworthy and honorable, and some of the white people said I could make greater crops than they could.

I had a wife and several children on a neighboring farm. She wished to leave for Canada, with the three youngest children. I gave her money and she got away into Canada safe enough. As soon as she was gone, I was seized and put in jail—her owners said, if they shut up the hen they could soon find the chickens. They asked me in the jail, "if I knew she was going?" I asked them "if they knew the height and size of my wife?" They said they did. "Well," I told them, "that is my life—and if your wife has done as many pretty things for you, as mine has for me, wouldn't you be willing to give her a little money to help her?" In a few days, I was let out. I still continued on the farm attending faithfully to my work—but my mistress' friends, suspecting that when she died, I would run off to rejoin my wife, persuaded her to sell me. One day, eighteen months after my wife left, I was sent for to the house. I went in, and asked my mistress what was wanting. "Oh, dear!" said she, "I don't know, Thomas." But I know what 'twas for. Said I, "When our Saviour was on earth, they could make out nothing against him, till they got false witnesses,—and there are false witnesses against me."

I was kept at the house that night, in charge of three men, but was not put into strict confinement. The next morning, one of them produced a pair of handcuffs connected with a long chain, and said, "we must put these on, Thomas." I said, "You will not put them on to me,—I have done nothing for which I should wear such things as them." "I'll tell you the truth, Thomas," said he, "we are going to send you down the river."

I was sitting at the grunsel, and as I sat, I carefully slipped off my boots, then jumped up and ran for the woods. They ran after me a short distance. I had thirty-five dollars in my coat pocket, which came in the way, running. I held it up in my hand, and as I did so, turned to look behind me. My mistress' son was at a fence, and he called out, "Thomas! o-o-h, Tho-o-mas!" pitifully. No one was now following me. I hid in the woods. I could not realize it—I sat down on a stump, and said to myself, "isn't this a dream?" I could not realize that *I* had done such a thing as to run away—it seemed so *low*. I—that had always been trusted, and had served faithfully—to be a *runaway* at last.

That night, I crossed the river to Cincinnati. From this place I sent a letter to a man in Kentucky, that if he would buy me, I would return and live with him. He showed the letter to my folks, and they wrote me to come back, promising a great many things. My letter was dated Cleveland, but I was in Cincinnati. I thought as I was now away from them, I might as well go on to Canada. I aimed for Toronto, but on my way fell in with a man on board the boat, who knew where my wife and children lived in Malden. I went there and joined them: and since that time, three others of my children have made their escape and are here.

I hired a piece of land in Malden for three years. It was not cleared,—I cleared it: then my lease was up, and I rented a farm fifty dollars a year for five years. When I took it, the fence was down. I fixed it up, and cleared more. Then I told my folks that I would have a piece of land of my own. They thought I could not pay for it. I told them if they put a piece of ice on a log in the sun, they would see the ice melt away,—so, said I, our strength is melting away. I took a piece of fifty acres, six acres cleared, at five dollars an acre, and I have got the clear deed of it. Others have done the same, and are doing it now. I don't want anybody to beg for me in the United States.

ELI JOHNSON

In slavery, we are goods and chattels, and have no surname: but slaves generally take their master's name.

I was born and raised in old Virginia, Orange Co., till I was thirty. My treatment there was only middling. After thirty, I was sold to a trader, and carried to Natchez. I was then sold at auction for $1,200,—put on a cotton farm, and allowed a peck of corn a week and three pounds meat,—was called sometimes an hour to day, sometimes less,—must be on hand else got the whip. If there was deemed sufficient cause, if there was any word, or the least thing they did not like, the man was staked down for four hundred lashes. I saw a man staked down and whipped one Sunday, until the blood lay in a pool on each side of him. It was through the fear of the Lord, that I endured the persecution put upon me,—I suffered a great deal there,—and but for the fear of the Lord and the worth of my own soul, I should have murdered the overseer. When I first went it was a warm climate: I had to drink the muddy water of the river, which made me sick and weakened me down. Every day I was threatened with seven hundred and fifty lashes, if I complained of being sick. I had to keep on: being of strong constitution I began to mend, and endured all they put on me for six years.

My wife was with me, and was made to suffer worse than I. I was in constant fear of the lash, but made out to plead off, although the whipping seemed to be sometimes, just to keep their hand in. Many men and women were punished with a paddle and whip. I had to make paddles with twelve holes in them. A block lay in the cotton yard over which they were placed to be paddled. I saw them take one man and paddle him, then they struck him with a handsaw, then with a bull whip: then they ordered me to lock the biggest log chain I could find on the place around his neck with the biggest lock, and keep him at my house until next morning. I went out in the field leaving him at the house, not believing him able to get out. The overseer gave me so many minutes to go and get him. I went back for him, and met him hobbling along with the chain. He had to work at chopping wood. Three weeks he wore the chain: then myself and another bailed him, and the chain was taken off: if he had run away, we were to wear the chain. Three days after the whipping, he was allowed no food. We gave him some of ours, but did not dare let it be known.

The whipping was because he ran away. He ran away, because the overseer appropriated his wife. The man threatened to do something about it,—the overseer threatened him with a whipping,—then he ran away. I know all this,—I saw the treatment with my own eyes. E—— was the overseer's name,—he stayed there three years.

While under E——, I was put on short allowance of food and made to work on the Sabbath, etc. I was then a professor and used to hold prayer-meetings Saturday night. One Saturday night, during meeting,

E—— sent for me. I went to him. He told me to stay until he had eaten breakfast next morning, then he would stake me down and give me five hundred lashes; for he wouldn't have such things as meetings carried on. I managed to slip off, and went to the cabins. I went back to him next morning while he was at breakfast: his wife was facing me, he was back to me. She pointed at me, and said, "there he is." I clapped my hands together and said, "In the name of God why is it, that I can't after working hard all the week, have a meeting on Saturday evening? I am sent for to receive five hundred lashes for trying to serve God. I'll suffer the flesh to be dragged off my bones, until my bones stare my enemy in the face, for the sake of my blessed Redeemer." He did not come to me,—he appeared startled at my appearance. He went into the house from the porch, got his gun and walked away. After he had gone I walked away.

I think the reason he did not punish me was, that once when it got to me that he said he would whip me, and his wife wished he would, I had said,—"If he whips me, I'll put him and his wife in hot water." I knew that he had been intimate with some of the slave women. He told me at one time to leave my cabin door, so he could get in, in the night, on account of one of two girls that were there. I left the door on the latch, and warned the girl. He came—but she struggled against him, got away, and came to the bed where were I and my wife. His wife heard what I said about "hot water," and sent for me, making an excuse about a partition. She placed a chair near me, "Well, Eli," she says, "what's that you was going to put me and my husband in hot water for?" I tried to turn it off. She insisted, and at last got mad because I wouldn't tell her, and said she'd make him make me tell. He made her believe, that he would make me tell, and he told me that he wouldn't for his right arm have his wife know. So I knew what grounds I stood on, and kept clear of the lash.

The next overseer was S——. He kicked a woman's eye out, the first day he came there. He asked her a question in the gin-house, which she did not understand. She said "No, Sir," at a venture. The answer was wrong—she was stooping down, and he kicked her face. It put her eye out. He went to the house for something to put on it. She cried out aloud. Said he, "Shut up! I've killed a great many better looking niggers than you, and thrown 'em in the bayou." This I heard him say myself. Nothing was done about the loss of the eye: the woman's husband dared say nothing about it. In three weeks' time, S—— whipped three women and nine men. The talk in the quarters was among some to put him to death; others were afraid to try it. He left before the month was up; another named W—— was then overseer.

He went on rather roughly. There had been an underhanded business done in selling cattle and wood off the place, from which master had no benefit, in consequence of which, I was privately made a sort of watchman over the place.

After W——, the next overseer, was my master's brother. At the end of two years, they fell out about settling—the master said he was broke: they drew knives, threatening each other, but did not use them. Master said he would take the best slaves off the place, and then sell the place, with the sorriest ones on it. Then he said he couldn't pay his brother in money, but his brother might take it in slaves. The brother picked out myself, wife, and two children and two others, which was too many. Master objected—then they drew the knives. Master gave him me, wife, and children. At night, fearing he might take the others, he took them himself, to his upper place, where he lived above Natchez.

My new master removed us to Kentucky. We were all the slaves he had. We raised tobacco, oats, etc. I considered my treatment worse than at any other place. They gave me great encouragement to come with them, promising me well. Among other things, he promised to pay me $10.25, earned by me at overwork chopping. After I got to Kentucky, I wanted a hat. I went and picked one out, and told the shopman I'd get the money of my master. I sent his son in to ask for it. He sent me word that if I mentioned money again, or told any person that he owed it, he would give me *five hundred lashes!* A while after, I asked him to *give* me a little money. "What do you want of money?" "To buy me a hat." "Isn't that hat good enough?" "It don't turn the water, and I see the colored people wearing respectable hats, and I want one to wear to meeting." He said "go to such a place, get a wool hat, and have it charged to me." I went and got it,—it was a poor thing, and cost one dollar. I did what he wanted as well as I could, to avoid punishment. I staid with him three years.

One day he had ordered me to draw some water on a sled: then he called me into the field. I stooped down to unloose a chain,—he hurried up to me with an axe in his hand. He says, "When I want you for one thing, you are sure to do another." I answered, "I've got to work till I die, and had as lief work at one thing as another." He threatened me with the axe—I didn't dodge. Then he threatened me that he would give me the five hundred lashes before many days. I thought he might finally undertake it, and that I'd better be off. I received assistance from kind friends, and reached Canada without difficulty about five years ago. I have had a serious time in my life.

I felt so thankful on reaching a land of freedom, that I couldn't express myself. When I look back at what I endured, it seems as if I had entered a Paradise. I can here sing and pray with none to molest me. I am a member of the Baptist Church, and endeavor to live a Christian life.

I rent a piece of land, and make out to live. My family are sickly, so that I have not been able to purchase land. But I am not discouraged, and intend to work on while I have health and strength, and to live such a life as I should wish when I come to die.

A CATALOG OF SELECTED
DOVER BOOKS
IN ALL FIELDS OF INTEREST

A CATALOG OF SELECTED DOVER
BOOKS IN ALL FIELDS OF INTEREST

CONCERNING THE SPIRITUAL IN ART, Wassily Kandinsky. Pioneering work by father of abstract art. Thoughts on color theory, nature of art. Analysis of earlier masters. 12 illustrations. 80pp. of text. 5⅜ x 8½. 23411-8

ANIMALS: 1,419 Copyright-Free Illustrations of Mammals, Birds, Fish, Insects, etc., Jim Harter (ed.). Clear wood engravings present, in extremely lifelike poses, over 1,000 species of animals. One of the most extensive pictorial sourcebooks of its kind. Captions. Index. 284pp. 9 x 12. 23766-4

CELTIC ART: The Methods of Construction, George Bain. Simple geometric techniques for making Celtic interlacements, spirals, Kells-type initials, animals, humans, etc. Over 500 illustrations. 160pp. 9 x 12. (Available in U.S. only.) 22923-8

AN ATLAS OF ANATOMY FOR ARTISTS, Fritz Schider. Most thorough reference work on art anatomy in the world. Hundreds of illustrations, including selections from works by Vesalius, Leonardo, Goya, Ingres, Michelangelo, others. 593 illustrations. 192pp. 7⅛ x 10¼. 20241-0

CELTIC HAND STROKE-BY-STROKE (Irish Half-Uncial from "The Book of Kells"): An Arthur Baker Calligraphy Manual, Arthur Baker. Complete guide to creating each letter of the alphabet in distinctive Celtic manner. Covers hand position, strokes, pens, inks, paper, more. Illustrated. 48pp. 8¼ x 11. 24336-2

EASY ORIGAMI, John Montroll. Charming collection of 32 projects (hat, cup, pelican, piano, swan, many more) specially designed for the novice origami hobbyist. Clearly illustrated easy-to-follow instructions insure that even beginning papercrafters will achieve successful results. 48pp. 8¼ x 11. 27298-2

THE COMPLETE BOOK OF BIRDHOUSE CONSTRUCTION FOR WOODWORKERS, Scott D. Campbell. Detailed instructions, illustrations, tables. Also data on bird habitat and instinct patterns. Bibliography. 3 tables. 63 illustrations in 15 figures. 48pp. 5¼ x 8½. 24407-5

BLOOMINGDALE'S ILLUSTRATED 1886 CATALOG: Fashions, Dry Goods and Housewares, Bloomingdale Brothers. Famed merchants' extremely rare catalog depicting about 1,700 products: clothing, housewares, firearms, dry goods, jewelry, more. Invaluable for dating, identifying vintage items. Also, copyright-free graphics for artists, designers. Co-published with Henry Ford Museum & Greenfield Village. 160pp. 8¼ x 11. 25780-0

HISTORIC COSTUME IN PICTURES, Braun & Schneider. Over 1,450 costumed figures in clearly detailed engravings–from dawn of civilization to end of 19th century. Captions. Many folk costumes. 256pp. 8⅜ x 11¾. 23150-X

STICKLEY CRAFTSMAN FURNITURE CATALOGS, Gustav Stickley and L. & J. G. Stickley. Beautiful, functional furniture in two authentic catalogs from 1910. 594 illustrations, including 277 photos, show settles, rockers, armchairs, reclining chairs, bookcases, desks, tables. 183pp. 6½ x 9¼.   23838-5

AMERICAN LOCOMOTIVES IN HISTORIC PHOTOGRAPHS: 1858 to 1949, Ron Ziel (ed.). A rare collection of 126 meticulously detailed official photographs, called "builder portraits," of American locomotives that majestically chronicle the rise of steam locomotive power in America. Introduction. Detailed captions. xi+ 129pp. 9 x 12.   27393-8

AMERICA'S LIGHTHOUSES: An Illustrated History, Francis Ross Holland, Jr. Delightfully written, profusely illustrated fact-filled survey of over 200 American lighthouses since 1716. History, anecdotes, technological advances, more. 240pp. 8 x 10¾.
                                                                        25576-X

TOWARDS A NEW ARCHITECTURE, Le Corbusier. Pioneering manifesto by founder of "International School." Technical and aesthetic theories, views of industry, economics, relation of form to function, "mass-production split" and much more. Profusely illustrated. 320pp. 6⅛ x 9¼. (Available in U.S. only.)   25023-7

HOW THE OTHER HALF LIVES, Jacob Riis. Famous journalistic record, exposing poverty and degradation of New York slums around 1900, by major social reformer. 100 striking and influential photographs. 233pp. 10 x 7⅞.   22012-5

FRUIT KEY AND TWIG KEY TO TREES AND SHRUBS, William M. Harlow. One of the handiest and most widely used identification aids. Fruit key covers 120 deciduous and evergreen species; twig key 160 deciduous species. Easily used. Over 300 photographs. 126pp. 5⅜ x 8½.   20511-8

COMMON BIRD SONGS, Dr. Donald J. Borror. Songs of 60 most common U.S. birds: robins, sparrows, cardinals, bluejays, finches, more—arranged in order of increasing complexity. Up to 9 variations of songs of each species.
                                                    Cassette and manual 99911-4

ORCHIDS AS HOUSE PLANTS, Rebecca Tyson Northen. Grow cattleyas and many other kinds of orchids—in a window, in a case, or under artificial light. 63 illustrations. 148pp. 5⅜ x 8½.   23261-1

MONSTER MAZES, Dave Phillips. Masterful mazes at four levels of difficulty. Avoid deadly perils and evil creatures to find magical treasures. Solutions for all 32 exciting illustrated puzzles. 48pp. 8¼ x 11.   26005-4

MOZART'S DON GIOVANNI (DOVER OPERA LIBRETTO SERIES), Wolfgang Amadeus Mozart. Introduced and translated by Ellen H. Bleiler. Standard Italian libretto, with complete English translation. Convenient and thoroughly portable—an ideal companion for reading along with a recording or the performance itself. Introduction. List of characters. Plot summary. 121pp. 5¼ x 8½.   24944-1

TECHNICAL MANUAL AND DICTIONARY OF CLASSICAL BALLET, Gail Grant. Defines, explains, comments on steps, movements, poses and concepts. 15-page pictorial section. Basic book for student, viewer. 127pp. 5⅜ x 8½.   21843-0

THE CLARINET AND CLARINET PLAYING, David Pino. Lively, comprehensive work features suggestions about technique, musicianship, and musical interpretation, as well as guidelines for teaching, making your own reeds, and preparing for public performance. Includes an intriguing look at clarinet history. "A godsend," *The Clarinet,* Journal of the International Clarinet Society. Appendixes. 7 illus. 320pp. 5$\frac{3}{8}$ x 8$\frac{1}{2}$. 40270-3

HOLLYWOOD GLAMOR PORTRAITS, John Kobal (ed.). 145 photos from 1926-49. Harlow, Gable, Bogart, Bacall; 94 stars in all. Full background on photographers, technical aspects. 160pp. 8$\frac{3}{8}$ x 11$\frac{1}{4}$. 23352-9

THE ANNOTATED CASEY AT THE BAT: A Collection of Ballads about the Mighty Casey/Third, Revised Edition, Martin Gardner (ed.). Amusing sequels and parodies of one of America's best-loved poems: Casey's Revenge, Why Casey Whiffed, Casey's Sister at the Bat, others. 256pp. 5$\frac{3}{8}$ x 8$\frac{1}{2}$. 28598-7

THE RAVEN AND OTHER FAVORITE POEMS, Edgar Allan Poe. Over 40 of the author's most memorable poems: "The Bells," "Ulalume," "Israfel," "To Helen," "The Conqueror Worm," "Eldorado," "Annabel Lee," many more. Alphabetic lists of titles and first lines. 64pp. 5$\frac{3}{16}$ x 8$\frac{1}{4}$. 26685-0

PERSONAL MEMOIRS OF U. S. GRANT, Ulysses Simpson Grant. Intelligent, deeply moving firsthand account of Civil War campaigns, considered by many the finest military memoirs ever written. Includes letters, historic photographs, maps and more. 528pp. 6$\frac{1}{8}$ x 9$\frac{1}{4}$. 28587-1

ANCIENT EGYPTIAN MATERIALS AND INDUSTRIES, A. Lucas and J. Harris. Fascinating, comprehensive, thoroughly documented text describes this ancient civilization's vast resources and the processes that incorporated them in daily life, including the use of animal products, building materials, cosmetics, perfumes and incense, fibers, glazed ware, glass and its manufacture, materials used in the mummification process, and much more. 544pp. 6$\frac{1}{8}$ x 9$\frac{1}{4}$. (Available in U.S. only.) 40446-3

RUSSIAN STORIES/RUSSKIE RASSKAZY: A Dual-Language Book, edited by Gleb Struve. Twelve tales by such masters as Chekhov, Tolstoy, Dostoevsky, Pushkin, others. Excellent word-for-word English translations on facing pages, plus teaching and study aids, Russian/English vocabulary, biographical/critical introductions, more. 416pp. 5$\frac{3}{8}$ x 8$\frac{1}{2}$. 26244-8

PHILADELPHIA THEN AND NOW: 60 Sites Photographed in the Past and Present, Kenneth Finkel and Susan Oyama. Rare photographs of City Hall, Logan Square, Independence Hall, Betsy Ross House, other landmarks juxtaposed with contemporary views. Captures changing face of historic city. Introduction. Captions. 128pp. 8$\frac{1}{4}$ x 11. 25790-8

AIA ARCHITECTURAL GUIDE TO NASSAU AND SUFFOLK COUNTIES, LONG ISLAND, The American Institute of Architects, Long Island Chapter, and the Society for the Preservation of Long Island Antiquities. Comprehensive, well-researched and generously illustrated volume brings to life over three centuries of Long Island's great architectural heritage. More than 240 photographs with authoritative, extensively detailed captions. 176pp. 8$\frac{1}{4}$ x 11. 26946-9

NORTH AMERICAN INDIAN LIFE: Customs and Traditions of 23 Tribes, Elsie Clews Parsons (ed.). 27 fictionalized essays by noted anthropologists examine religion, customs, government, additional facets of life among the Winnebago, Crow, Zuni, Eskimo, other tribes. 480pp. 6$\frac{1}{8}$ x 9$\frac{1}{4}$. 27377-6

FRANK LLOYD WRIGHT'S DANA HOUSE, Donald Hoffmann. Pictorial essay of residential masterpiece with over 160 interior and exterior photos, plans, elevations, sketches and studies. 128pp. 9¼ x 10¾.   29120-0

THE MALE AND FEMALE FIGURE IN MOTION: 60 Classic Photographic Sequences, Eadweard Muybridge. 60 true-action photographs of men and women walking, running, climbing, bending, turning, etc., reproduced from rare 19th-century masterpiece. vi + 121pp. 9 x 12.   24745-7

1001 QUESTIONS ANSWERED ABOUT THE SEASHORE, N. J. Berrill and Jacquelyn Berrill. Queries answered about dolphins, sea snails, sponges, starfish, fishes, shore birds, many others. Covers appearance, breeding, growth, feeding, much more. 305pp. 5¼ x 8¼.   23366-9

ATTRACTING BIRDS TO YOUR YARD, William J. Weber. Easy-to-follow guide offers advice on how to attract the greatest diversity of birds: birdhouses, feeders, water and waterers, much more. 96pp. 5³⁄₁₆ x 8¼.   28927-3

MEDICINAL AND OTHER USES OF NORTH AMERICAN PLANTS: A Historical Survey with Special Reference to the Eastern Indian Tribes, Charlotte Erichsen-Brown. Chronological historical citations document 500 years of usage of plants, trees, shrubs native to eastern Canada, northeastern U.S. Also complete identifying information. 343 illustrations. 544pp. 6½ x 9¼.   25951-X

STORYBOOK MAZES, Dave Phillips. 23 stories and mazes on two-page spreads: Wizard of Oz, Treasure Island, Robin Hood, etc. Solutions. 64pp. 8¼ x 11. 23628-5

AMERICAN NEGRO SONGS: 230 Folk Songs and Spirituals, Religious and Secular, John W. Work. This authoritative study traces the African influences of songs sung and played by black Americans at work, in church, and as entertainment. The author discusses the lyric significance of such songs as "Swing Low, Sweet Chariot," "John Henry," and others and offers the words and music for 230 songs. Bibliography. Index of Song Titles. 272pp. 6½ x 9¼.   40271-1

MOVIE-STAR PORTRAITS OF THE FORTIES, John Kobal (ed.). 163 glamor, studio photos of 106 stars of the 1940s: Rita Hayworth, Ava Gardner, Marlon Brando, Clark Gable, many more. 176pp. 8⅜ x 11¼.   23546-7

BENCHLEY LOST AND FOUND, Robert Benchley. Finest humor from early 30s, about pet peeves, child psychologists, post office and others. Mostly unavailable elsewhere. 73 illustrations by Peter Arno and others. 183pp. 5⅜ x 8½.   22410-4

YEKL and THE IMPORTED BRIDEGROOM AND OTHER STORIES OF YIDDISH NEW YORK, Abraham Cahan. Film Hester Street based on *Yekl* (1896). Novel, other stories among first about Jewish immigrants on N.Y.'s East Side. 240pp. 5⅜ x 8½.   22427-9

SELECTED POEMS, Walt Whitman. Generous sampling from *Leaves of Grass*. Twenty-four poems include "I Hear America Singing," "Song of the Open Road," "I Sing the Body Electric," "When Lilacs Last in the Dooryard Bloom'd," "O Captain! My Captain!"—all reprinted from an authoritative edition. Lists of titles and first lines. 128pp. 5³⁄₁₆ x 8¼.   26878-0

THE BEST TALES OF HOFFMANN, E. T. A. Hoffmann. 10 of Hoffmann's most important stories: "Nutcracker and the King of Mice," "The Golden Flowerpot," etc. 458pp. 5⅜ x 8½. 21793-0

FROM FETISH TO GOD IN ANCIENT EGYPT, E. A. Wallis Budge. Rich detailed survey of Egyptian conception of "God" and gods, magic, cult of animals, Osiris, more. Also, superb English translations of hymns and legends. 240 illustrations. 545pp. 5⅜ x 8½. 25803-3

FRENCH STORIES/CONTES FRANÇAIS: A Dual-Language Book, Wallace Fowlie. Ten stories by French masters, Voltaire to Camus: "Micromegas" by Voltaire; "The Atheist's Mass" by Balzac; "Minuet" by de Maupassant; "The Guest" by Camus, six more. Excellent English translations on facing pages. Also French-English vocabulary list, exercises, more. 352pp. 5⅜ x 8½. 26443-2

CHICAGO AT THE TURN OF THE CENTURY IN PHOTOGRAPHS: 122 Historic Views from the Collections of the Chicago Historical Society, Larry A. Viskochil. Rare large-format prints offer detailed views of City Hall, State Street, the Loop, Hull House, Union Station, many other landmarks, circa 1904-1913. Introduction. Captions. Maps. 144pp. 9⅜ x 12¼. 24656-6

OLD BROOKLYN IN EARLY PHOTOGRAPHS, 1865-1929, William Lee Younger. Luna Park, Gravesend race track, construction of Grand Army Plaza, moving of Hotel Brighton, etc. 157 previously unpublished photographs. 165pp. 8⅞ x 11¾. 23587-4

THE MYTHS OF THE NORTH AMERICAN INDIANS, Lewis Spence. Rich anthology of the myths and legends of the Algonquins, Iroquois, Pawnees and Sioux, prefaced by an extensive historical and ethnological commentary. 36 illustrations. 480pp. 5⅜ x 8½. 25967-6

AN ENCYCLOPEDIA OF BATTLES: Accounts of Over 1,560 Battles from 1479 B.C. to the Present, David Eggenberger. Essential details of every major battle in recorded history from the first battle of Megiddo in 1479 B.C. to Grenada in 1984. List of Battle Maps. New Appendix covering the years 1967-1984. Index. 99 illustrations. 544pp. 6½ x 9¼. 24913-1

SAILING ALONE AROUND THE WORLD, Captain Joshua Slocum. First man to sail around the world, alone, in small boat. One of great feats of seamanship told in delightful manner. 67 illustrations. 294pp. 5⅜ x 8½. 20326-3

ANARCHISM AND OTHER ESSAYS, Emma Goldman. Powerful, penetrating, prophetic essays on direct action, role of minorities, prison reform, puritan hypocrisy, violence, etc. 271pp. 5⅜ x 8½. 22484-8

MYTHS OF THE HINDUS AND BUDDHISTS, Ananda K. Coomaraswamy and Sister Nivedita. Great stories of the epics; deeds of Krishna, Shiva, taken from puranas, Vedas, folk tales; etc. 32 illustrations. 400pp. 5⅜ x 8½. 21759-0

THE TRAUMA OF BIRTH, Otto Rank. Rank's controversial thesis that anxiety neurosis is caused by profound psychological trauma which occurs at birth. 256pp. 5⅜ x 8½. 27974-X

A THEOLOGICO-POLITICAL TREATISE, Benedict Spinoza. Also contains unfinished Political Treatise. Great classic on religious liberty, theory of government on common consent. R. Elwes translation. Total of 421pp. 5⅜ x 8½. 20249-6

MY BONDAGE AND MY FREEDOM, Frederick Douglass. Born a slave, Douglass became outspoken force in antislavery movement. The best of Douglass' autobiographies. Graphic description of slave life. 464pp. 5⅜ x 8½. 22457-0

FOLLOWING THE EQUATOR: A Journey Around the World, Mark Twain. Fascinating humorous account of 1897 voyage to Hawaii, Australia, India, New Zealand, etc. Ironic, bemused reports on peoples, customs, climate, flora and fauna, politics, much more. 197 illustrations. 720pp. 5⅜ x 8½. 26113-1

THE PEOPLE CALLED SHAKERS, Edward D. Andrews. Definitive study of Shakers: origins, beliefs, practices, dances, social organization, furniture and crafts, etc. 33 illustrations. 351pp. 5⅜ x 8½. 21081-2

THE MYTHS OF GREECE AND ROME, H. A. Guerber. A classic of mythology, generously illustrated, long prized for its simple, graphic, accurate retelling of the principal myths of Greece and Rome, and for its commentary on their origins and significance. With 64 illustrations by Michelangelo, Raphael, Titian, Rubens, Canova, Bernini and others. 480pp. 5⅜ x 8½. 27584-1

PSYCHOLOGY OF MUSIC, Carl E. Seashore. Classic work discusses music as a medium from psychological viewpoint. Clear treatment of physical acoustics, auditory apparatus, sound perception, development of musical skills, nature of musical feeling, host of other topics. 88 figures. 408pp. 5⅜ x 8½. 21851-1

THE PHILOSOPHY OF HISTORY, Georg W. Hegel. Great classic of Western thought develops concept that history is not chance but rational process, the evolution of freedom. 457pp. 5⅜ x 8½. 20112-0

THE BOOK OF TEA, Kakuzo Okakura. Minor classic of the Orient: entertaining, charming explanation, interpretation of traditional Japanese culture in terms of tea ceremony. 94pp. 5⅜ x 8½. 20070-1

LIFE IN ANCIENT EGYPT, Adolf Erman. Fullest, most thorough, detailed older account with much not in more recent books, domestic life, religion, magic, medicine, commerce, much more. Many illustrations reproduce tomb paintings, carvings, hieroglyphs, etc. 597pp. 5⅜ x 8½. 22632-8

SUNDIALS, Their Theory and Construction, Albert Waugh. Far and away the best, most thorough coverage of ideas, mathematics concerned, types, construction, adjusting anywhere. Simple, nontechnical treatment allows even children to build several of these dials. Over 100 illustrations. 230pp. 5⅜ x 8½. 22947-5

THEORETICAL HYDRODYNAMICS, L. M. Milne-Thomson. Classic exposition of the mathematical theory of fluid motion, applicable to both hydrodynamics and aerodynamics. Over 600 exercises. 768pp. 6⅛ x 9¼. 68970-0

SONGS OF EXPERIENCE: Facsimile Reproduction with 26 Plates in Full Color, William Blake. 26 full-color plates from a rare 1826 edition. Includes "The Tyger," "London," "Holy Thursday," and other poems. Printed text of poems. 48pp. 5¼ x 7. 24636-1

OLD-TIME VIGNETTES IN FULL COLOR, Carol Belanger Grafton (ed.). Over 390 charming, often sentimental illustrations, selected from archives of Victorian graphics–pretty women posing, children playing, food, flowers, kittens and puppies, smiling cherubs, birds and butterflies, much more. All copyright-free. 48pp. 9¼ x 12¼. 27269-9

PERSPECTIVE FOR ARTISTS, Rex Vicat Cole. Depth, perspective of sky and sea, shadows, much more, not usually covered. 391 diagrams, 81 reproductions of drawings and paintings. 279pp. 5⅜ x 8½. 22487-2

DRAWING THE LIVING FIGURE, Joseph Sheppard. Innovative approach to artistic anatomy focuses on specifics of surface anatomy, rather than muscles and bones. Over 170 drawings of live models in front, back and side views, and in widely varying poses. Accompanying diagrams. 177 illustrations. Introduction. Index. 144pp. 8⅜ x11¼. 26723-7

GOTHIC AND OLD ENGLISH ALPHABETS: 100 Complete Fonts, Dan X. Solo. Add power, elegance to posters, signs, other graphics with 100 stunning copyright-free alphabets: Blackstone, Dolbey, Germania, 97 more–including many lower-case, numerals, punctuation marks. 104pp. 8⅛ x 11. 24695-7

HOW TO DO BEADWORK, Mary White. Fundamental book on craft from simple projects to five-bead chains and woven works. 106 illustrations. 142pp. 5⅜ x 8. 20697-1

THE BOOK OF WOOD CARVING, Charles Marshall Sayers. Finest book for beginners discusses fundamentals and offers 34 designs. "Absolutely first rate . . . well thought out and well executed."–E. J. Tangerman. 118pp. 7¾ x 10⅝. 23654-4

ILLUSTRATED CATALOG OF CIVIL WAR MILITARY GOODS: Union Army Weapons, Insignia, Uniform Accessories, and Other Equipment, Schuyler, Hartley, and Graham. Rare, profusely illustrated 1846 catalog includes Union Army uniform and dress regulations, arms and ammunition, coats, insignia, flags, swords, rifles, etc. 226 illustrations. 160pp. 9 x 12. 24939-5

WOMEN'S FASHIONS OF THE EARLY 1900s: An Unabridged Republication of "New York Fashions, 1909," National Cloak & Suit Co. Rare catalog of mail-order fashions documents women's and children's clothing styles shortly after the turn of the century. Captions offer full descriptions, prices. Invaluable resource for fashion, costume historians. Approximately 725 illustrations. 128pp. 8⅜ x 11¼. 27276-1

THE 1912 AND 1915 GUSTAV STICKLEY FURNITURE CATALOGS, Gustav Stickley. With over 200 detailed illustrations and descriptions, these two catalogs are essential reading and reference materials and identification guides for Stickley furniture. Captions cite materials, dimensions and prices. 112pp. 6½ x 9¼. 26676-1

EARLY AMERICAN LOCOMOTIVES, John H. White, Jr. Finest locomotive engravings from early 19th century: historical (1804–74), main-line (after 1870), special, foreign, etc. 147 plates. 142pp. 11⅜ x 8¼. 22772-3

THE TALL SHIPS OF TODAY IN PHOTOGRAPHS, Frank O. Braynard. Lavishly illustrated tribute to nearly 100 majestic contemporary sailing vessels: Amerigo Vespucci, Clearwater, Constitution, Eagle, Mayflower, Sea Cloud, Victory, many more. Authoritative captions provide statistics, background on each ship. 190 black-and-white photographs and illustrations. Introduction. 128pp. 8⅞ x 11¾. 27163-3

LITTLE BOOK OF EARLY AMERICAN CRAFTS AND TRADES, Peter Stockham (ed.). 1807 children's book explains crafts and trades: baker, hatter, cooper, potter, and many others. 23 copperplate illustrations. 140pp. 4⅝ x 6.   23336-7

VICTORIAN FASHIONS AND COSTUMES FROM HARPER'S BAZAR, 1867–1898, Stella Blum (ed.). Day costumes, evening wear, sports clothes, shoes, hats, other accessories in over 1,000 detailed engravings. 320pp. 9⅜ x 12¼. 22990-4

GUSTAV STICKLEY, THE CRAFTSMAN, Mary Ann Smith. Superb study surveys broad scope of Stickley's achievement, especially in architecture. Design philosophy, rise and fall of the Craftsman empire, descriptions and floor plans for many Craftsman houses, more. 86 black-and-white halftones. 31 line illustrations. Introduction 208pp. 6½ x 9¼.   27210-9

THE LONG ISLAND RAIL ROAD IN EARLY PHOTOGRAPHS, Ron Ziel. Over 220 rare photos, informative text document origin (1844) and development of rail service on Long Island. Vintage views of early trains, locomotives, stations, passengers, crews, much more. Captions. 8⅞ x 11¾.   26301-0

VOYAGE OF THE LIBERDADE, Joshua Slocum. Great 19th-century mariner's thrilling, first-hand account of the wreck of his ship off South America, the 35-foot boat he built from the wreckage, and its remarkable voyage home. 128pp. 5⅜ x 8½.
40022-0

TEN BOOKS ON ARCHITECTURE, Vitruvius. The most important book ever written on architecture. Early Roman aesthetics, technology, classical orders, site selection, all other aspects. Morgan translation. 331pp. 5⅜ x 8½.   20645-9

THE HUMAN FIGURE IN MOTION, Eadweard Muybridge. More than 4,500 stopped-action photos, in action series, showing undraped men, women, children jumping, lying down, throwing, sitting, wrestling, carrying, etc. 390pp. 7⅞ x 10⅝.
20204-6 Clothbd.

TREES OF THE EASTERN AND CENTRAL UNITED STATES AND CANADA, William M. Harlow. Best one-volume guide to 140 trees. Full descriptions, woodlore, range, etc. Over 600 illustrations. Handy size. 288pp. 4½ x 6⅜.   20395-6

SONGS OF WESTERN BIRDS, Dr. Donald J. Borror. Complete song and call repertoire of 60 western species, including flycatchers, juncoes, cactus wrens, many more–includes fully illustrated booklet.   Cassette and manual 99913-0

GROWING AND USING HERBS AND SPICES, Milo Miloradovich. Versatile handbook provides all the information needed for cultivation and use of all the herbs and spices available in North America. 4 illustrations. Index. Glossary. 236pp. 5⅜ x 8½.
25058-X

BIG BOOK OF MAZES AND LABYRINTHS, Walter Shepherd. 50 mazes and labyrinths in all–classical, solid, ripple, and more–in one great volume. Perfect inexpensive puzzler for clever youngsters. Full solutions. 112pp. 8⅛ x 11.   22951-3

PIANO TUNING, J. Cree Fischer. Clearest, best book for beginner, amateur. Simple repairs, raising dropped notes, tuning by easy method of flattened fifths. No previous skills needed. 4 illustrations. 201pp. 5⅜ x 8½. 23267-0

HINTS TO SINGERS, Lillian Nordica. Selecting the right teacher, developing confidence, overcoming stage fright, and many other important skills receive thoughtful discussion in this indispensible guide, written by a world-famous diva of four decades' experience. 96pp. 5⅜ x 8½. 40094-8

THE COMPLETE NONSENSE OF EDWARD LEAR, Edward Lear. All nonsense limericks, zany alphabets, Owl and Pussycat, songs, nonsense botany, etc., illustrated by Lear. Total of 320pp. 5⅜ x 8½. (Available in U.S. only.) 20167-8

VICTORIAN PARLOUR POETRY: An Annotated Anthology, Michael R. Turner. 117 gems by Longfellow, Tennyson, Browning, many lesser-known poets. "The Village Blacksmith," "Curfew Must Not Ring Tonight," "Only a Baby Small," dozens more, often difficult to find elsewhere. Index of poets, titles, first lines. xxiii + 325pp. 5⅜ x 8¼. 27044-0

DUBLINERS, James Joyce. Fifteen stories offer vivid, tightly focused observations of the lives of Dublin's poorer classes. At least one, "The Dead," is considered a masterpiece. Reprinted complete and unabridged from standard edition. 160pp. 5³⁄₁₆ x 8¼. 26870-5

GREAT WEIRD TALES: 14 Stories by Lovecraft, Blackwood, Machen and Others, S. T. Joshi (ed.). 14 spellbinding tales, including "The Sin Eater," by Fiona McLeod, "The Eye Above the Mantel," by Frank Belknap Long, as well as renowned works by R. H. Barlow, Lord Dunsany, Arthur Machen, W. C. Morrow and eight other masters of the genre. 256pp. 5⅜ x 8½. (Available in U.S. only.) 40436-6

THE BOOK OF THE SACRED MAGIC OF ABRAMELIN THE MAGE, translated by S. MacGregor Mathers. Medieval manuscript of ceremonial magic. Basic document in Aleister Crowley, Golden Dawn groups. 268pp. 5⅜ x 8½. 23211-5

NEW RUSSIAN-ENGLISH AND ENGLISH-RUSSIAN DICTIONARY, M. A. O'Brien. This is a remarkably handy Russian dictionary, containing a surprising amount of information, including over 70,000 entries. 366pp. 4½ x 6⅛. 20208-9

HISTORIC HOMES OF THE AMERICAN PRESIDENTS, Second, Revised Edition, Irvin Haas. A traveler's guide to American Presidential homes, most open to the public, depicting and describing homes occupied by every American President from George Washington to George Bush. With visiting hours, admission charges, travel routes. 175 photographs. Index. 160pp. 8¼ x 11. 26751-2

NEW YORK IN THE FORTIES, Andreas Feininger. 162 brilliant photographs by the well-known photographer, formerly with *Life* magazine. Commuters, shoppers, Times Square at night, much else from city at its peak. Captions by John von Hartz. 181pp. 9¼ x 10¾. 23585-8

INDIAN SIGN LANGUAGE, William Tomkins. Over 525 signs developed by Sioux and other tribes. Written instructions and diagrams. Also 290 pictographs. 111pp. 6⅛ x 9¼. 22029-X

ANATOMY: A Complete Guide for Artists, Joseph Sheppard. A master of figure drawing shows artists how to render human anatomy convincingly. Over 460 illustrations. 224pp. 8⅜ x 11¼. 27279-6

MEDIEVAL CALLIGRAPHY: Its History and Technique, Marc Drogin. Spirited history, comprehensive instruction manual covers 13 styles (ca. 4th century through 15th). Excellent photographs; directions for duplicating medieval techniques with modern tools. 224pp. 8⅜ x 11¼. 26142-5

DRIED FLOWERS: How to Prepare Them, Sarah Whitlock and Martha Rankin. Complete instructions on how to use silica gel, meal and borax, perlite aggregate, sand and borax, glycerine and water to create attractive permanent flower arrangements. 12 illustrations. 32pp. 5⅜ x 8½. 21802-3

EASY-TO-MAKE BIRD FEEDERS FOR WOODWORKERS, Scott D. Campbell. Detailed, simple-to-use guide for designing, constructing, caring for and using feeders. Text, illustrations for 12 classic and contemporary designs. 96pp. 5⅜ x 8½. 25847-5

SCOTTISH WONDER TALES FROM MYTH AND LEGEND, Donald A. Mackenzie. 16 lively tales tell of giants rumbling down mountainsides, of a magic wand that turns stone pillars into warriors, of gods and goddesses, evil hags, powerful forces and more. 240pp. 5⅜ x 8½. 29677-6

THE HISTORY OF UNDERCLOTHES, C. Willett Cunnington and Phyllis Cunnington. Fascinating, well-documented survey covering six centuries of English undergarments, enhanced with over 100 illustrations: 12th-century laced-up bodice, footed long drawers (1795), 19th-century bustles, 19th-century corsets for men, Victorian "bust improvers," much more. 272pp. 5⅝ x 8¼. 27124-2

ARTS AND CRAFTS FURNITURE: The Complete Brooks Catalog of 1912, Brooks Manufacturing Co. Photos and detailed descriptions of more than 150 now very collectible furniture designs from the Arts and Crafts movement depict davenports, settees, buffets, desks, tables, chairs, bedsteads, dressers and more, all built of solid, quarter-sawed oak. Invaluable for students and enthusiasts of antiques, Americana and the decorative arts. 80pp. 6½ x 9¼. 27471-3

WILBUR AND ORVILLE: A Biography of the Wright Brothers, Fred Howard. Definitive, crisply written study tells the full story of the brothers' lives and work. A vividly written biography, unparalleled in scope and color, that also captures the spirit of an extraordinary era. 560pp. 6⅛ x 9¼. 40297-5

THE ARTS OF THE SAILOR: Knotting, Splicing and Ropework, Hervey Garrett Smith. Indispensable shipboard reference covers tools, basic knots and useful hitches; handsewing and canvas work, more. Over 100 illustrations. Delightful reading for sea lovers. 256pp. 5⅜ x 8½. 26440-8

FRANK LLOYD WRIGHT'S FALLINGWATER: The House and Its History, Second, Revised Edition, Donald Hoffmann. A total revision–both in text and illustrations–of the standard document on Fallingwater, the boldest, most personal architectural statement of Wright's mature years, updated with valuable new material from the recently opened Frank Lloyd Wright Archives. "Fascinating"–*The New York Times*. 116 illustrations. 128pp. 9¼ x 10¾. 27430-6

CATALOG OF DOVER BOOKS

PHOTOGRAPHIC SKETCHBOOK OF THE CIVIL WAR, Alexander Gardner. 100 photos taken on field during the Civil War. Famous shots of Manassas Harper's Ferry, Lincoln, Richmond, slave pens, etc. 244pp. 10⅝ x 8¼. 22731-6

FIVE ACRES AND INDEPENDENCE, Maurice G. Kains. Great back-to-the-land classic explains basics of self-sufficient farming. The one book to get. 95 illustrations. 397pp. 5⅜ x 8½. 20974-1

SONGS OF EASTERN BIRDS, Dr. Donald J. Borror. Songs and calls of 60 species most common to eastern U.S.: warblers, woodpeckers, flycatchers, thrushes, larks, many more in high-quality recording. Cassette and manual 99912-2

A MODERN HERBAL, Margaret Grieve. Much the fullest, most exact, most useful compilation of herbal material. Gigantic alphabetical encyclopedia, from aconite to zedoary, gives botanical information, medical properties, folklore, economic uses, much else. Indispensable to serious reader. 161 illustrations. 888pp. 6½ x 9¼. 2-vol. set. (Available in U.S. only.)
Vol. I: 22798-7
Vol. II: 22799-5

HIDDEN TREASURE MAZE BOOK, Dave Phillips. Solve 34 challenging mazes accompanied by heroic tales of adventure. Evil dragons, people-eating plants, blood-thirsty giants, many more dangerous adversaries lurk at every twist and turn. 34 mazes, stories, solutions. 48pp. 8¼ x 11. 24566-7

LETTERS OF W. A. MOZART, Wolfgang A. Mozart. Remarkable letters show bawdy wit, humor, imagination, musical insights, contemporary musical world; includes some letters from Leopold Mozart. 276pp. 5⅜ x 8½. 22859-2

BASIC PRINCIPLES OF CLASSICAL BALLET, Agrippina Vaganova. Great Russian theoretician, teacher explains methods for teaching classical ballet. 118 illustrations. 175pp. 5⅜ x 8½. 22036-2

THE JUMPING FROG, Mark Twain. Revenge edition. The original story of The Celebrated Jumping Frog of Calaveras County, a hapless French translation, and Twain's hilarious "retranslation" from the French. 12 illustrations. 66pp. 5⅜ x 8½. 22686-7

BEST REMEMBERED POEMS, Martin Gardner (ed.). The 126 poems in this superb collection of 19th- and 20th-century British and American verse range from Shelley's "To a Skylark" to the impassioned "Renascence" of Edna St. Vincent Millay and to Edward Lear's whimsical "The Owl and the Pussycat." 224pp. 5⅜ x 8½. 27165-X

COMPLETE SONNETS, William Shakespeare. Over 150 exquisite poems deal with love, friendship, the tyranny of time, beauty's evanescence, death and other themes in language of remarkable power, precision and beauty. Glossary of archaic terms. 80pp. 5³⁄₁₆ x 8¼. 26686-9

THE BATTLES THAT CHANGED HISTORY, Fletcher Pratt. Eminent historian profiles 16 crucial conflicts, ancient to modern, that changed the course of civilization. 352pp. 5⅜ x 8½. 41129-X

THE WIT AND HUMOR OF OSCAR WILDE, Alvin Redman (ed.). More than 1,000 ripostes, paradoxes, wisecracks: Work is the curse of the drinking classes; I can resist everything except temptation; etc. 258pp. 5⅜ x 8½. 20602-5

SHAKESPEARE LEXICON AND QUOTATION DICTIONARY, Alexander Schmidt. Full definitions, locations, shades of meaning in every word in plays and poems. More than 50,000 exact quotations. 1,485pp. 6½ x 9¼. 2-vol. set.
Vol. 1: 22726-X
Vol. 2: 22727-8

SELECTED POEMS, Emily Dickinson. Over 100 best-known, best-loved poems by one of America's foremost poets, reprinted from authoritative early editions. No comparable edition at this price. Index of first lines. 64pp. 5³⁄₁₆ x 8¼. 26466-1

THE INSIDIOUS DR. FU-MANCHU, Sax Rohmer. The first of the popular mystery series introduces a pair of English detectives to their archnemesis, the diabolical Dr. Fu-Manchu. Flavorful atmosphere, fast-paced action, and colorful characters enliven this classic of the genre. 208pp. 5³⁄₁₆ x 8¼. 29898-1

THE MALLEUS MALEFICARUM OF KRAMER AND SPRENGER, translated by Montague Summers. Full text of most important witchhunter's "bible," used by both Catholics and Protestants. 278pp. 6⅝ x 10. 22802-9

SPANISH STORIES/CUENTOS ESPAÑOLES: A Dual-Language Book, Angel Flores (ed.). Unique format offers 13 great stories in Spanish by Cervantes, Borges, others. Faithful English translations on facing pages. 352pp. 5⅜ x 8½. 25399-6

GARDEN CITY, LONG ISLAND, IN EARLY PHOTOGRAPHS, 1869–1919, Mildred H. Smith. Handsome treasury of 118 vintage pictures, accompanied by carefully researched captions, document the Garden City Hotel fire (1899), the Vanderbilt Cup Race (1908), the first airmail flight departing from the Nassau Boulevard Aerodrome (1911), and much more. 96pp. 8⅞ x 11¾. 40669-5

OLD QUEENS, N.Y., IN EARLY PHOTOGRAPHS, Vincent F. Seyfried and William Asadorian. Over 160 rare photographs of Maspeth, Jamaica, Jackson Heights, and other areas. Vintage views of DeWitt Clinton mansion, 1939 World's Fair and more. Captions. 192pp. 8⅞ x 11. 26358-4

CAPTURED BY THE INDIANS: 15 Firsthand Accounts, 1750-1870, Frederick Drimmer. Astounding true historical accounts of grisly torture, bloody conflicts, relentless pursuits, miraculous escapes and more, by people who lived to tell the tale. 384pp. 5⅜ x 8½. 24901-8

THE WORLD'S GREAT SPEECHES (Fourth Enlarged Edition), Lewis Copeland, Lawrence W. Lamm, and Stephen J. McKenna. Nearly 300 speeches provide public speakers with a wealth of updated quotes and inspiration–from Pericles' funeral oration and William Jennings Bryan's "Cross of Gold Speech" to Malcolm X's powerful words on the Black Revolution and Earl of Spenser's tribute to his sister, Diana, Princess of Wales. 944pp. 5⅜ x 8⅜. 40903-1

THE BOOK OF THE SWORD, Sir Richard F. Burton. Great Victorian scholar/adventurer's eloquent, erudite history of the "queen of weapons"–from prehistory to early Roman Empire. Evolution and development of early swords, variations (sabre, broadsword, cutlass, scimitar, etc.), much more. 336pp. 6⅛ x 9¼.
25434-8

AUTOBIOGRAPHY: The Story of My Experiments with Truth, Mohandas K. Gandhi. Boyhood, legal studies, purification, the growth of the Satyagraha (nonviolent protest) movement. Critical, inspiring work of the man responsible for the freedom of India. 480pp. 5⅜ x 8½. (Available in U.S. only.) 24593-4

CELTIC MYTHS AND LEGENDS, T. W. Rolleston. Masterful retelling of Irish and Welsh stories and tales. Cuchulain, King Arthur, Deirdre, the Grail, many more. First paperback edition. 58 full-page illustrations. 512pp. 5⅜ x 8½. 26507-2

THE PRINCIPLES OF PSYCHOLOGY, William James. Famous long course complete, unabridged. Stream of thought, time perception, memory, experimental methods; great work decades ahead of its time. 94 figures. 1,391pp. 5⅜ x 8½. 2-vol. set. Vol. I: 20381-6 Vol. II: 20382-4

THE WORLD AS WILL AND REPRESENTATION, Arthur Schopenhauer. Definitive English translation of Schopenhauer's life work, correcting more than 1,000 errors, omissions in earlier translations. Translated by E. F. J. Payne. Total of 1,269pp. 5⅜ x 8½. 2-vol. set. Vol. 1: 21761-2 Vol. 2: 21762-0

MAGIC AND MYSTERY IN TIBET, Madame Alexandra David-Neel. Experiences among lamas, magicians, sages, sorcerers, Bonpa wizards. A true psychic discovery. 32 illustrations. 321pp. 5⅜ x 8½. (Available in U.S. only.) 22682-4

THE EGYPTIAN BOOK OF THE DEAD, E. A. Wallis Budge. Complete reproduction of Ani's papyrus, finest ever found. Full hieroglyphic text, interlinear transliteration, word-for-word translation, smooth translation. 533pp. 6½ x 9¼. 21866-X

MATHEMATICS FOR THE NONMATHEMATICIAN, Morris Kline. Detailed, college-level treatment of mathematics in cultural and historical context, with numerous exercises. Recommended Reading Lists. Tables. Numerous figures. 641pp. 5⅜ x 8½. 24823-2

PROBABILISTIC METHODS IN THE THEORY OF STRUCTURES, Isaac Elishakoff. Well-written introduction covers the elements of the theory of probability from two or more random variables, the reliability of such multivariable structures, the theory of random function, Monte Carlo methods of treating problems incapable of exact solution, and more. Examples. 502pp. 5⅜ x 8½. 40691-1

THE RIME OF THE ANCIENT MARINER, Gustave Doré, S. T. Coleridge. Doré's finest work; 34 plates capture moods, subtleties of poem. Flawless full-size reproductions printed on facing pages with authoritative text of poem. "Beautiful. Simply beautiful."–*Publisher's Weekly.* 77pp. 9¼ x 12. 22305-1

NORTH AMERICAN INDIAN DESIGNS FOR ARTISTS AND CRAFTSPEOPLE, Eva Wilson. Over 360 authentic copyright-free designs adapted from Navajo blankets, Hopi pottery, Sioux buffalo hides, more. Geometrics, symbolic figures, plant and animal motifs, etc. 128pp. 8⅜ x 11. (Not for sale in the United Kingdom.) 25341-4

SCULPTURE: Principles and Practice, Louis Slobodkin. Step-by-step approach to clay, plaster, metals, stone; classical and modern. 253 drawings, photos. 255pp. 8⅛ x 11. 22960-2

THE INFLUENCE OF SEA POWER UPON HISTORY, 1660–1783, A. T. Mahan. Influential classic of naval history and tactics still used as text in war colleges. First paperback edition. 4 maps. 24 battle plans. 640pp. 5⅜ x 8½. 25509-3

CATALOG OF DOVER BOOKS

THE STORY OF THE TITANIC AS TOLD BY ITS SURVIVORS, Jack Winocour (ed.). What it was really like. Panic, despair, shocking inefficiency, and a little heroism. More thrilling than any fictional account. 26 illustrations. 320pp. 5⅜ x 8½.
20610-6

FAIRY AND FOLK TALES OF THE IRISH PEASANTRY, William Butler Yeats (ed.). Treasury of 64 tales from the twilight world of Celtic myth and legend: "The Soul Cages," "The Kildare Pooka," "King O'Toole and his Goose," many more. Introduction and Notes by W. B. Yeats. 352pp. 5⅜ x 8½.
26941-8

BUDDHIST MAHAYANA TEXTS, E. B. Cowell and others (eds.). Superb, accurate translations of basic documents in Mahayana Buddhism, highly important in history of religions. The Buddha-karita of Asvaghosha, Larger Sukhavativyuha, more. 448pp. 5⅜ x 8½.
25552-2

ONE TWO THREE . . . INFINITY: Facts and Speculations of Science, George Gamow. Great physicist's fascinating, readable overview of contemporary science: number theory, relativity, fourth dimension, entropy, genes, atomic structure, much more. 128 illustrations. Index. 352pp. 5⅜ x 8½.
25664-2

EXPERIMENTATION AND MEASUREMENT, W. J. Youden. Introductory manual explains laws of measurement in simple terms and offers tips for achieving accuracy and minimizing errors. Mathematics of measurement, use of instruments, experimenting with machines. 1994 edition. Foreword. Preface. Introduction. Epilogue. Selected Readings. Glossary. Index. Tables and figures. 128pp. 5⅜ x 8½.
40451-X

DALÍ ON MODERN ART: The Cuckolds of Antiquated Modern Art, Salvador Dalí. Influential painter skewers modern art and its practitioners. Outrageous evaluations of Picasso, Cézanne, Turner, more. 15 renderings of paintings discussed. 44 calligraphic decorations by Dalí. 96pp. 5⅜ x 8½. (Available in U.S. only.)
29220-7

ANTIQUE PLAYING CARDS: A Pictorial History, Henry René D'Allemagne. Over 900 elaborate, decorative images from rare playing cards (14th–20th centuries): Bacchus, death, dancing dogs, hunting scenes, royal coats of arms, players cheating, much more. 96pp. 9¼ x 12¼.
29265-7

MAKING FURNITURE MASTERPIECES: 30 Projects with Measured Drawings, Franklin H. Gottshall. Step-by-step instructions, illustrations for constructing handsome, useful pieces, among them a Sheraton desk, Chippendale chair, Spanish desk, Queen Anne table and a William and Mary dressing mirror. 224pp. 8⅛ x 11¼.
29338-6

THE FOSSIL BOOK: A Record of Prehistoric Life, Patricia V. Rich et al. Profusely illustrated definitive guide covers everything from single-celled organisms and dinosaurs to birds and mammals and the interplay between climate and man. Over 1,500 illustrations. 760pp. 7½ x 10⅛.
29371-8

Paperbound unless otherwise indicated. Available at your book dealer, online at **www.doverpublications.com**, or by writing to Dept. GI, Dover Publications, Inc., 31 East 2nd Street, Mineola, NY 11501. For current price information or for free catalogues (please indicate field of interest), write to Dover Publications or log on to **www.doverpublications.com** and see every Dover book in print. Dover publishes more than 500 books each year on science, elementary and advanced mathematics, biology, music, art, literary history, social sciences, and other areas.